# MEDITATIONS FOR MEN WHO DO NEXT TO NOTHING

### (AND WOULD LIKE TO DO EVEN LESS)

# MEDITATIONS FOR MEN WHO DO NEXT TO NOTHING

## (AND WOULD LIKE TO DO EVEN LESS)

### LEE WARD SHORE

**WARNER BOOKS**

A Time Warner Company

Copyright © 1994 by N. K. Peske and B. J. Pennacchini
All rights reserved.

Warner Books, Inc., 1271 Avenue of the Americas, New York, NY 10020

**w** A Time Warner Company

Printed in the United States of America
First Printing: June 1994
10  9  8  7  6  5  4  3  2  1


Library of Congress Cataloging-in-Publication Data
Shore, Lee Ward.
    Meditations for men who do next to nothing  :  and would like to do
even less / Lee Ward Shore.
        p.    cm.
    ISBN 0-446-39525-0
    1. Men—Conduct of life—Humor.   I. Title.
PN6231.M45S5   1994
818'.5402—dc20                                                          93-48955
                                                                          CIP

*Cover design by Diane Luger*

*Cover illustration by Carter Goodrich*

*Book design by L. McRee*

To Nicky and Shiva,
*the masters of creative inertia*

# ACKNOWLEDGMENTS

Thanks to all who made this book possible:
Mary Yost, Joann Davis, Grace Sullivan, Sona Vogel,
and Tom Pennacchini.

# INTRODUCTION

Choices. Decisions. Responsibilities. As modern men in today's complex world, we face the stress of having to make a vast number of decisions every day, decisions that can have far-reaching, serious effects on our health and happiness, and how often we score with the babes—or, indeed, if we ever do. The sheer volume of choices to make and duties to perform can overwhelm us, especially when we're preoccupied with the hooters on the new gal in Purchasing.

On top of our responsibilities to job, home, and relationships, we can't neglect ourselves. We are challenged to set personal boundaries, to take inventory of ourselves and review old patterns, to let go of the clutter left over from dysfunctional childhoods in our families of origin, to work through the pain, fear, and anger that cause us to be reactors rather than actors. Faced with difficult decisions, like picking point spreads for this weekend's game, we may become paralyzed, dwelling on negative inner dialogues and distorted beliefs that have kept us from connecting in a nurturing, loving way to our inner child and the outer world. Which is a long way of saying our self-absorption is totally justified. Personally, I like to think of myself as a victim of a cold and mechanical society, which is just the kind of deep, introspective thought that impresses chicks at 12 Step meetings (if you haven't discovered them yet, they're a great place for hitting on babes).

Speaking of women, I get exhausted watching the women in my life scurry around like mice, trying to juggle it all. They call themselves Women Who Do Too Much. And they call me a lazy SOB.

Sadly, these gals haven't learned the value of time-out, as we Men Who Do Next to Nothing have. Activity-addicted women try to make us feel guilty for not doing the dishes, participating in child rearing, or stirring from our prone position in front of the tube until the smell of supper hits our nostrils. They demand action. We demand our MTV.

Face it, making choices and decisions is like hitting a pothole on the running track of life. How we handle these unplanned pockmarks in the course will determine the outcome of the race. Do we stumble in the hole? Do we avoid the obstacle in a looping, circuitous detour that costs us valuable time? Do we courageously leap over the hole and risk injury? Or do we stop midcourse, take stock of our situation, and realize that races are stupid: that competition and victory are hollow and what we really want to do is sit down, crack a frosty, turn on the tube, and watch some other loser run the race?

Our course becomes clear when we have the courage to face ourselves, when we dare to be truth speakers. Decisions become easier to make. We accept that it is healthier to follow our nature and shirk responsibility whenever possible than to bow down to the demands of modern life. Of course we would rather golf than clean the garage, rather check out the comic book convention than get that report done for work, rather recreate for five days and work for two—it's certainly more fun than the other way around! Without question, we prefer sitting down to standing up and enjoy lying down best of all. We must

*x*

listen to our inner voices, which are reflective of a Higher Power telling us to stop and smell the barbecue.

What we need is validation on a daily basis. Hence, I decided to write *Meditations for Men Who Do Next to Nothing (And Would Like to Do Even Less)*, a book that would inspire us to fight the good fight, to remain true to ourselves and steadfast in the conviction that the elimination of all activity and decision making from our lives will grant us the serenity we seek.

These meditations include affirmations that will replace those negative tapes in our heads that tell us to work harder, faster, more diligently. Each meditation begins with a quotation, follows with a brief discussion of a personal issue for the day, and concludes with a reminder to help us stay the course.

I decided to use only quotations from men, not because women haven't contributed immensely to our cultural dialogue, but because, oddly enough, I couldn't find any quotations from women on the virtue of inactivity. I used a variety of quotations from men of different ages, cultures, eras, and philosophies. This gathering of men's quotations has proved to me that some of the greatest men of history knew a great deal about doing next to nothing.

This book of meditations was written to inspire men, but I hope that women will read it as well, particularly women who project their own patterns of frenzied workaholism onto their mates. I hope female readers will gain a new understanding of the peace that comes through procrastination and introduce a little inertia into their own hectic routines.

If you do not respond to a particular meditation, bag it and switch on the tube. That's probably what I did when I was writing it. After all, life is meant to be lived at a 180-degree angle.

# MEDITATIONS FOR MEN WHO DO NEXT TO NOTHING

(AND WOULD LIKE TO DO EVEN LESS)

# STRESS/PRESSURE

*Consider the lilies of the field, how they grow; they toil not, neither do they spin. Yet even Solomon in all his splendor was not arrayed like one of these.*

Matthew 6:28–29

We Men Who Do Next to Nothing can find the beginning of a new day a perplexing and difficult time. All around us people are making agendas, setting lunch dates, and writing "to do" lists. The pressure that the workaholics who inhabit our world exert upon us to join them in their frantic struggle—to get it right, to get up off the couch, to switch off the ball game and lose the beer gut, to spend more time with the family—can be overwhelming.

At trying times like these, it is important to remember that we are fashioned in God's image and perfect just as we are.

**Just for today, give me the willingness to do nothing at all.**

# GETTING AHEAD/
# GOAL ORIENTATION

*Give me a roof over my head and something to drink, I've got
    all I need.*

                                                    Slash

It is only the second day of the work week, but already we
Men Who Do Next to Nothing are feeling the pressure to
improve ourselves, to make today more productive than yesterday.

Getting ahead is an exacting business that demands sacrifices like getting up in the morning, showering, and putting on
a suit. Success requires that we put work before everything else
in our lives . . . including football. It insists that we compete
and compromise and put off our first beer until noon.

It is time to stop and see what happens to us when we live a
goal-oriented life. Are we the men we want to be or the wimps
our wives wished they'd married?

**I wonder if I am the kind of guy I'd want to sit down and
have a beer with?**

# DISHONESTY

*Father, I cannot tell a lie . . .*

George Washington

Dishonesty is a milepost on the road to self-deception. When we allow ourselves to give in to deception, we alienate ourselves and those close to us.

Think about it. The last time you swore to your girlfriend that you were finally going to clean the leaves out of the gutters, and then you didn't and the rain backed up and collapsed the ceiling over the cedar closet where her winter wardrobe is stored, what was the result? Negativity? Conflict? An erosion of intimacy?

Although we are surrounded by a society where dishonesty runs rampant, we Men Who Do Next to Nothing must dare to be truth speakers. Be honest. Tell your wife you have no intention of cleaning the gutters or anything else . . . ever. We are the only ones who can choose truth over deception.

**There is an old saying, "What's done is done," so why make excuses?**

# RESPONSIBILITIES/OPTIONS

*All work and no play makes Jack a dull boy.*

James Howell

We are counseled from the time we are children that work must come before play. Before we can watch cartoons or go to the movies, the chores have to be done. All sorts of cruel and inhuman restrictions are imposed in the name of responsibility. If we want that hot-fudge sundae, we must eat every last lima bean.

We Men Who Do Next to Nothing have learned that work, once begun, is never finished and so is better never begun at all. We have learned how to break the intergenerational chain of the work ethic. We can decide to be different. We can have dessert before dinner. We can read the latest *Playboy* before *The Wall Street Journal*. We can let her bring home the bacon. We have choices.

**Let go, let God, let somebody else.**

# DISCOVERY/INFLEXIBILITY

*He was a very valiant man who first adventured on eating of oysters.*

James I

Crazy thinking involves the belief that things are better when they are in place, in order, and permanently fixed. So much energy is wasted trying to Super Glue life, but what is inflexible can break. When we become rigid, we lose touch with the rushing creek of life.

Be flexible. Let things lie where they fall. Dirty socks don't always have to go in a hamper. Dinner doesn't always have to be eaten at a table. Where is it written that one must always sleep in a bed at night? What's wrong with a desk top at noon? Why must we always work during the week and rest over the weekend? Why not vice versa?

When we stop experimenting, stop looking, stop asking new questions, it is time to die.

**Am I dead, or alive at a 180-degree angle?**

# WIT/WISDOM

*Take my wife . . . please!*

Henny Youngman

Wit is a weapon against the onslaught of life. There is nothing like a chuckle to perk up our day, particularly when it is at someone else's expense. Humor, like the miniskirt, is one of the few good reasons to get out of bed each morning.

Sometimes, though, we lose the ability to find the fun in life. We cannot see the humor in ourselves or, more important, in others. If our mates complain that we don't make a living, participate in parenting, or share the housework, and we feel that they are personally attacking us, putting us down, calling us heels, we must reassess our negative thinking.

In moments of personal crisis, humor helps us cope, so try making a funny. Everybody loves a cut-up, and doesn't she always say that your sense of humor is one of the reasons she married you?

**Today, I will laugh in the face of adversity, my wife, my boss, or anyone or anything that tries to crush my playful inner child.**

# SPONTANEITY

*Many a man's profanity has saved him from a nervous break-down.*

Henry S. Haskins

Have you ever noticed how much of your day is spent doing two things at once? We lead busy lives: we watch TV and eat dinner, we have sex and watch TV, we eat and breathe, we breathe and watch TV. We are so distracted by our many overlapping activities that we forget how to live in the moment. We forget to savor the simple pleasures that life provides us, inhaling, exhaling, bellowing at the tops of our lungs, or excreting extraneous intestinal gas. This is our human inheritance. Is it wrong to revel in it?

We need to fully experience these simple moments, to feel the fullness of our life force. It is in these personal moments of self-expression that we are truly alive.

**Today, let me not only go with the flow, but celebrate it.**

# ANGER

*I never work better than when I am inspired by anger.*

Martin Luther

Anger is a hotbed of controversy for us Men Who Do Next to Nothing. Although we understand that anger is not only a healthy outlet but a great motivator, our mates take our anger personally and often react with a host of painful emotional blows that interrupt our peaceful enjoyment of life.

Remember the last time your wife asked you to fix the washer on the kitchen sink and you pulled out your four-hundred-and-fifty-dollar faucet-washer repair kit, but all you managed to do was scratch the stainless steel and break your left index finger? And then you started screaming so loud that she grabbed the wrench out of your hand and in twenty seconds flat fixed the washer, but then refused to sleep with you for a week?

What does this teach us? When our rage brims over the lip of our self-control at the petty annoyances of life, should we bottle it up? Should we seal ourselves off emotionally? Should we give up and call in a professional? No! Anger is our friend, and a wife is cheaper than a plumber.

**Anger is not the problem. My wife is.**

# AFFIRMATION/NEGATION

*How can they say my life is not a success? Have I not for more than sixty years got enough to eat and escaped being eaten?*

Logan Pearsall Smith

We Men Who Do Next to Nothing should give ourselves more credit. Although the world will tell us that our beer glass is perpetually half-empty, we must remind ourselves that it doesn't much matter because there's half a case left in the fridge.

Workaholics who measure their lives in laundry lists of meaningless accomplishments cannot understand the perfect bliss of utter inactivity. Isn't existing, in and of itself, an art? Isn't regressing to a vegetative state, in fact, a perfect union of man and nature? What does your lawn accomplish each day? It looks happy, doesn't it? No one tells turf to get a job. And it costs a lot of money to maintain.

Take a few moments to applaud the wonder of yourself. In fact, take a few hours. Hell, take a long weekend.

**Today is realization day for what I have not accomplished. Celebrations may be in order. Gimme a beer.**

# PRESENTS

*A wise lover values not so much the gift of the lover as the love of the giver.*

Thomas à Kempis

It was your anniversary. And you forgot. So you didn't come home with a dozen long-stem roses. You didn't say it with diamonds. Does this mean that you are a bad partner? Isn't it enough that you simply came home? Isn't your very presence enough evidence of your devotion? Doesn't she know what a great catch you are?

What we do with our lives is up to us, and the gift of sharing our destiny with our significant other is the finest present we men can offer. Recite these truths to yourself when she demands more than you can give, when she insists on going out to eat at a restaurant that doesn't accept two-for-one coupons or traveling to a place that does not honor AAA discounts. Don't let her attitude wound your generous inner spirit. All of us have resentments to work through. Just be patient. She'll get over it.

**Help me to remember that I am God's gift.**

# FAILURE

*A man's life is interesting primarily when he has failed—I well know.*

Georges Clemenceau

When I read a passage like the one above, I am inspired. I just want to read it over and over again, to remind myself of how I sometimes suppress everything that is unique and special in myself in order to accomplish a goal. Usually I end up sick and sorry with effort, not realizing that everything I need is right here beside me: my cable guide, my remote control, and my family size bag of Doritos.

This passage is beautiful testimony to the fruits of failure. Do you think successful guys have time to contemplate what is truly interesting in life, like which bar to hit tonight, who should be on the All-Madden team this year, or how to pick up that hot new babe in Purchasing? Of course not. They're too busy working.

**Help me to remember that still waters run deep.**

# FELLOWSHIP/AFFECTION

*Love and do what you will.*

St. Augustine

It is impossible to watch the ball game and be intimate at the same time. It takes energy to be intimate, to express fellowship and affection, to do what is necessary to communicate with our mates. Being together is a lot of work.

Surprisingly, our significant others don't seem to understand this. They demand that we reach out, reach in, reach over, and reach through. Just the words alone are enough to exhaust us.

We must explain to those we love that intimacy with another is not possible unless we have achieved intimacy with ourselves. This requires taking the time to rest, to contemplate, to reorganize our collection of athletic socks, or to put a sixth coat of Turtle Wax on the Mustang. In order to merge spiritually with my spouse, I must first become my own best friend. And so I must ask myself, what would my best friend do for me to express his devotion? Certainly tickets to the next pennant race would be a good start.

**Intimacy, like a hangover, begins at the ball park.**

# PRODUCTIVITY/CREATIVITY

*We will sell no wine before its time.*

Ernest and Julio Gallo

Many people believe that it is the workaholics in this world who are the most fruitful, the most productive, and the most creative. Not so! We Men Who Do Next to Nothing realized long ago that overextended deadlines and frantic, anxiety-ridden activity never produce anything of quality. True creativity, like most of the finer things in this world, must be allowed to age sufficiently, and we are experts at that.

So the next time your mother asks you what you think you are doing sleeping your life away, or shrieks that you haven't moved for a week and are stinking up the family room, or demands that you strap on your tool belt and complete that kitchen addition you began eighteen months ago, tell her that you are ripening, fermenting, and will get up only when you have reached your peak flavor. Otherwise, your vintage bouquet may be severely compromised. Men, like fine wine, require absolute stillness in dark cool rooms to achieve peak performance.

**Rome wasn't built in a day, so why should your kitchen addition be any different?**

# GRUDGES

*The only things one never regrets are one's mistakes.*

Oscar Wilde

Nurturing grudges seems to be the favorite pastime of some people. So you forgot to pick up your mother after her doctor's appointment and she had to take three buses through the seediest neighborhood in town. She got home okay, so why dwell on it? What's she gonna do, disinherit you?

And so you forgot to tell your wife about the night crawlers you were storing in the empty dip container until she tried to serve it at her Lamaze class get-together. It's not all that different from sushi, so what's the big deal? Pregnant women are always throwing up anyway. Or perhaps you left the "Dear Fuck-face" salutation in your most recent report to the stockholders. Computer glitches happen all the time.

When faced with the consequences of your actions or inactions you can hold on to the pain, the shame, and the blame, or you can utter the magic words *I'm sorry* and move on. Recognize that grudges serve no purpose, and those who hold them are simply victims of their own inability to chill out. What a shame! Thank goodness we aren't stuck in a victim mentality.

**Forgiveness is a gift you give yourself.**

# CIVILIZED BEHAVIOR

*Labor is the curse of the world, and nobody can meddle with it
without becoming proportionately brutified.*

Nathaniel Hawthorne

Has civilization really progressed? Our prehistoric ancestors
risked their lives hunting to provide food for the clan. Today,
we risk the L.A. freeways at rush hour. The ancient tribes of
Europe, Asia, and Africa slaughtered each other to secure their
enemies' land and resources for themselves. Today, we park in
loading zones and Handicapped Only spaces to get a jump on
anybody else who was thinking of buying a few cases of
antifreeze at the Walgreens dollar day sale.

It seems we are still engaged in a ruthless, barbarous struggle to increase our riches and engine temperature at the expense
of our fellow beings. Wouldn't it be more civilized to avoid
contributing to those bad vibes on the freeway and just sleep in
today? And if parking is a problem, send your little sister on her
bike to pick up your lottery tickets and Alka-Seltzer. Park yourself on the porch, where you can't do any harm.

**If it's here today, it'll be here tomorrow, so what's your
hurry?**

# IDENTITY

*I do not know myself, and God forbid that I should.*
                                                Johann Wolfgang von Goethe


As men, we have been conditioned to define ourselves in relation to the outside world. We have been conditioned to identify ourselves in terms of what we do rather than what we are. No wonder we feel pressured to do something beyond moving our bowels on a regular basis.

An important part of recovery is finding out who we really are, beyond what others expect of us, beyond what we do, beyond what we earn.

Who is this person I call me? Am I the guy who schlepps to the office every morning to sell the gadgets that mechanically screw the tops onto tubes of toothpaste, or am I a secret agent in a red Alfa-Romeo with a Rolex watch and a beautiful blonde on each arm? Maybe I'm a lead guitarist for a heavy metal band, in a red Alfa-Romeo with a Rolex watch and a beautiful blonde on each arm. I mean, maybe I'm not, but the possibilities are certainly worth considering. Besides, self-discovery is a lot more fun than working.

**Today, I will begin an inner journey of self-discovery that, with any luck, will last the rest of my life, or at least until happy hour.**

# HUMOR

*What's a perfect ten?*
  *A three-foot-tall girl with no teeth and a flat head so you*
  *can put your beer down.*

Ricardo Panadero

I love jokes like the one above. They have such a refreshing way of cutting right through to the meat of things.

How often have we had whimsical, youthful thoughts yet have prevented ourselves from enjoying them because we are in mixed company. We think of a funny but do not share it because we are repressed. People curl their lips at us and hiss that we are politically incorrect. This is of course infinitely preferable to having a martini thrown in our faces, but it still can be embarrassing at a get-together.

What people, especially the people our girlfriends invite to cocktail parties, have forgotten is that to be male is to be politically incorrect. It's a package deal. We come naturally by a mischievous, boyish sense of fun. We should not be shamed into swallowing our punch lines. Which reminds me of the one about the sword swallower and the stallion.

Why can't everybody lighten up?

**F—— 'em if they can't take a joke.**

# LIVING LIFE FULLY

*He who draws upon his own resources easily comes to the end
of his wealth.*

William Hazlitt

We can get so obsessed with possessing things that we often find ourselves being possessed rather than possessing the trappings of a successful life. We can get so caught up in the need to own things—a house; a laser disc player; a thirty-inch, high-resolution television; a self-sharpening combination band saw and electric sander; a portable CD player with a belt attachment—that we end up slaves to our definitions of success.

We need to teach ourselves and our girlfriends that men are like pigeons. All pigeons do is hang around in parks all day, yet have you ever seen a skinny one? No? And why? Because they are free to live off other people's crumbs, other people's possessions, and therefore have no need to acquire their own, with the exception, of course, of the laser disc player, which, pigeons or not, I'm buying first thing next week.

**Am I content to fully appreciate what I do not possess? I think so. Although if I get the laser disc player, I guess I'll have to go ahead and get some laser discs. And my speakers are shot. What good is a laser disc player without good speakers? And my receiver really rots. What I really need is a whole new setup.**

# GOALS

*Let's face it, the first tours the Beatles did, the main essential thing was scoring chicks.*

Paul McCartney

In trying to reach our goals, we can develop tunnel vision. We visualize the end of our efforts and become obsessed with the finish line or the bottom line. We forget that the real reward comes when we remove all lines from our lives and just concentrate on the bottoms, in every sense of the word.

When we rush, rush, rush, we can forget that true enjoyment comes from the process. We overlook the violets along the path. We forget about the position that guy in the locker room was describing. Where was her left leg supposed to go again?

**In a perfect world, there would be no finish lines and all women would be double-jointed.**

# DECISION MAKING

*When a man hasn't a good reason for doing a thing, he has a
good reason for letting it alone.*

Sir Walter Scott

How often as Men Who Do Next to Nothing do we feel ourselves pressured to hurry up and make a decision, like which brand of garden weasel to buy or what to do with our lives?

Of course the problem is once we make those decisions, we come under pressure to act on them. Once we go ahead and buy our weasel of preference, we may actually have to weed. Once we decide what to do with our lives, the implication is that we go ahead and do it.

Isn't it much easier to avoid making any decisions in the first place? Isn't it healthier to avoid asking leading questions of ourselves or, in fact, asking any questions at all, of anybody, at any time? If we avoid thinking about the issues in our lives, we stay clear of the activity danger zone.

**If an issue falls in the forest and I'm not there to hear it, does it exist? Who cares? I hate hiking.**

# QUIET TIME

*Edith, stifle!*

Archie Bunker

Every day we are bombarded by renegade channels assaulting our own personal networks. We're distracted by traffic, the neighbors, our girlfriends, the neighbors' girlfriends. And everybody wants to discuss something just when your favorite shows are coming on. Your wife wants to talk about your relationship, your boss wants to discuss the ten grand missing from the Anderson account. Why can't they wait until a more convenient time, like the next Ice Age, for example?

We even have difficulty sleeping because we're constantly interrupted by clients calling during business hours.

We have to tune out the complaints, the ultimatums, and the threats of violence or legal action and tune in to ourselves. After all, we've got the best fall lineup going.

**Quiet time lets me star in my own life.**

# WISDOM/KNOWLEDGE

*Tomorrow a stranger will say with masterly good sense pre-
cisely what we have thought and felt all the time.*

Ralph Waldo Emerson

Oh, how we underestimate our own wisdom. Then that
stranger comes by and reminds us of what we knew all along
but temporarily forgot because, of course, short-term memory
loss is an unavoidable part of living.

Of course we understand those new memo-routing proce-
dures at work. We understand the president's new economic
plan. We knew you're not supposed to put aluminum foil in the
microwave.

Deep down, we know. We know that we know, even though
we forgot. That tax advice our friend gave us, you know, that
bit about mailing your return before April 15? We knew that.
That suggestion Dad gave us about approaching the boss with
a smile and a handshake instead of an automatic weapon? We
knew that. The stuff that professor at Joe's party was saying
about quantum physics and its relationship to time and matter
in a spatial universe? We knew that, too. We just need a little
memory jog now and again.

**Buried deep in my subconscious lie the answers to life's
greatest questions. Anybody got a shovel?**

# FAMILY

*Get away from me, kid, you bother me.*

W. C. Fields

Years ago, Mom and Pop, Grandma and Grandpa, and all the little children gathered together in front of the radio to laugh with Jack Benny or Uncle Milty, to wonder wide-eyed how the Shadow always knew or who that masked man really was.

But now with a television in every room, urban alienation, and the ability to put physical and emotional miles between families and their offspring, the parlor of yesteryear is considerably quieter. Thank God.

But we can still share quality time with the little kiddies. If they want to watch *Three's Company* and then see the Giants take on Phoenix, they can hang out, as long as they keep quiet and bring their own bag of Chee-tos. I mean, that's life, right? They're gonna have to learn eventually that they don't get to call the channels when there is someone bigger than them holding the remote control, and they better come equipped to provide for their own nourishment. These are invaluable lessons of modern life that I am duty bound to impart to my kids.

**Football is a metaphor for life.**

# HOPES AND DREAMS

*Hope is independent of the apparatus of logic.*
                                                    Norman Cousins

As boys, we had high hopes for the future. As men we are told that the future is now, so we better forget about that Stratocaster we've always wanted or those vintage Spiderman comic books and start locking in interest rates on long-term CDs.

Now this really enrages my inner child. I was really getting close to buying that guitar. It's electric purple, with orange flames climbing up the neck. The guy told me Jimi Hendrix once sat on that guitar because somebody had left it lying on a chair, and Jimi just sat on it because he was so distracted because he was right at that moment mentally composing "Purple Haze." See, the song was originally called "Purple Bass," on account of he was sitting on my guitar, but the record company made him change it on the LP.

When you think of it, it's really an investment. A guitar like that is bound to go up more than 2.3 percent compounded monthly.

**To hell with the future, I want my guitar.**

# SELF-AWARENESS

*Any desire for self-improvement is petty.*

J. Krishnamurti

In the race to get ahead, get better, get successful, we risk the danger of not appreciating fully the things that truly make life worth living, like lunch or dinner. In fact, working, rushing around, leaves us little time to be fully conscious of what our bodies are telling us, which is usually one of three things: I'm hungry, I'm thirsty, or I'm in the mood.

The work world would have us think of our bodies as nonexistent, but what could be more important? Who would work when he could drink instead, or eat, or excrete? Doesn't the ultimate appreciation of life reside in our bodies? Isn't it a crime against nature to turn a deaf ear to the most basic demands of our physical selves?

**I better take the time to listen and respond to my body's demands. It's the only fun I'm going to get out of life.**

# CURIOSITY/TAKING IT TO THE LIMIT

*Curiosity is one of the permanent and certain characteristics of a vigorous intellect.*

Samuel Johnson

As I look back on my greatest adventures in life, I realize that most of them would never have happened had I stuck to the straight and narrow. Like the time I wandered into the Sail and Rail down by the freight yard, a real man's kind of bar where your elbows stick to the tables and the smell of fine draft blends congenially with industrial disinfectant. And they don't serve frozen daiquiris.

I sat down next to an old salt who sucked down Wild Turkey like he was born with bourbon for blood, and after about the eighth round, he got kind of talkative. He told me about his stint as the owner of a Shanghai bordello, a profitable establishment very similar in style to the Sail and Rail, which had been financed for him by some guy named Vic the Throat. He never told me how Vic had earned his name. I was only on my fourth bourbon, and perhaps he deemed me unworthy. And I never did get the moral of the story, but he taught me a great card trick, which I use all the time at poker parties.

**Life is full of wonderful mysteries for those willing to check out the side streets. Just be sure to set your car alarm.**

# BEING IN CHARGE

*It is a fine thing to command, even if it be only a herd of cattle.*
Miguel de Cervantes

As born leaders, we think that we must do it all. How self-centered of us to think we are the only ones who can get it done and get it done right!

Of course, I'm not talking about highly complex tasks calling for an expertise that only we can bring to bear on a particular project, like grilling burgers. I'm talking about jobs that we could delegate. Like hot dogs; it's impossible to screw those up. I mean, they're precooked.

The thing with hot dogs is if you cut them in half, then you've got it knocked. It's pretty much a matter of even heat distribution, and that's it. Burgers, on the other hand, have to be finessed, or they go dry on the outside and raw on the inside. Also, you have to be pretty handy with a spatula to turn those quarter pounders without leaving an eighth of a pound still stuck to the grill.

So the idea is, leave yourself free to focus all your attention on the tough stuff, like burgers, and be man enough to let your wife turn the dogs.

**Besides, if she screws it up, she's gonna eat them anyway. I'm certainly not going to. Do you have any idea what they put in those things?**

# INTEGRITY

*[T]his above all: to thine own self be true . . .*

William Shakespeare

I wonder. Have I sacrificed my integrity in the race to get ahead? Am I opting for peace in the home over peace of mind? Am I listening to my mate when I should be listening to myself? Am I going to give in and paint the ceiling, or stand firm and go golfing like I planned?

Every day presents another opportunity to betray myself. Do I get up when my alarm rings or stay in bed until I'm not tired anymore? Do I get on the train to work, even though I'd rather stick needles in my eyes than commute one more day? Do I buy Billy braces or that rookie Ernie Banks card? Do I wear the new starched oxford or the soft flannel, with the precisely engineered ventilation system in the elbows, that I've spent fifteen years weathering to perfection? Do I live my life sitting up, when I'd much rather be lying down?

It is easy to forget to listen to myself. I gobble up these bits of integrity slippage like potato chips, and no one can eat just one. How important it is to stop and look at what I'm doing. What a relief to realize that underneath the pile of orthodontist bills, I can still find my self-respect ready to reconnect with me just as soon as I am willing to sit down and take a load off.

**So what if my life resembles a garbage dump? I like it that way.**

# FEELING OVERWHELMED/ DISAPPEARING

*In managing human affairs, there is no better rule than self-restraint.*

Lao-tse

From the moment we wake up till we drift off to sleep hours or minutes later, we are bombarded with information to be processed. We begin to feel machinelike, computing it all: Which side of the street can I park on this morning? Is this recycling day, or tomorrow? Is today clean underwear day, or is it next Tuesday?

Then we reach for the morning paper, and there is nothing but more bad news. John Elway still hasn't won a Super Bowl. Another supermodel is dating a rock star instead of us. Rain is predicted for Saturday and Sunday. It's a bleak forecast all the way around; no wonder we feel overwhelmed.

As Men Who Do Next to Nothing, we are only just taking baby steps toward learning the process of prioritizing, allowing ourselves to block out the trivia, to exercise self-restraint in our encounters with reality. Is it really important to know the name of our senator or if there is right on red in this state? I don't think so.

**When we clean our mental houses, we find serenity, along with a half-dozen dust bunnies and last month's Visa bill.**

# REALITY/FANTASY

*Ever let the fancy roam,*
*Pleasure never is at home.*

John Keats

People who are "experts" on the subject tell us that one of the danger signals of poor mental health is losing the ability to distinguish between reality and fantasy. A sick man, they tell us, builds a fantasy and then moves right in.

We Men Who Do Next to Nothing must learn to ask ourselves and our mates, "Yeah, and so what?" What is wrong with living a fantasy? Who would rather live real life as a systems analyst when he could live a fantasy life as Eddie Vedder? Who needs to sweat real blood to make the mortgage payments on a prefab suburban dump when he could live in a fantasy palace of his own design, rent free? What is the big deal about reality, anyway?

**It's not that we don't perceive reality, we just choose not to live in it.**

# SILENCE/INNER PEACE

*Silence is deep as Eternity; speech is shallow as Time.*
                                        Thomas Carlyle

When we still our minds, we may find inner peace that renews and strengthens us. Or, if you're like me, you'll catch a few much needed, well-deserved winks, which is certainly far more valuable than some abstract spirituality thing.

Frankly, few things stimulate my spirituality more than my wife talking to me. Somehow she inspires me to clear my mind of thoughts, still my brain waves, and cease all mental activity. I enjoy this inner peace, and I am calm as I bond with my Higher Power within, at least until she severs my cosmic line of communication and demands that I actually answer her.

**Silence is the sound of our Higher Power calling us. Noise is usually my wife.**

# RESPONSIBILITY

*Is life worth living?*

Samuel Butler

As men, we have been raised to take care of our families. Yet down deep, we often have a secret wish that someone else would take care of us. Frequently, we wish we could be stowaways instead of ticketed passengers on the garbage scow of life. Who wants to pay for a ticket on a trash barge, anyway? Come to think of it, they should pay us to ride. We ought to get a salary just for agreeing to exist.

Unfortunately, life is a nonprofit organization supported solely by volunteers, but as volunteers we do have options. For one thing, we can exercise some choice over our destination. We can demand that the scow go someplace besides, say, New Jersey. For another thing, we have the right to pick and choose the tasks we undertake. For instance, we can decline to scrub between our toes or, in fact, to scrub anything at all. We don't have to separate glass and cans, and they can't make us provide for our families or contribute to a more humane global economy. We're volunteers, so what are they gonna do . . . fire us? Dock our pay?

**To participate in our lives does not mean that we have to go to New Jersey.**

# ANGER

@#*!! +@**%#@!!

Axl Rose

Anger is a powerful force. When we become truly enraged we may feel overwhelmed by the force of our feeling and attempt to bottle up our emotions. Inevitably, though, our anger builds to the boiling point, and we explode, often with disastrous results. We get fired. We get thrown out of bars. We get blood on the carpet.

How much better it is to express anger at the moment we begin to experience it. There are so many opportunities to let off steam and avoid nuclear meltdown, if only we would avail ourselves of them.

Say your secretary misspells a client's name or misplaces a preposition. Say your wife serves your dinner and the broccoli's cold. Let them have it. You'll all be better off in the long run if you get those feelings out. And the best part is that next time your broccoli will be hot.

**It is the angry young man who gets the multimillion-dollar recording contract and the groupies.**

# TRANQUILLITY

*Periods of tranquillity are seldom prolific of creative achieve-
ment.*

Alfred North Whitehead


Sometimes people confuse peace and tranquillity with catatonia. In fact, although many of the outward symptoms are similar, they are very different states of being.

Tranquillity comes after watching eight solid hours of NBA
playoff action, during which you move nothing more than two
eyeballs, a right index finger, and occasionally a vocal cord or
two. Peace comes when we still our minds and our bodies,
when our jaw hangs slack, when our boxers bag down along
with our hopes for the future. Peace comes when we relax, let
go of the guilt and most of the sensory awareness of our surrounding environment.

**Come to think of it, we might be giving catatonia a bum
rap.**

# FOCUS/CONCENTRATION/ PRIORITIES

*My hobbies are hooking up stuff to see if it works, and beer.*
Joe Walsh

Have you ever watched Minnesota Fats play pool? He has total focus. He knows he has to block out everything around him so he can sink that next shot. He knows what his priorities are.

When we try to focus like this in our own lives, people around us tell us we are rude and inattentive. They don't appreciate the intense concentration it requires to work out the Sunday *Times* puzzle, tie a fly, or eat a chili burrito properly, savoring every bit and feeling it work its way through our lower intestine.

Of course we didn't notice we knocked over the ashtray, and now the cat is chewing on last night's cigarette butts and tracking ashes all over the new carpet. Actually, we hadn't noticed that burn mark in the middle of it, either. Or the mud we must've tracked in—it is mud, isn't it?

The point is, we've got to focus to get important tasks done. These magical moments when we give our complete and undivided attention to a task put us in touch with our Higher Power. We can get in touch with the carpet cleaner tomorrow.

**Focusing allows me to be at one with myself and my own little world. I think I'll stay there for a while. I think the rent's cheaper.**

# EXPLORATION

*. . . to boldly go where no man has gone before.*
Mission of the USS *Enterprise*

Not just to go, but to go boldly. I think that means never asking for directions. It means that when faced with new adventures in life or major decisions, such as whether to go left or to go right, we must boldly go left, without relying on maps or lame instructions from gas station workers who can't even navigate gas through a hose.

We must not be afraid of the unexpected intersections of life, even if we've passed one three times in the last half hour. This could be a new shortcut. In a sense, we know where we are going. I mean, knowledge is relative, as are the directions to Aunt Sally's. Funny, but I don't remember passing that burned-out building last time or circling the airport parking lot three times, but memory, too, is relative.

**Life is what happens while you're circling the airport.**

# SELFLESSNESS

*He who undervalues himself is justly undervalued by others.*
William Hazlitt

The arrogance of our disease fools us into thinking that self-lessness means denying our own egos. But if we give up our egos, what is left?

How can we offer anything to anybody if we abandon ourselves? And think of what a loss to the world it would be if we could no longer offer it our unique and special gifts.

Who would keep our wives in line, curb their spending, instruct them in how to stack the refrigerator so that nothing ever drips on our beer cans? Who would tell our secretaries that "occasional" has two *c*'s and one *s*? Who would tell our kids that a liberal arts education is a waste of time? Without us, they'll be studying useless stuff like Shakespeare or something they call "communication," which, it seems to me, no college in the world can teach you.

Obviously, without our intervention the world would run amok. I'm going to speak up more often.

**I have a lot to offer others, and I'm going to make sure they know about it.**

# THOUGHTS/OPINIONS

*To lie still and think little is medicine for the soul.*
Friedrich Nietzsche

How many times have we heard it said that we men are creatures of the mind, that we are logical, linear, rational, and left-brained? Could this be true? Are we truly better thinkers than women? It is certainly nice to think so.

Maybe, as heirs to this intellectual tradition of men, we should put our minds to use. Maybe we should work toward envisioning and creating a better world. Maybe we should fulfill our potential as intellectual adventurers, cognitive conquerors, mental world movers. But then again . . . maybe not.

**Today, I will not clutter my mind with thoughts.**

# INTEGRATION/SELFHOOD

*To love oneself is the beginning of a life-long romance.*
Oscar Wilde

People tell me I'm selfish because I put my needs before the needs of others. She doesn't like it when I opt to watch the bout on Tuesday night instead of going to Aunt Marilyn's funeral. She gets incensed because I like to save old boxes in case I have to move in a hurry one day. She grows irate because I saw no harm in borrowing the shower curtain to use as a tarp on a camping weekend. Hey, water's water, right? She disapproves because I figure if you can't see it, it's not there, so why clean it or pay for it? Who cares what's behind the refrigerator? When am I going to use medical insurance?

As a result of this impervious and all-inclusive disapproval, we Men Who Do Next to Nothing can sometimes get the idea that we are unappreciated. Guilt can rain on our parade of confidence and self-esteem. But men are more than the sum of their character flaws, and the world would be a pretty dull place if there were no secrets behind the refrigerator. We are like rainbows, adding contrast and excitement to a world of women workaholics who have never had the guts or the imagination to sleep under the stars on a shower curtain.

**Today, I own up to myself. I own myself, and I could own a lot more if Aunt Marilyn had left me something in the will.**

# GROWTH

*[T]he crooked roads without improvement are roads of genius.*
William Blake

Somehow, we all harbor the secret hope that if we can just get ourselves together, if we can finally work out all our issues, plumb the depths of our strengths and weaknesses, and get a grip, then at last, life will leave us alone to catch a few solid *z*'s before the bout starts.

What a shock it is to realize that, like my wife, life never lets up, never leaves me alone, no matter how much money I make, no matter if I clean the garage five times a weekend and finish every household project I've begun in the last ten years—it never, ever, has the common human decency to leave me alone for just five minutes. Just when I think I'm free and clear, and I've settled back onto the couch, it's something else again, like the lawn, or the plugged-up chimney, or the unpaid electric bill, or a new sin tax. It's always something.

How much easier it would be to just avoid growth altogether, to toss away our emotional twin blade and remain spiritually unshaven.

**To grow and to change is the normal state for human beings. I am a human being. Maybe there's something I can do to change that.**

# HINDRANCE/COMPLETION

*God keep me from ever completing anything.*

Herman Melville

We are often told that there is a purpose behind life's tribulations. There are people who would have us believe that we grow from the challenges that confront us and that every obstacle we hurdle increases our character. These people are women.

We Men Who Do Next to Nothing know that there is no use slugging it out with what is obviously preordained anyway. These things are prearranged by our Higher Power. Who are we to question what is obviously in the cards?

Women don't understand this kind of reasoning. They think that if we don't get a promotion, swing the vacation time, or finance the mortgage, it's our fault. "You got yourself into this, now you can get yourself out" is a common catchphrase, as if we had something to do with what is going on around us. As if it is really within our power to confront the forces at work in our lives.

It is best at times like these to tread a line of least resistance. True, life isn't fair, but neither are women, so nod your head, grunt occasionally, but if she insists on action, let her do it.

**An obstacle isn't an obstacle until you try to overcome it.**

# COURAGE

*Of all the thirty-six alternatives, running away is best.*

Chinese proverb

How true. And what a perfect formula for a happy life, if only we can find the spiritual serenity to put down our pens, our fists, our memos, and our cellular phones and run like hell to the nearest corner bar.

What has ever been accomplished through competition? Ulcers, high blood pressure, rampant anxiety, urban blight. Are these the legacies we wish to leave to the future? Would we rather say to our grandchildren, "Yes, I stayed, I fought, I worked my whole life in order to retire and live on a fixed income that won't even let me buy the brand of toilet paper with the baby oil on it"? Or would we rather say, "No, I refused, I laid down on the couch, I turned on the television, and now I live on the same fixed income, but I don't need the brand of toilet paper with the baby oil on it because I avoided the stress and don't have to contend with irritated-bowel syndrome"?

**Brave men take naps where workaholics fear to tread.**

# BEAUTY

*The most beautiful subjects? The simplest, and the least clad.*
Anatole France

How long has it been since we have allowed ourselves to rejoice in a beautiful woman? How long has it been since we have allowed ourselves to tip back our head, to break the crisp morning air with a heartfelt wolf whistle, to follow our fancy, trotting just beside that gorgeous, big-haired brunette headed in the opposite direction of our office? Be honest with yourself. How long has it really been? Two, maybe three days? This is a good indication that your priorities are out of order.

When we live and work in cities, or even when we don't, there are endless opportunities to appreciate the gifts Mother Nature has bestowed upon us. There are tall gifts and short gifts, blonde gifts and redheaded gifts. There are gifts that are built like brick shit houses. We must remember where our priorities truly lie. We must learn to look away from that computer screen and take in the miracles around us.

If we want to appreciate beauty more, we are going to have to work less.

**I long for the awareness to say, "Oh, what a glorious piece of ass."**

# FINANCIAL SECURITY

*I spend money on, what—snakes, guitars, and cars.*

Slash

It's okay to have money. It's best to have a lot of it if possible. In fact, no matter how much we have, it's never enough. Money, of course, is simply an abstract concept, but it can change into anything we desire: Porsches, imported Scotch, or state-of-the-art electronic equipment. Most important, though, money can buy leisure. Money means you can pay somebody else to shovel your walk, fix your car, paint your apartment, raise your kids, or even occupy your wife for an afternoon if there's a good football game on. Just tell her to go shopping. Women love that.

Of course, earning money is another matter. Actually working for the stuff can turn into a dangerous and frantic need to labor, accumulate, and hoard. A man may deny himself and his conscience in a lifelong, heedless pursuit of hollow capital gain, so it you can, arrange to inherit a fortune or, if you cannot, marry one.

**Financial security is okay as long as I don't have to work for it.**

# SERIOUSNESS/ RESPONSIBILITY/PRIORITIES

*I never go jogging, it makes me spill my martini.*

George Burns

Straighten that tie. Haul that ass. Get that job, because it's been six years since you earned a decent living. How many of these tapes play over and over again in our minds?

When we hear the negative inner voices or, more often, the negative outer ones nagging at us to get our act together, to grow up, to get serious, we can become tempted to chuck our carefully cultivated patterns of avoidance and become just like everybody else, productive and miserable.

Stop! Stop it right now! Smell those roses. Breathe in that fresh country air. Breathe in carbon monoxide fumes if you have to. Anything's better than becoming an activity addict.

There are only twenty-four hours in each day, and you've already spent half of them asleep. Do you want to spend the other half in a mind-deadening occupation? If you died tomorrow, would you regret that promotion you didn't get because you called in sick forty-seven times in six months, or would you regret that you never hit the road on that Harley you've always dreamed of, with that leggy blonde out of your wildest bondage fantasies clinging to your leather fringe?

**Which would you rather have for lunch, a hot dog or a hot hog? Set your priorities and stick to them. It's later than you think.**

# RISK TAKING

*I'm a Sagittarian . . . half man, half horse, with a license to shit
   in the streets.*

Keith Richards

Safety, boredom, monogamy. Sometimes I think they're all
one and the same. Crazy thinking tells us that if we take risks,
we will get caught, but that's our disease talking.

We can take risks. We can flirt with disaster, with danger,
with the babe in Purchasing. We can ride that untamed mechanical stallion at Cow Chip Charlie's. We don't fear reprisal. The
phone is broken at Cow Chip's, so how can she expect us to
call home?

If we weren't meant to drive any faster than 55 MPH, then
how come they make Mustangs that can hit 85 in 40.4 seconds
on a straightaway? Besides, the cops are mostly in Chevys, so
they can't catch you, and if they can't catch you, how are they
going to give you a ticket?

We can dance with the devil. We can dance with Linda and
Evelyn and Suzanne. We can live like outlaws, at least until last
call at Cow Chip's.

**I have courage, I have conviction, I have a damn good
lawyer.**

# IN TOUCH/AWARENESS/ LIVING IN THE MOMENT

*Hey, Rog, what's happening?*

Rerun

What's happening indeed? What's the scoop, the skivvy, the lowdown? Who's in, who's out, who has been benched for the season for having pine tar on his glove? When is Elway going to win a Super Bowl? Is Bud Dry really drier? How many Bon Jovi fans really did keep the faith?

Caught up in our dis-ease, we forget that there's a world going on out there while we're at work. Each day for eight hours plus, we're out of the loop. We don't know what's happening. We don't know who was on Arsenio last night. What's with Darryl Hannah and John-John? When did they take all the music videos off MTV? When did they start putting headlights on sneakers?

Let's face it, the world is a rapidly changing and complicated mosaic of events and personalities. It's a full-time job just keeping up with current events. Who has time to earn a living?

**I'd rather be in the swing than in a sling.**

# REPENTANCE/WISDOM

*To repent nothing is the beginning of wisdom.*

Ludwig Börne

Wouldn't it be boring if our lives were completely predictable? How tiresome to resolve each and every crisis right when it happens. Life's little surprises can be enlivening affirmations of existence.

Yet how easy it is to become resentful when old skeletons we have long ago shut in a closet and forgotten about suddenly resurface, rattling ancient bones. How unpleasant it can become when events that happened at a panty raid on a sorority house after twelve tequilas when we were twenty-seven suddenly resurface when we are forty, signaling us that they need to be worked through or, at the very least, compensated monetarily.

At moments of crisis like this I ask myself, Can I really believe my inner processes were responsible? I mean, after all, how could she have recognized me with a pair of panties over my head?

**There is something within me that knows more than I do. Hopefully, it won't tell anyone else.**

# CONTROL/ATTITUDE

*To be crazy is not necessarily to writhe in snake pits or converse with imaginary gods. It can sometimes be not knowing what to do in the morning.*

Christopher Lehman-Haupt

Slowly but surely we are recovering. We are learning to live one day at a time, to not expect too much of ourselves, to take life easy, to smell the dandelions. But sometimes, come nine-fifteen on a traffic-choked freeway, those old panic patterns set in.

I should've gotten up by 8:30 like I planned. It takes longer than twelve minutes to go twelve miles at rush hour. I should've finished writing that presentation I have to give this morning. Do I have the papers I need for the meeting? Did I leave them in that hotel room? What was her name again? She was over eighteen, wasn't she? Why won't this traffic move, for God's sake?

It's probably a bus. It's always a bus. There should be mandatory sentences for drivers who wreck their buses. They should get the chair for causing this kind of mayhem when people are trying to get to work on time. But they don't, they get a coffee break. The guy's probably standing there, having his coffee and doughnut. He doesn't have to get to work. He's at work. He's getting paid to stand there with his coffee and his Boston cream. He's laughing at me. He's dunking his doughnut and laughing at me.

**If I cannot control the world, how can they expect me to get to work on time?**

# EXPECTATIONS/FAILURES

*There is much to be said for failure. It is more interesting than success.*

Max Beerbohm

When we experience failure, this is usually a good indication that our goals were too high. Lower your expectations, preferably beneath what you know to be your level of achievement, and success is virtually guaranteed.

The fact is the world is a cutthroat, coldhearted place where nice guys usually finish last, so why plan on finishing at all? Why not run half the race, quit before you're winded, and join the babes in the stands watching the other schmucks limp through the finish line? When the race is over, all those babes are gonna be looking for some attention, attention that the guys who finished the race aren't going to be able to give them because they're too tuckered out from all that senseless race running.

Okay, so the egghead back in school who always ruined the grade curve, that jerk in Finance who always works until eight o'clock at night, and the brownnoser who sucks up to the boss instead of throwing bar dice with us real men is gonna run a better race come eight A.M. But what are they going to get for their efforts, ultimately? Bad knees and fallen arches.

**I'd rather do without the gain. I have a low threshold for pain, and I'm kind of fond of my arches.**

# DESPAIR/HOPELESSNESS

*Show me a good loser and I'll show you a loser.*

Jimmy Carter

Do you remember the day you hit bottom? It was raining, so you pulled out your umbrella, the cabana-size one with the fancy logo that you went to such pains to pinch from the VP of Finance at last year's Christmas party. And guess what? It leaked. All that trouble for a leaky umbrella.

That was the moment you realized that all your hard work and sacrifice would ultimately get you nowhere. The depths of despair were so low that you realized there was nowhere to go but up, and since you knew you weren't going there, you suddenly realized that there was nowhere to go at all.

That's when the sun came out. The clouds lifted, and the sky grew bright and blue. You pulled out the lawn chair of life, the suntan lotion of hope, cranked up the boom box of self-esteem, and basked in the sunshine of self-love. Having nowhere else to go, you began to live in the process. You accepted your powerlessness and forgave yourself for working all those years. You let despair dissipate into the stratosphere and bagged some serious rays.

**If the way to the top is uphill, I'll set up camp down here at the bottom.**

# UNIQUENESS/FEELING SPECIAL

*If there is such a thing as genius—which is what . . . what the fuck is it?—I am one, and if there isn't, I don't care.*

John Lennon

Am I normal? Am I crazy? Am I an overlooked genius who by some stroke of terrible luck got stuck with this job, this apartment, this hairline? What hidden wonders lie beneath my hair plugs?

Perhaps in a former life I was a great warrior, a dragon slayer, a pharaoh, or a lusty priest.

Perhaps in this life I am actually a slayer of hearts, even though nobody knows it yet. Maybe I am meant to be pursued by Kathy Ireland, Naomi Campbell, and Cindy Crawford all at once. It's only that they've never happened by the Starlight Lanes in Cincinnati on a Friday night and seen me in action.

Out of five billion human beings on this planet, there is only one me, perhaps because the world isn't big enough for two. My insights and opinions are worth as much as the next man's, probably even more. I could write a novel or not. I could host my own successful television talk show. Who knows what awesome destiny I am meant to fulfill.

**I'm special just because I'm me. My mom said so.**

# MATURITY/SOPHISTICATION

*I'm extremely careful. I've never turned blue in someone else's bathroom. I consider that the height of bad manners.*
Keith Richards

Face it, one man's sushi is another man's fish bait. So you'd much rather go have an egg in the skillet at the Short Stop than chateaubriand at Laffite's. So you'd rather watch football than have sex with your wife. So she insists you look stupid in leather fringe. She's not exactly Sharon Stone, either.

How often we are told that we're acting foolish, immature, or boorish because we don't fit someone else's narrow-minded definition of sophistication or maturity? But this is because we're rebels, unappreciated trailblazers who do not fear the disapproval of the cultural elite or the culturally bankrupt.

We know there's nothing worth watching on PBS. We know it doesn't matter what we eat or how we eat it; it all winds up in the same place eventually. Well, more or less. And hey, Road Runner is still the funniest damn thing on TV and we're not afraid to admit it.

**If my inner child says it's cool, it's cool. End of discussion.**

# HOSTING/BUSYNESS

*Every man likes the smell of his own farts.*

Icelandic proverb

Whenever I have visitors, I find myself so busy playing the good host that I forget to enjoy their company. I forget that they came over to see me, not to sit on a chair or drink beer out of a glass. This is unfortunate, because as I have neither furniture nor drinking glasses, sometimes I can get to feeling pretty bad about my hospitality.

I've got to remember that being close to somebody means letting them feel right at home. That's why I've started to allow Mom to stop by and clean the oven, as long as she closes the kitchen door while she's going it, because those fumes can be carcinogenic and cause birth defects in future generations. Mom's already had all her kids, but she ought to be more considerate about my reproductive capabilities. After all, I'm still a young man.

I can hear her murmuring to herself contentedly, and when she emerges, flushed with enthusiasm, I know she's pleased that I've given her the chance to express her love for me and to be at home in my world.

**Next month, maybe I'll give her a big kick and rent a carpet steam cleaner. I'll probably have to get a hotel room for myself that weekend, though. Those things are known to cause tumors in lab rats.**

# BALANCE/RESPONSIBILITIES

*I have a tendency to get really drunk and then I get to the hotel and I'll pick the first chick that I can get. . . . You'd be surprised at some of the chicks I've picked up. . . . What you do is you go up to the room and just drink till they look good.*

Slash

Okay, okay, so I screwed up. It's not like I meant to call her Anne instead of Shirley. It just slipped out. And it's not like I intentionally forgot to bring a condom. So I forgot to mention that I'm married. It's an understandable omission, given the heat of the moment.

What can I say? I'm a whimsical, impetuous kind of a guy. I'm fun loving and free. I'm a live wire.

So occasionally I slip up on the minor details. I forget to cross my *t*'s and dot my *i*'s. I miss a few deadlines and cut a few corners when it comes to annoying details like health, hygiene, income taxes, and federal regulations governing the use of controlled substances. I'm worth it.

**I'd rather be fun than done.**

# TRAVEL

*A good traveler is one who does not know where he is going.*
                                                          Lin Yutang


What a thrill it is when the world stretches before us like an open highway! What a sensation to go where no man has gone before, or at least never when he was sober.

Men are born explorers. Women sometimes think that they are explorers, too, but it is best to discourage them from subscribing to this theory because they may get ideas about coming along and spoiling the fun.

Our explorations take many forms. We may take a road trip across town to the new go-go joint on the county line. We may test the limits of our boss's patience or the grace period on our auto insurance.

Whatever the territory, we Men Who Do Next to Nothing must not shrink from boldly probing into unknown nooks and crannies.

**If Columbus had listened to his wife and gotten a real job, he never would have discovered America.**

# BEAUTY

*When I'm in the studio and I'm creating beauty, I'm six foot*
*nine and look like Cary Grant. And then I see that reduced*
*to this nebbishy little guy with a double chin.*

Billy Joel

When I get to feeling badly about my success with the babes,
I remind myself that Christie Brinkley married Billy Joel. She
has great legs. I try to imagine myself surrounded by legs: long
legs; short legs; legs with chubby knees connected to ripe,
fleshy little thighs; or bony knees, blending gracefully into
long, lush thighs that seem to go all the way up to her belly button . . . and beyond. . . .

I usually start to feel a lot better when I realize that legs are
a large part of my life. Not only the gams on the babe in the
Purchasing department but other gams, on other babes, in other
departments, in other buildings, in other cities all across the
country.

When I get discouraged, I remind myself that there is beauty before, behind, below, and if I'm lucky, even above me.

**Boots were made for more than just walking.**

# TRUTH

*Pay no attention to the truth.*

Jules Renard

We live in a dishonest society. Everybody lies: politicians, businessmen, the bartender who says he's out of those little pigs in blankets even though Happy Hour is only half over. In business, in politics, and in bars, it seems the successful communicator is the one who can talk the best game, regardless of whether or not he's telling the truth. The prize goes to the best bullshitter.

Clearly, our world is more concerned with winning than truth telling, and as Men Who Do Next to Nothing, we have learned that to try to fight fairly, to point out that we should have been alerted to the pigs in blankets shortage before being poured our fourth Johnnie Walker, gets us nowhere. Still, we argue with ourselves until we are so exhausted that we cannot stay awake long enough to catch *Muffy Goes to Boarding School* on the Playboy channel. Maybe we should learn that in this world we are going to have to bend a little, and if a guy twice our size tells us he's out of pigs in blankets, we're just going to have to settle for a chili dog at Cow Chip Charlie's.

**The truth hurts, but so does Scotch on an empty stomach.**

# SECRETS

*No one needs to know anything.*

Jean Paul

The 12 Step program teaches that we are as sick as the secrets we keep. Secrets are like an acid eating away at ourselves and our relationships. When we keep a secret we sacrifice a piece of ourselves, and ultimately we are devoured, thread by thread, very much like an edible sheet.

An essential ingredient of recovery is to give up our secrets and live our lives in the open. Let your neighbors see you sleeping in the hammock at noon on a Tuesday. Those sneers are probably just because they're jealous. Let them see you taking a leak in your bushes. It's your hedge, and it looks damn healthy. Let your lawn grow. Don't shave. Don't change your shirt for a week. Refuse to shower. These are the outer manifestations of the inner man and should be displayed proudly like a medal of honor, not hidden beneath a well-manicured exterior, cowering beneath layers of pima cotton and Aramis for men.

**The French say, "He who eats sheets before bedtime wakes up with cotton mouth."**

# SATISFACTION

*I can't hardly sing, you know what I mean? I'm no Tom Jones
and I don't give a fuck.*

Mick Jagger

Sometimes satisfaction seems unattainable. Yet to be satisfied with ourselves is like a warm Jacuzzi with the jets angled just so. It is so peaceful and cleansing to be truly content with who we are and where we are at this moment.

Often, we equate contentment and satisfaction with stagnation. This is absolutely true, and when this occurs to us we must congratulate ourselves for being on the right track.

After all, which is more peaceful, a still pond or a rushing stream? Can anything truly be said to grow in white water? Can fish eat lunch in it?

Satisfaction is a stagnant pond of quietude, a lunch break from the rapids of life, but it gets kind of crowded at the noon hour, so make your reservations early.

**Men, like algae, flourish in standing water.**

# MALE BONDING

*One's friends are that part of the human race with which one
can be human.*

George Santayana

One of the devastating consequences of the constant and
hectic froth of activity in our lives is that we have less and less
contact with our friends. Friendship is a time for letting our hair
down, for reveling in the differences and similarities that have
drawn and kept us together. Friendship is a time to remember
common histories and to be young bucks frolicking in the fields
once more.

When did you last spend time with a friend? Can you even
remember the last time you went to a hot-oil wrestling match
or hung out on a street corner with a pal, smoking cigarettes
and discussing automobiles, women, and condom sizes, not
necessarily in that order?

What a shame that as employed adults we have placed work
over friendship and have come to treat our friends the way our
wives treat us—kind of like stale bread that we haven't gotten
around to making into croutons yet.

**Strike a blow for brotherhood. Organize a circle jerk.**

# WONDER

*He's intercepted the ball at the forty-five-yard line. He's bro-*
*ken away, ten, thirty, forty-five yards for the touchdown.*
*He's really earned his twelve point five million today.*
                                                      John Madden


I hear the above passage, and I feel lost in wonder at the beauty of athletic competition. As I listen, I envision a brisk fall afternoon, cold beer, and bleachers. I can hear the roar of the crowd and glimpse the cartwheeling cheerleaders in those cute little pleated numbers, with their thighs pink from the cold, straining against gravity as they hurl themselves heavenward; up and up they go, along with their skirts and those cute little cropped sweaters that play peekaboo with me and everyone else in the first four rows.

I wonder at the grace and command of the quarterback, the salaries these guys make, and all the poontang they must nail.

At moments like this, the workaday world seems far away, which is where it belongs.

**Wonder is a gift of real living—real living is a gift of the NFL.**

# SELF-LOVE

*Self-love, my liege, is not so vile a sin as self-neglecting.*
William Shakespeare

We are so accustomed to doing what others want us to do, or doing what is right, or doing what earns us money, that we have lost touch with our inner selves. We have grown so used to listening to the "shoulds" that we can no longer hear the "would if we coulds." In the fight to meet our responsibilities, we have stopped knowing ourselves. We have denied our own needs and have come down with such a severe case of blue balls that we may never recover.

Imagine starting each day with the question, "What would I do today if I could?" What would be your answer? I'll give you a hint. It probably has nothing to do with getting out of bed and going to work. Just as an exercise, try shutting off that alarm clock. Try missing the 8:07. Try out that new pair of chamois gloves the girlfriend got you for Christmas.

Try to visualize what your inner self is saying. If you're like the rest of us Men Who Do Next to Nothing, it's probably saying, "Jeez, why didn't I think of these gloves before?"

**Do they make Playtex gloves for men?**

# SELF-ESTEEM/SELF-ABUSE

*Of course we revel in our own fucking genius. Why the hell
    not? Self-indulgence is what we're full of and we're proud
    of it.*

Johnny Rotten (Lydon)

Our feelings of unworthiness often lead us to abuse ourselves. One of the most common forms of self-abuse is work.
Another is marriage. Many Men Who Do Next to Nothing are
beginning to see that it is abusive to the self to keep so busy that
we have no time to experience those things in life that make us
feel good, like forests, or sunsets, or wet T-shirt nights at the
Hell Hole.

It is abusive to the self to be so busy taking care of others that
we neglect our own needs. And when we are unkind to ourselves it is inevitable that we will be unkind to others, which is
an excellent argument for not visiting your in-laws. Try it out
next Thanksgiving.

**Although self-abuse is okay for some people, I do not
believe that it is right for me.**

# HELPLESSNESS

*Sitting is better than standing, lying is better than sitting.*

Indian proverb

Me? Helpless? An empty skid on the loading dock of life? You bet! Is this bad? I don't think so. I know that when I struggle to achieve and succeed, I feel ragged around the edges, my personal life takes a beating, and all I end up with for my pains is a paycheck eaten up by the government, interest payments, and dial 900-HOT-BABE.

Maybe I need to accept my helplessness, my utter lack of control over my own success or failure, and realize that if my life does need something, it'll turn up eventually, and if it doesn't, I probably didn't need it anyway.

**Just finding a reason to get up in the morning is enough of a challenge. What was that 900 number again?**

# INTIMACY/ISOLATION

*If it weren't for pickpockets I'd have no sex life.*
                                            Rodney Dangerfield

Human beings were not made to live in isolation. If we were, there would be no such thing as stadium concerts with festival seating. I like to get close, real close, to my fellow human beings. Women, I mean. I find that a bus at rush hour is a great place to achieve intimacy. So they usually don't look as good as Barbara Dare, but they have one thing going for them. They're three-dimensional.

It's just not enough to watch all the time. Sometimes I have to get involved, as long as that involvement is confined to the eight-block stint on the crosstown express.

**I deserve a soul mate. I deserve two. Preferably at the same time.**

# NEEDS/DESIRES

*I've looked on a lot of women with lust.*

Jimmy Carter

Have you ever heard a fog horn? It's that low and mournful sound, penetrating the mist, leading blind ships ashore. For me, that baritone wail sounds the depths of despair and puts me in mind of the desolation of the human heart when it hasn't gotten laid in a month and a half.

When I feel despairing and alone, caught in the heavy grayness of my existence, I find that duplicating the sounds of the fog horn can lead me safely to shore. I groan, I whine, I howl into the night, and before you know it, light appears in the midst of my murkiness, red flashing lights, coming to find out who is making all the racket in 2B.

**In the stillness I can hear the sound of my needs demanding to be met. So can my neighbors.**

# FEAR

*A man who has learned not to feel fear will find the fatigue of daily life enormously diminished.*

Bertrand Russell

Fear is often the first link in a chain of emotions that can lead to activity. Fear can make us do all sorts of exhausting things. Fear makes us put our tails between our legs or hang our heads in shame. A final warning at work leads us at last to write up those reports that were due six months ago. An ultimatum from our wife or girlfriend spurs us to run to the nearest jeweler and pop for some overpriced bauble. All needless, fear-motivated activity.

We must learn to suppress our fears before they lead us to actions that embarrass us. When we feel that familiar knot beginning to form in the pit of our stomach, we must ignore it and wait for it to go away. It's bound to eventually. And if it doesn't, pound a fistful of Tums and forget about it.

**What's wrong with repression? It works.**

# EXPECTATIONS

*Blessed is the man who expects nothing, for he shall never be
disappointed.*

Alexander Pope

Expectations are the worst! They are setups for disappointment and misunderstanding, particularly when other people are expecting something from us.

Many a pleasant evening has been sacrificed at the altar of expectation. Remember last Friday night when you took that fox from Purchasing out for Chinese, after which you expected to take her home and test out your edible sheets, but before this she expected to discuss the future of your relationship? What was the result? Disappointment? Misunderstanding? Certainly nobody was biting any sheets that night.

Be alert to the dangers of expectations. The next time she expects a relationship, or even dinner, explain to her that expectations are an illusion of control, which ought to be stamped out before being allowed to screw up another Friday night.

**When we are tied to expectations, we usually don't get laid. Besides, who needs dinner when you've got edible sheets?**

# NATURE/MASCULINITY

*Like, peace and love, motherfucker, or you're gonna die! I'm gonna kick your ass if you fuck with my garden.*

Axl Rose

Deep down inside each of us is a wild man, a guttural, visceral, irascible being who if turned loose would call in sick tomorrow morning and see who is on *Live with Regis & Kathie Lee*.

Who is this wild man, this virile beast within, who bays at the moon and at girls wearing those thong things? Could this possibly be me? God, I hope so.

Imagine a world where your wild man can roam free as the tide, where you don't have to hide, where you can live as free as the wind, unfettered by the expectations of others, or condoms. Imagine a world where beauty surrounds you, where women take you to dinner and then expect something in return. Imagine that you are born free.

**Wild men, like lions, need nothing more than a grassy knoll and a large plain tree to be utterly fulfilled.**

# FREEDOM

*Bo bo bo b'do bo . . .*

The Cream

Addiction to activity is a progressive disease, which, if allowed to fester unattended, can rob us of our reason and even our enjoyment of life. We begin innocently enough, changing a light bulb, mending a roof leak, and the next thing we know projects like cleaning the gunk caked up around the base of the toilet or scrubbing petrified bits of food clinging to the walls of the sink begin to suggest themselves. Consider this: Would we have even seen the gunk or the petrified bits if we had not changed that light bulb in the first place?

We must embrace the freedom that exists in the semidarkness. We must recognize the inherent threat to our being in that first step toward doing. We must cast off the chains of guilt and duty that bind us and recognize that we are free men, if we choose to be.

**Freedom's just another word for nothing left to do.**

# ACTION

*He who acts, spoils; he who grasps, lets slip.*

Lao-tse

If there is anything we Men Who Do Next to Nothing have learned in our recovery, it's how to avoid getting things done. We have become experts at avoidance. We have an unswerving instinct for looking in the opposite direction whenever things need to be done. It's a way of life and one we are proud of.

Sometimes, though, we forget to celebrate how important our practical, everyday avoidances are. We long for some monumental task to shirk, some huge, all-important oversight. Yet our lives are made up of ordinary chores that need to be ignored: getting to work every morning, paying the bills, fixing the furnace. These common, routine avoidances can seem small and insignificant, yet they are not as meaningless as they might seem, as you will find out next winter, so we must remember to recognize them.

**If they cut off my heat, my pipes will burst, which means I won't have to bathe anymore. There is a positive side to everything, if we look in the right place.**

# FOOLISH BEHAVIOR

*A fool has a fine world.*

Yiddish proverb

The harder we strive to avoid working, the more flak we take from the unenlightened majority who actually think that work is important. We Men Who Do Next to Nothing know that although the grasshopper and the ant lead very different lives—one a creature of leisure, the other a creature of endless toil—they come to the same end, either squashed under somebody's boot or fried by a kid with a magnifying glass. So why work so hard? Why work at all?

So some people call us fools. Why? Because we don't have a six-figure salary, a stock portfolio, or furniture in our apartment? But while we're gorging on Little Debbie cakes and perusing the new swimsuit edition, what are all those wise guys doing? They're working. So we must ask ourselves: Who is the fool, and who is the wise man?

**What good is furniture if you're too busy to sit on it?**

# COMPETITION

*Nice guys finish last.*

Leo Durocher

May the best man win. Sounds fair, unless of course you're not the best man. What if you're the second-best guy, or the third or the fourth? What if you're not even in the wedding party?

What if we don't have an uncle on the board of directors, a friend who is sleeping with the professor, or a girlfriend with a mortgage? What if we are underemployed? What if, in the race of life, we are saddled with lead Nikes?

The point is, when we stop worrying about winning races, these things don't matter. We no longer have to compare ourselves with that jerk down the hall who takes his girlfriend to the Bahamas twice a year and still has enough left over to not only pay rent, but purchase Minoxidil on a regular basis.

Besides, we've got a lot to offer when we think about it. How about that belching thing or our 10 percent employee discount on recreational rifles? That's pretty good.

**I'm doing the best I can, and that's all that really matters.**

# PROCESS

*I can't be forced to do anything.*

Sid Vicious

Process. I instinctively cringe when I hear that word. I imagine myself plodding along in endless toil toward some long-term abstract goal, like death.

But process is simply a term for the way we do things, like washing only the tops of our dinner plates. I mean, that's the side you eat off of, right? Why wash the bottoms? Or like walking the dog at night so you don't have to scoop the poop. What are they gonna do? Dust for fingerprints?

When our processes help us save time, money, or, more important, precious personal energy resources, they are invaluable. Take a moment today to cut a new corner. Drink straight from the milk carton of life and leave the refrigerator door open while you're doing it.

**The shortest distance between two points is usually a creative maneuver, best done out of the sight of a police officer.**

# PURPOSE/MEANING/
# FEELING NEEDED

*Act if you like, but do it at your peril.*

Ralph Waldo Emerson

So often the world places a high premium on being needed, being useful, and having a purpose. Things that do not meet these rigid criteria are tossed away, dismissed, discarded, donated to a local charity, or left to languish in the back of the fridge until they ferment into food for cockroaches—unless your ex-mother-in-law decides to come over for dinner, in which case you'll cut off the blue stuff and serve it to her on toast.

Are we to become fodder for lower life forms before our time? No! This is why it is so very important to keep breathing and have a detectable pulse at all times, even when in a turkey-and-football coma.

We must also remember that life is its own justification. Like the cockroach, we are our own very special link in the food chain, and it's going to take more than boric acid to stop us from following our natural instincts.

**Between the past and the present, I am the missing link.**

# EMPTINESS

*B'deeya, b'deeya, b', that's all, folks!*

Porky Pig

We all remember, don't we? That terrible moment when we looked around and realized, This is it. This is the end of the road, the final frontier, the whole shooting match. This is my life, my home, my woman, my inferior stereo system. This is all I'll ever be, do, have, and let's face it, it's been a downhill slide since high school. I'm just another nobody, a dust mote in the cosmic scheme of things, a zero, a bum, a loser.

But then it hit us, didn't it? Like a blast of fresh air on a clear adolescent autumn afternoon with a dog and a brew and a whole squad of sweet-thighed high school cheerleaders crying out our name 'cause we just aced the big game against those meatballs from Central.

In that moment of despair, we suddenly remembered that the new Kim Basinger movie is on HBO in twenty minutes and that Domino's Pizza delivers.

**Attitude adjustment is a lot easier than life adjustment.**

# DISAPPOINTMENT

*Have the neighborhood kids been right all along? Am I truly*
*nothing?*

Al Bundy

Disappointment. Remorse. Regret for the roads not taken.
When these feelings of sadness and insecurity overwhelm us,
we begin to reassess the decisions we have made in life and to
reflect upon what might have been had we chosen differently.

Maybe it is a good idea to really experience the depth of
regret lying fallow in our stagnant minds. Maybe we ought to
lie down to get the full effect. Once we are lying down, though,
and the couch pillow is supporting our neck just so, holding our
gaze in perfect alignment with the fifty-yard line while main-
taining our mouth at enough of an angle to be able to sip out of
a can without raising our head, we feel validated. We remember why we have chosen to be Men Who Do Next to Nothing
and remember, too, that regret is something that women invented to make men go to work every day.

As we let ourselves experience our grief and pain, particularly when we experience it at a 180-degree angle, it all begins
to feel like something else, something along the lines of eupho-
ria.

**When life gets you down, lie down. What's the point in**
**fighting gravity?**

# CONTENTMENT

*We are happy from possessing what we like, not from possessing what others like.*

La Rochefoucauld

Happiness is an elusive and spontaneous thing. Often we fool ourselves into thinking that if we had a better handle on our lives—if, for instance, we had a nice car, a better job, or some idea of how we were going to pay the rent next month—then we would be happy. Of course, when we actually do pay the rent we feel depressed because we've thrown all that money out the window for some cheap dump right next door to an old bat who calls the cops every time you turn up your stereo above level five. What a witch. Then we wonder why we can never feel contentment or happiness. We wonder where we have gone wrong.

The first mistake we made was in listening to the woman who told us that we'd feel better once we had a better job and could pay our bills. These material things don't bring us happiness. Happiness cannot be planned or purchased. Maybe it's time we begin to question the woman who taught us that possessions and power can bring us contentment. Maybe she owes us a six-pack for dishing out such rotten advice. Come to think of it, it may be the same woman who keeps calling the cops. Something should be done about her.

**Happiness comes from within, and occasionally from Anheuser-Busch.**

# SUCCESS

*Success has ruined many a man.*

Benjamin Franklin

Perhaps it isn't success itself but the way in which we define it that causes us so many problems. If we define success as having a job, a house, or a car with a functional transmission, then we are bound to feel like losers.

If, on the other hand, we say that success is the ability to live healthy, contented lives, or if, for instance, we define success as getting through a day without suffocating or getting mugged on the subway, how much more comfortable would we be with ourselves?

Starting today, I'm going to learn to be happy with each and every accomplishment and reward myself accordingly. When I wake up and get out of bed tomorrow, first I'm going to congratulate myself and then, as a reward, I'm going to lie right back down. I could go on like that for weeks.

**I am as successful as I think I am.**

# TRAVEL

*The soul of a journey is liberty . . .*

William Hazlitt

One of our strong points as Men Who Do Next to Nothing is our understanding of the value of vacations in the process of recovery. Vacations mean a break in routine, a time of rest and renewal, a time to pamper ourselves. When we travel, we open ourselves up to new experiences, new women, new athletic teams, and different kinds of beers on tap. The change in scenery vacuums out the cobwebs of monotony, restores our spirit, and makes us feel brand spanking new. Which reminds me of that weekend in Tijuana. But that was a different kind of spanking, although I did feel new afterward.

How sad that we must relegate this expansive experience to a mere two weeks out of each year. How weary and irritable we become with the dull routine of our lives. Perhaps it is time to ask ourselves some difficult questions. Isn't it time to look into taking a permanent vacation? Shouldn't we be looking into how unemployment benefits work? Couldn't we get by on her salary?

Vacations don't have to be expensive. Cerveza's dirt cheap in Tijuana.

**If I buy a case of Dos Equis, maybe I could have a vacation right here on my couch.**

# HIGHER POWER

*One with God is a majority.*

Adam Clayton Powell

How easy it is to forget that our Higher Power is always there to give us strength and courage. How else would we find the courage to say, "No! I will not go to the store just to buy toilet paper. If I can do without it, so can she!" Where else can we find the inner strength to say, "Yes! I like the grayish half-light created by the soot caked to my window, and I will not clean it off."

When we are in touch with our Higher Power, we see the Zen-like beauty in all things. Like that pile of old papers and empty Roach Motel boxes on top of the VCR. Is it garbage? Is it art? Certainly it's worth thinking about for a few more weeks.

When we are in touch with our Higher Power we know what we are about and can stand up to those who question our priorities, like our bosses, who place budget meetings over office football pools, or our friends, who think we should pay them the fifty bucks we owe them before springing for a new pair of Ray-Bans.

When we are truly one with our Higher Power, we are at peace, we are cool, we are credible, and best of all we are probably unemployed.

**I wouldn't want to mess with God's will.**

# LONELINESS

*Solitude would be ideal if you could pick the people to avoid.*
                                                        Karl Kraus

It's funny, but even when we are surrounded by people, we can find ourselves feeling alone, separated from the rest of mankind, out of place, and out of the loop.

We need to share special moments of connection with others. We need to feel we are not alone in thinking there's a big difference between Miller Lite and Genuine Draft. We need to know that someone else thinks the "Trouble with Tribbles" *Star Trek* episode is overrated. We need to be comforted that someone else understands the devastating ramifications of instant replay and truly needs his MTV.

When we feel lonely we must reach out. Wouldn't it be nice to share our most intimate thoughts with that hot A&P checkout girl with the awesome pair of cupcakes?

Today, I will not dwell on my feelings of aloneness. I will make new friends and keep the old, for one is silver and the other gold.

**Reach out and touch someone. Just be sure you can't get arrested for it.**

# TOIL

*[W]e have toiled all the night, and have taken nothing. . . .*
Luke 5:5

This quotation is so aptly reflective of the ultimate emptiness of the oppressive system of enforced labor in which we live. It is a system subtly imposed by women and one we have learned to conform to in order to get laid.

This is not reality, it is a conspiracy, perpetrated by workaholic women and perpetuated by us helpless addicts who would do anything in exchange for the wild thing.

Fortunately, if we are courageous, there are other options. and not all of them cause blindness.

**One in the hand is worth two in the office.**

# HOUSEWORK

*A good housewife is of necessity a humbug.*

W. M. Thackeray

They say there are two inevitabilities in life: death and taxes. Taxes, though, are easily avoided—just refuse to work. And death doesn't worry me much because it only happens once, and it doesn't cost money. But there is a third inevitable curse that they habitually forget to mention: housework.

No matter how many times you clean, you always have to do it again. As an experiment, I tried to get around the fruitlessness of housework by living nude in an empty apartment and eating all my meals out. But one morning, lying naked on the floor in my sanctuary, I saw it—dust on my baseboards, dust on my light fixtures, dust on the floors and windowsills. There was even dust on me. That fateful morning I realized that no matter where you go, there is always going to be dust. There is no lint-free corner to retreat to, no place where you are completely safe from housework.

That is the day I decided to move in with my girlfriend.

**A woman's work is never done, so what difference will a few more loads of laundry make?**

# CHANGE

*I can't change the laws of physics, Captain.*

Scotty

I must accept that no matter how hard I try, some things will never change. In fact, most things won't. My salary, for instance, my future prospects, that rattling in the radiator of my Pontiac, male-pattern balding. It's a discouraging list.

Of course another thing I can't change is that some things are going to change, like my marital status, which has proved extremely mercurial, as has my place of employment. My TRS report is in constant flux. Sometimes nightmares that look just like good opportunities come my way and change my bank balance.

Let's face it: changing or not changing, it's all one giant, miasmic, disastrous, infinitely collapsible world in which a guy is better off just grabbing a pillow and ducking for cover.

**If opportunity knocks, don't answer the door. Let her get it.**

# POWER

*Power without abuse loses its charm.*

Paul Valéry

As we begin to recover, to get in touch with our true selves and to accept who we genuinely are, we begin to get the idea that we may in fact be all-powerful beings.

We begin to sense that awesome power first in relation to others, like when we scream at our families, neighbors, co-workers, or employers. Next we are screaming at whole teams of guys much larger than us on the television, and soon we are screaming at large institutions, like the Department of Motor Vehicles, or the Office of Unemployment, or even the entire U.S. government, but usually only over the telephone. The government can't afford caller ID.

Gradually we begin to feel that power glowing and radiating within ourselves. We uncover the Spartan warrior within us, standing our ground at Thermopylae, combing our luxuriant locks in calm defiance of the invading Athenians. We flex, we grimace, we don't change our underwear for a week.

**Today, I will assert my power. After all, I'm a taxpayer. At least in theory.**

# RELATIONSHIPS/
# COMMITMENTS

*Promises and pie-crust are made to be broken.*

Jonathan Swift

Our fathers thought they had it all figured out. Get a good job, and you get a good woman. Take care of her financially, and she'll take care of you physically and emotionally. What this amounts to is that for a little chicken soup during flu season, clean shirts, and an occasional (very occasional, to hear my father tell it) afternoon quickie, our fathers allowed themselves to become success objects.

We modern Men Who Do Next to Nothing have other options. Modern morality makes it possible for us to escape the success trap. People live with each other now before getting married; women work. These new advances in gender relations can be used to our advantage. There are women out there who, in exchange for an occasional Hallmark card and a few vague references to future commitment, will contribute to our lives not only emotionally and physically, but financially as well.

**Never say "I do" when you can get away with "I might."**

# CONFUSION

*Lack of understanding is a great power. Sometimes, it enables
    men to conquer the world.*

Anatole France

So often, we Men Who Do Next to Nothing are expected to
be rational. Yet so much of our life just doesn't make sense.
When we struggle for logic and clarity, we get confused and
irritable. We become the kind of man who kicks small animals,
becomes a nuisance at cocktail parties, and demands to know
things like how bombs can be called peacekeepers or what the
purpose of monogamy is in an overpopulated world.

In our recovery, we have learned that no matter how hard we
try, nothing is going to make sense. We can't understand
what's going on because invariably women are involved somewhere in the process, and they remain one of life's eternal rid-
dles.

**If you don't know an answer, skip it and go on to the next
question.**

# COURTESY

*Good manners are made up of petty sacrifices.*
Ralph Waldo Emerson

We Men Who Do Next to Nothing are constantly feeling the pressure to be nice, to be courteous, to mind our manners and do our fair share. Many of us have given in to this restrictive mandate and have experimented with politeness. We found out that being polite is not only dishonest and detrimental to our recovery, but a lot of unnecessary effort that doesn't pay off in the long run.

Those of us trying to get clearer with ourselves must face the fact that courtesy is a deception. Real men don't really say "Excuse me." They don't write thank-you notes. They don't volunteer to help with the dishes. They don't get up and leave the room when they have to fart. So why lie to ourselves and those close to us?

**If we want to be honest with ourselves and others, we have to be willing to let go of niceness along with excess intestinal gas.**

# COMPARISON

*Comparisons are always odious and ill taken.*
Miguel de Cervantes

How beautiful and joyful it is to accept ourselves the way that we truly are. How sad that women so often have difficulty appreciating the purity of our visceral selves. How unfortunate that they must always compare us with others, like Arnold Schwarzenegger, Donald Trump, or the guy next door with a full-time job.

Held to impossibly high standards, of course we don't measure up. We are too short, too tall, too fat, too passive, too underemployed. But to compare human beings is to miss out on the unique splendor of each individual. Who else could name from memory every RBI in Babe Ruth's final season? And not just anybody could drink forty-seven kamikazes without blowing chunks. All these are indeed special gifts.

**Imagine a day—today, for example—when you express your unique splendor and are appreciated. Go ahead, demonstrate that trick with the shot glass and the condom.**

# UNITY/ONENESS

*All for one, one for all.*

Alexandre Dumas

Part of our disease is thinking that it is up to us to do something about our situation in life and that we are all alone in a cold and unfriendly universe. What a relief to reassure ourselves that our Higher Power, our wife, or some significant other is there to take control and sort out our dirty from our clean, our whites from our brights, our dry cleaning from our hand washables. What a serene pleasure to know that we just have to sit back and let it happen.

When we recognize that the forces outside of ourselves are actually much better at this sort of thing than the force within, we begin to heal. When a man realizes that his mate is merely an extension of himself, a more capable extension that never fades his colors, then he can sit back, turn the showerhead to massage, and revel in the unity of the universe.

Healing is the experience of the oneness of all things. Therefore, in a unified universe, my mate is the same as myself, so if she goes to work, then so do I, even though I'm at the arcade playing air hockey.

**What is mine is hers, so let her wash it.**

# FEELINGS

*Feel slightly, think little, never plan.*

Benjamin Disraeli

So often we are told that we must express our feelings in order to be modern men. This is a twofold dilemma. First, we must actually have these feelings, and then, as if that weren't enough, we are supposed to talk about them.

At the urging of our significant others, we have attended weekend seminars, therapy sessions, relationship classes, couples retreats, and 12 Step meetings. We've tried to tap into, get in touch with, embrace, cherish, and communicate our innermost feelings. Why is it at these times we are unable to communicate that the strongest emotion we feel is irritation that we must get in touch with deep-seated emotions we don't have?

This is a lot of effort in the service of self-deception. Today, if someone asks you "How are you feeling?" tell them you are feeling absolutely nothing. Even if this isn't entirely true, insist upon it anyway. You'll save a fortune in therapy bills and keep your weekends free for the only effective mental medicine yet invented, Saturday afternoon football and a case of Bud.

**Denial ain't just a river in Egypt.**

# TRANSITION/STABILITY

*Any very great and sudden change is death.*

Samuel Butler

There is no hiding from the fact that transition is traumatic. Change feels like a direct, personal attack because, very often, it is.

Remember last week when your favorite plaid velour chair that you've loved ever since you stole it from outside Vito's Calzone King to put in your dorm room had simply vanished? And for what reason? Because she thinks it's ugly? Because she doesn't care if it is comfortable, it still clashes with the carpet? Because she's got connections down at the Salvation Army and can get next day, curbside pickup service?

No! It's because you moved in with your girlfriend. You changed your place of residence. It's because change means movement, transformation, readjustment. Change means work, and work means getting up out of that favorite chair, leaving it vulnerable to diabolical designers who would color-coordinate your comfort right out of existence.

**If it isn't broken, don't fix it. In fact, even if it is broken, don't bother. It's fine the way it is.**

# SECRETS

*He who tells the truth should have one foot in the stirrup.*
                                                    Arab proverb

Our current culture instructs us that only total honesty will pave the way to intimacy. This is because the culture is currently being manipulated by women who don't know what's good for them.

They don't really want to know where you were last Wednesday night. And when she asks you if you think she's getting fat, there's only one right answer.

Let's face it, truth is not always the best solution. If women were really being honest with us and themselves, they wouldn't ask questions that they already know the answers to just to trick us into saying something that's going to make them feel morally justified in withholding sex for two weeks.

In reality, confessions are best entrusted to priests, bartenders, and, if a large payment is involved, the tabloids. After all, if you're rich, you can buy intimacy.

**I refuse to answer on the grounds that I may incriminate myself.**

# WORK/RELATIONSHIPS

*Work is the curse of the drinking classes.*

Oscar Wilde

Why are women always objectifying things? Why do they make so many demands on us? And what is all this nonsense about relationships being work? I mean, every time you see her lately she has another reference to some form of enforced relationship labor, and she was the one who insisted on calling what was a perfectly good casual fling a relationship in the first place. There's emotional work, personal work, inner work. There's work to share more of yourself, express your inner feelings. There's being-somewhat-less-of-a-lazy-son-of-a-bitch-and-get-up-off-the-couch-while-you're-at-it-and-vacuum-something work and, of course, the ever-popular you-should-appreciate-me-more work.

This is not what you planned on when you caught that first look at her in Purchasing and asked her out for Chinese. This was not what you went through twelve pairs of edible sheets for. If you wanted to work, you would have kept your job. At least you got paid twice a month and had your weekends and holidays free.

**If a relationship was meant to be work, they'd have to pay you to be in one.**

# ENTHUSIASM

*Enthusiasm is very wearing.*

Robert Louis Stevenson

Several weeks ago, I made a fundamental decision for myself. I decided that I would do only work that I was enthusiastic about. Since then I have been unemployed.

I was a barrel reamer in a munitions plant then. I decided not to ream any barrels about which I was unenthusiastic. I would not put in any hours, sweep any metal shavings, or oil any pistons just because of the money.

I resolved that I would only do things that put me in touch with myself, like reading magazines in the men's room, or watching the babe in Purchasing bend over to pick up the pencils I dropped by her desk. After I got fired, I decided to devote myself exclusively to those things that seemed related to the meaning and purpose of my life, like watching television or judging bikini contests or napping frequently.

**I feared I would end up a derelict. I feared I would starve. Thank goodness she has a job.**

# ATTITUDE/PERCEPTION

*We don't give a shit about inner attitude, just as long as it sounds good.*

Johnny Rotten (Lydon)

I have spent the major portion of my life feeling like an empty bucket, a skinny pig, a barren field, a troutless stream. In fact, for most of my adult life, a good chunk of my childhood, and all of my adolescence, I've felt completely auxiliary to life.

Fortunately, adulthood has brought its compensations. Whenever I find myself feeling empty, I remind myself I'm alive by throwing a temper tantrum. I find these outbursts to be a valuable release that rids me of excess emotional gas. And there's always something handy to get irate about: the leaky bathroom faucet, the pants your girlfriend didn't pick up at the cleaners, the price of tea in China.

After an explosion I feel valued, I feel feared, and best of all, I feel that good kind of tired.

**I'm not really empty. Even my girlfriend tells me I'm full of it.**

# LOVE/FORGIVENESS

*Love means not ever having to say you're sorry.*
Erich Segal, *Love Story*

I like to think of love as one giant eraser, rubbing out all the suffering, sorrow, and ugliness between people.

When you love someone you see their scars as stars and rub until the beautiful surface that lies beneath the emotional scribbling of pain, shame, and blame shines through and you can see your own reflection. Like a weathered barn, a smooth piece of driftwood, a kitchen counter with perfect ring-shaped coffee stains, love makes everything seem beautiful.

I tried to explain this to my roommate last month when my rent check bounced, but unfortunately, to her, love is an indelible marker, you know, the kind that not even all-temperature Cheer or a nuclear holocaust can wipe out, so my love eraser didn't stand much of a chance.

I stood my ground. I told her that someone who really loved me would accept me for who I am, rubber checks and all. They would accept my inner child, my innocence, and my bad credit rating, but all she would accept was my key and a promise to have my things out by Monday.

**I forgive myself for my past. I'm sure others will forgive me, too, and if they don't, I can move cross country, grow a beard, and get an unlisted phone number.**

# CARETAKING/PROVIDING

*You'll be lucky to save your own ass, let alone somebody else's.*
Axl Rose

In our diseased families of origin, we were told to eat our spinach and to drink our milk so we would grow up and be big strong men who could take care of our families. A fringe benefit, we were promised, was that we would be able to finally take care of the muscle-headed jerk on the beach who has been putting sand in our trunks since we were four.

Well, here we are, all grown up, and we aren't all Arnold Schwarzeneggers, are we? No. It all turned out to be just another deception, perpetrated by a generation of parents who all must have owned serious interest in the spinach industry.

As for taking care of our families, well, it's pretty hard to support a vice president of Purchasing in the style to which she is accustomed on a barrel reamer's salary. So I gave up.

I did cling to one goal, however. I am certain that with hard work and determination I can finally turn the tables on that muscle-headed jerk on the beach and dump a whole bucket full of sand down his trunks.

**I will break the intergenerational chain of unrealistic expectations. I will never again eat spinach, and I am boycotting Popeye.**

# IMPRESSION MANAGEMENT

*I despise making the most of one's time. Half of the pleasures
of life consist of the opportunities one has neglected.*

Oliver Wendell Holmes

I must. I should. I ought to. I damn well better. It's that
stinkin' thinkin' again, telling us we aren't real men unless we
behave like explorers or continent conquerors sailing the high
seas of adventure, or at least the high seas of minimum wage
employment.

That all sounds great on paper or in movies starring guys like
Mel Gibson, who would actually look good in one of those pert
little brimmed numbers with the red-and-white checkerboard
bands and the buttons that say "Have It Your Way."

Taking risks calls for energy, a steel will, and good insurance
coverage, none of which I have, so I try to stay home or as close
to it as possible. Sticking my neck out and going on job inter-
views, traveling to places without a Burger King or cable, all
cause more stress than I can deal with.

I have learned to push those "shoulds" right out of my mind.
I'm no Indiana Jones, and that's just fine with me and Mutual
of Omaha.

**I'm into the modern mental machismo that doesn't
require additional casualty insurance.**

# JOY

*Yabba dabba do.*

Fred Flintstone

Joy is spontaneous and unexpected. Joy cannot be planned for. It springs up and flowers on its own. What a comfort to realize that even if I never weed or water, I too can raise a crop of happiness.

What a relief to realize that we need not toil lovelessly for a mountain of materialistic mirth. We can just lie back and let joy happen. As long as we don't set our sights too high, joy will pop up unexpectedly and uncontrollably, like dandelions in a new lawn or like mushrooms on a cow pie.

Remember when that girl down the block that you've been in love with since you were twelve and suggested a game of strip Twister? Or remember when you called in sick and then realized there was a Three Stooges festival on TV and you hadn't even realized it before you called in? Remember when you discovered that you actually can put Tupperware in the dishwasher? What did you feel? Joy, right? Or at least something slightly more pleasant than the usual swift kick in the ass?

Next time you're thinking about shelling out the fifty bucks for a dozen roses to smell, smell a dandelion instead. They don't cost anything and require only minimal maintenance. Of course, they don't really smell, either, but what self-respecting man wants to smell a flower, anyway?

**Given enough fresh compost, I can grow anything.**

# LEARNING

*His knowledge of books had in some degree diminished his
knowledge of the world.*

William Shenstone

I forgive myself for not reading. I used to feel kind of bad
about it, but then I realized that life's most important lessons
are not to be found in books.

Take my bullterrier, Pizzahead. Pizza taught me the sheer
joy of beef by-products, telephone poles, and bitches in heat.
Now that's what I call a life lesson. I can still see his little tail
wagging as he made a beeline for the neighbor's poodle. God,
that poodle was ripe. Her legs were shaved really close, except
for two little balls at her hips and feet. And she had this pink
bow cocked at a coquettish angle just above her lovely azure
eyes.

Pizza taught me to love life, to forget about my responsibilities and just cut loose, ears flapping in the wind, stopping only
to sniff at life's marvelous mysteries and relieve myself whenever I feel the need. I sure wish those guys who work at the
state park could understand that.

Maybe if we stop thinking about education as something we
find in books, we'll actually learn something.

**The world is my classroom, my poodle, and my toilet.**

# WHOLENESS/UNITY

*Life just is. You have to flow with it. Give yourself to the moment. Let it happen.*

Governor Jerry Brown

We are all like fluid. We are off on a journey to our oceans of origin. All of us, ultimately, rejoin the universal wholeness from which we have sprung and to which we will return.

Some of us begin like crisp, sparkling champagne, others like day-old Coors. Ultimately we are all consumed by some poor, bleary-eyed slob trying to get a buzz on. We all proceed through this everyman's inner processes and are expelled once more into sewer systems that deposit us into rivers and streams whose swollen and degraded banks guide us safely back to our nascent seas.

**Given the similarity between men and fluid, I would think twice about swimming in the ocean.**

# ESTEEM/COURAGE

*There is no such thing as bravery, only degrees of fear.*
John Wainwright

We're never good enough, are we? We're always looking for outside validation, believing we aren't worthy of feeling good about ourselves unless we live up to ridiculously high standards that have been set for us, like steady employment, retaining our driving privileges, or moving out of Mom and Dad's by the time we're forty.

We deserve a positive self-image regardless of our external accomplishments. So we still live at home and Mom still washes our socks and makes our beds every morning. So we don't have insurance, paid vacations, or a pension plan. So unemployment compensation has run out again. So the government is threatening to garnish wages we don't even earn anymore. Are these reasons for feeling like a loser?

We don't need to rescue people from burning buildings to feel like heroes. Waking up every morning with a will to survive takes a hell of a lot of courage.

**I believe in a better tomorrow. I just prefer not to think that far ahead.**

# CONFLICT

*It is a good rule in life never to apologize.*

P. G. Wodehouse

Painful as it can be, conflict does sometimes arise. Of course, conflict takes a great deal of energy, and as we grow stronger in our conviction to do next to nothing, we must inevitably face the fact that this includes fighting, even if we are in the right.

We must always bear in mind that while conflict can be healthy (unless of course somebody is armed), there are easier, less tiring ways of getting our point across. We can reason our way to resolution. We can tell them the check is in the mail, the load is on the truck. We can tell them that we didn't mean anything by that last remark, some of our best friends are Polish. Spontaneous sleep is another option. It doesn't look good to hit a narcoleptic. Feigned drunkenness works. So does actual drunkenness. Pretend you've temporarily taken leave of your senses, lost your ability to swallow properly. Nobody wants to get drooled on just to make a point. The glasses thing doesn't work anymore, but nobody hits a blind man. There are always alternatives to conflict.

**Peace on earth begins with me.**

# AGING/YOUTH

*One of the things at my age is to avoid strain.*
Arnold Bennett

I once met a guy in his fifties who shared with me what an awesome revelation it was when he discovered Grecian Formula for Men. "I can just lather and rinse," he told me, "and I don't have to deal with all that weird energy coming from babes who are old enough to be my wife."

Another guy in his forties told me that the way to stay young is to jog five miles a day. I have stopped returning his phone calls because I suspect that he has gone insane.

Why would anybody jog when they could just lather and rinse? It doesn't make sense. All that effort, and for what? Lower back and knee problems in later life, and it doesn't even change your hair color.

It seems to me that life is hard enough, what with breathing and bipedal locomotion and all, so why push it?

**If man were meant to go three miles a day, he would have been born with a turbo engine.**

# BEAUTY/SELF-IMAGE

*It is better to look good than to feel good.*

Fernando

In our visually conscious culture, we feel the pressure to put aside those activities that give us pleasure because we are worried about looking good. We don't eat that sixth Twinkie, we forgo the family size bag of Doritos, because we are worried about our appearance.

We start to feel self-conscious when we compare ourselves to guys like Mel Gibson, Lawrence Taylor, or Jon Bon Jovi. We begin to dread looking in the mirror. We begin to measure ourselves against every guy on TV, computing in inches, in quarter inches, or in metric if it sounds bigger.

What we have to remember is that while women have to be beautiful, we Men Who Do Next to Nothing can rely on something called "character." We can be "distinguished" or "quirky," we can have loads of "personality," a big bank balance, or just enough room on our credit cards to make it look convincing.

Look at Keith Richards, Refrigerator Perry, Donald Trump. These are real men who are seeing major action in the trenches, and do you imagine that they are worried about an extra Twinkie here or there?

**Dieting is for wimps. Does Dunkin' Donuts deliver?**

# RELATIONSHIPS

*Relations stop nowhere.*

Henry James

We Men Who Do Next to Nothing know more than we might think about healthy relationships. Even though most of our models for relationships are based on the unhealthy examples set by our dysfunctional parents, and even though our girlfriends have told us that we wouldn't know a good relationship if it came up and bit us on the butt, we have to realize that we have learned a thing or two about the endless opportunities available for new and better ways to relate to a whole variety of women.

Too often, relationships are looked at as some kind of eternal fix, like Super Glue. We are told that a relationship is a structure that gives form and shape to the bond between two people. Without it, we are like Jell-O without a mold. So what's wrong with putting Jell-O in other places, like in the bathtub, for example? Green Jell-O, about three hundred quarts of it, kept at room temperature, so it kind of squishes when you step into it and oozes into every available orifice and gets real interesting when you turn on the whirlpool jets, although this usually requires the presence of a competent plumber.

**I'm Jell-O and you're glue. Whatever slides off me sticks to you. Sounds like fun.**

# JEALOUSY/LOST OPPORTUNITIES

*Whenever a friend succeeds, a little something in me dies.*

Gore Vidal

I admire a man who can own up to jealousy. It's an ugly emotion, and when we recognize ourselves turning green, we feel ashamed, particularly as it clashes with the couch.

It's only natural to resent those who have succeeded where we have failed, which means we Men Who Do Next to Nothing resent just about everybody, although only on alternate Thursdays because that much angst is just too exhausting on a daily basis.

It's hard to accept our station in life when we see where other guys are who have less on the ball than we do. I mean, can Schwarzenegger act? Can Dylan sing? No. And neither can we. So why aren't we making the same kind of money they are? It just isn't fair.

**Nobody said life was fair, but I at least thought I was going to be graded on a curve.**

# PERSONAL SPACE/
# GETTING AWAY

*Unless we have a war or a big disease or a famine, there's just too many people, and they're gonna have to get off the planet.*

Paul Kantner

Sometimes we just have to get away from everyone and everything to recharge our batteries. If we don't have a mountaintop retreat, or a summer home, since she got it in the divorce, we may have to find sanctuary elsewhere.

There are many spaces we can call our own. My favorite bat cave is the last booth at the Pleasure Chest. There I can get in touch with my inner self, my life force. As I slide in my fortieth quarter of the afternoon, I feel assured that there is a special place in the world just for me, and when you work it out, it comes to a lot less than the mortgage on that place in the Berkshires.

**All I want is a room somewhere with a clap on, clap off light switch and a VCR.**

# GIVING CREDIT

*He who believes in himself is always good.*

Montesquieu

Do I devalue myself? Do I forget to give myself enough credit? Do I forget my positive qualities and focus only on the negative?

Today I will make a list of all that is good about me. I'm not on death row. The student loan people haven't garnished my wages . . . yet. I can tell a good joke. I can remember the names and ages of all my kids. I remembered to give my mother a card on Mother's Day last year. Or was that two years ago? Once I told a girlfriend that her new hairdo was nice even though it looked like her neck just threw up.

If I think hard enough, I can come up with many wonderful, positive qualities that I possess. If I think even harder, I might be able to come up with something I've accomplished since graduating, or at least outline a plan for something I'm going to do eventually that my mom can put in her Christmas newsletter.

**Today I will give myself credit not only for what I have done, but for what I would like to do someday.**

# IDENTITY

*I use heavy-gauge strings, tune low, play hard, and floor it.*
                                              Stevie Ray Vaughan


Did you ever see Stevie Ray Vaughan's guitar? What a beautiful piece of work. So well-worn there's hardly any finish left. Deep, sweat-stained grooves in the neck, nicks and burns from years of hard use.

Like me. I'm sweat-stained and deeply grooved also. I have nicks and burns from that time when I tried to use a soldering iron. Hell, I even have calluses from years of strenuous league bowling, and I can't even see my feet anymore when standing erect. Now that's hard use!

When I think of the life I've lived, and the scars I bear, the blues I've wished I could sing but can't because my voice is shot, too, I see that I am one beautiful instrument.

**If I paint myself purple and attach some strings at my neck, maybe Susanna Hoffs will want to strum me.**

# COURAGE

*I am the greatest.*

Muhammad Ali

Face it: if you can say it, and mean it, then you can be it. Live any theory, even a wrong one, long enough and it becomes true. It worked for Ali. It works for the majority of monarchs and all politicians.

Go ahead, say it, just once. Say, Dammit, I am one hell of a guy. I am an all-around, happening kind of dude. I'm the big cheese, the bee's knees, the cat's pajamas. Despite what my ex-wife, my kids, and even my mother are saying about me lately, I am the crème de la crème, passing through life, imparting that ineffable je ne sais quois to everyone and everything around me. I am an apotheosis of myself. I am my own best friend, my comrade in arms. I am my own hero.

**Honk if you love yourself.**

# SELF-ACCEPTANCE

*It's not the meat, it's the motion.*

Bulgarian proverb

I am just right! Sometimes I have suspected otherwise. Others have tried to tell me that I am too much. Like the time I tried to get my date to pay for dinner by declaring that I was a feminist and therefore felt that gender specifications with regard to dinner tabs was a slap in the face of liberated women everywhere. After she paid up (I left the tip—hey, I'm not a total slouch) I asked her in for a nightcap. That's when she told me I was too much. One time a date told me I was too little, but I don't like to talk about that.

What a relief to realize that I am just right, neither too much nor too little, but a healthy, respectable, undisputable, substantial, well-orchestrated, intensely mobile, neither understated nor overstated, neither diminutive nor pronounced, but a considerably well-rigged, well-maintained, and well-balanced five inches.

**Today, I will sit and be just right. Then tomorrow, maybe I'll be just right with that girl in the French-cut bikini who sells foot-long hot dogs on the corner. I mean, how's she gonna tell the difference in the dark?**

# ALTERNATIVES/WORK

*It's no credit to anyone to work too hard.*

E. W. Howe

Contrary to popular belief, we Men Who Do Next to Nothing are constantly doing something. Just because we're not getting paid for it doesn't mean that we aren't making excellent use of each and every day.

There's the lost episodes of Spiderman to catch up on, the sock drawer to organize, and I could wax the Mustang, too, even though it doesn't run right now. Still, that car's a classic, and I've got to protect the finish, because I'm gonna sell that baby for some serious dollar someday, and then I'm gonna buy a guitar and start a rock and roll band and tour the world and make zillions of dollars and get laid every single night by beautiful babes in fish-net stockings who all have alter egos that are German and look really good in midnight blue leather.

Then I'll be really busy, but until then, I have plenty here to occupy my time. I could hang up a hammock in the other corner of the yard, in case Dad is using this one when I feel like lying down.

**I wonder how much guitar lessons cost?**

# CREATIVITY

*Every man of genius sees the world at a different angle from his fellows.*

Havelock Ellis

I love the image of the back door. All men of vision approach the world from new directions. I, for instance, always make my approach through the back door. I love the thought of secret, out-of-the-way entrances. I love spending the afternoon contemplating what wonderful and surprising sensations await me on the other side of that unexplored gate.

I suppose the real idea is not the back door per se; it's the willingness to explore new paths, to go in through the out door.

I need more back doors in my life.

**Getting in the back door may not be easy, but if they don't see you coming, they can't stop you at the gate or collect the price of admission.**

# INSPIRATION

*Inspiration is never genuine.*

Samuel Butler

Sometimes we forget that to do our work well, no matter what it is, we must be inspired. This is true for any kind of work, be it paid or otherwise, which explains why I haven't been able to do any for quite some time now. Inspiration is the piston in our cylinder, the spark in our plugs, and as I haven't had a tune-up in about eight months now, inspiration is just about entirely out of the question.

I don't know why my mother doesn't understand this. I try to explain this to her. And I also add that inspiration does not come on demand. Like any process, it is a mystery and does not answer when called, but comes, uninvited, and expects not only a beer, but a beer glass.

Inspiration is a real pain in the ass and somebody I'd never willingly sit down and have a beer with, 'cause you just can't depend on him. I mean, you give him a beer, you turn around to slap him on the back, where is he? He's disappeared, and you're sitting there, a dumb schmuck, with a dirty glass, and when you go to the fridge you realize the beer's all gone. I mean, what kind of a guest is that?

**When I wait for inspiration, I always end up making another beer run.**

# INSTINCT/ANIMAL NATURE

*Mglfwabogtrmslztsff.*

Kurt Cobain

Any man who has sat in the park and watched a dog lift his leg on a tree, any man who has witnessed this unabashed and free-flowing expression of masculinity, knows the beauty of animal instinct.

How often do our own pure instincts become clouded with civility and politeness? How easy it is to lose sight of the men we truly are. What a far better world it would be if we allowed ourselves to express our essential selves.

Who we are is inextricably linked with what we are. We are men and like the spaniel must lift our legs often to mark our territory, to write our names proudly in the snow, and to claim every bitch on this side of the avenue as our property.

**To be a man I have to pee.**

# PANIC/FATIGUE

*Jane, stop this crazy thing!*

George Jetson

Living our lives can be so exhausting. Writing down phone messages, parking only in designated areas, and leaving the toilet seat down can be monumental burdens. Sometimes it feels like life is one responsibility after another, leaving us drained and despondent, and, in return, granting us only an illusion of control.

We are caught on a treadmill, strapped to a rowing machine, chained to a Stairmaster, with no big-breasted, Spandex-clad aerobics instructor in sight. Could it be that we are creating our own inner turmoil, that conflicts and crises do not just happen to us, but are self-perpetuated? Wouldn't it be better to admit that we are totally out of control?

Isn't it preferable to leave your shoes untied, your zipper unzipped, or better yet, just not to get dressed at all? Might not the elimination of all activity from our lives grant us the serenity we seek?

**I hope I will allow myself to see that an illusion of control is not worth the effort.**

# ROMANCE

*Love'll get you like a case of Bovine Encephalitis.*

Croatian shepherd's saying

Sometimes, when I'm feeling particularly lonely and unlovable, my mother takes the opportunity to tell me that there's a trick to attracting women. She says that if I put on a nice suit, shave, and get a haircut, or a job, this will make others love me. I don't think so.

I mean, she's my mother, what does she know about love? She probably hasn't had any in about two hundred years. My father went into a walking coma back around 1969, the year we lost the pennant race by one run, and he hasn't uttered a sound since. He can still do the important things, like operate the BarcaLounger and the remote control, but let's face it, his Don Juan days are over. She drove him to it, always insisting that he put on a suit, shave, and get a haircut or a job. She did it to him, and now she's doing it to me. It's just like her, too, to choose these moments when I'm feeling down to sink her hooks into me and try to get me to conform to her expectations.

Loving is letting go of expectations and letting people be who they are. If my mother really loved me, she'd get off it already and start baking me some of the miniwienies wrapped in the Poppin' Fresh rolls. Now that would be helpful and loving.

**In a world with miniwienies, who needs love?**

# HOLIDAYS

*Bah . . . humbug!*

Charles Dickens

Christmas is coming, and already I feel exhausted and over-whelmed. It is so difficult to maintain my daily rituals and rou-tines when she's in a frenzy of gift buying, decorating, baking, entertaining, and just generally running around being cloying-ly annoying. All that stuff was okay when I was a kid, but why does she have to bother now? I'm not five years old anymore, and I'm beginning to suspect that I'm allergic to tinsel because every time I walk by that damn tree I get hives. Besides, I can't afford Christmas on an ex–barrel reamer's unemployment ben-efits, so why does she have to go and rub it in?

I have to face it. I am dreading the holiday season. Perhaps it is time for me to take stock and reevaluate whether or not it is truly important to me to have to go through this every year. Is all of the mind-bending activity around here really worth the vented boxer shorts and the eight-pack of tube socks that is always waiting for me under the tree?

**Maybe I should check into the YMCA for a week. Wait, did I pay them yet for last Christmas?**

# BECOMING A MAN

*The fox condemns the trap, not himself.*

William Blake

In our shallow, materialistic society, so much emphasis is placed upon financial success that we have very few role models for manliness. Without any instruction manual, we are suddenly expected to be men and have the wage ceiling and bank balance of our fathers.

In a society that knows absolutely nothing about it (or if they do, they're certainly not telling us), there is the assumption that one is a little boy, and then suddenly one is a systems analyst. In our bourgeois, hedonistic, brutalizing culture, becoming a man is linked with making a lot of money. But manhood is much more than a pay stub or a bank balance. Manhood is about hanging out in bars drinking dollar drafts and talking about sports, and Rocky, and the Terminator, and the Dallas Cowboys cheerleaders. Manhood is vintage Mustangs, and pre-CBS Fender guitars, heavy metal, and fly girls. Manhood is telling my mother that I won't turn down the TV, shave, or go job hunting tomorrow because I don't need those external yardsticks to measure my value as a man.

**I am just being a man, so get off my case.**

# WOMEN

*Nowadays, we're more into staying in our rooms and reading Nietzsche.*

Robert Plant

Sex has become very complicated, even for rock stars. I myself decided to stay away from professional women because I was sick and tired of feeling like a slave to success. I wanted to avoid that trap. Lately I've found that any woman can become a trap, whether she's a homemaker, aerobics instructor, toll collector, cocktail waitress, vice president of Finance or Purchasing, or my mother. They're all the same.

I need to recognize that all of them, regardless of what they do, are ultimately part of the "materialistic" world. Even when they start out on the bottom of the professional ladder, like as a purchasing clerk, next thing I know, she's getting promoted and demanding that I do the same.

And does she care if I was working for a fascist who didn't care if it took all night as long as I met my barrel quota? Does she care if I worked for an abusive tyrant who didn't care if I was sick or tired and who didn't think twice about insisting that I work overtime and miss the heavyweight championship fight on Pay-Per-View, even though I already paid for it? What was I supposed to do? I had to quit. My honor was at stake. But did she understand? No. And what's worse, my mother is on her side. She's always on her side.

**This isn't a third world country, this is America, and oppression costs more than $4.35 an hour.**

# LAUGHTER

*To laugh means to love mischief.*

Friedrich Nietzsche

One of my better moments was when I was invited to give that presentation to the board of directors at my old company. I was a little anxious, so right before going on stage I went to the executive lounge to expel all of my anxieties. I came out feeling pretty cocky. And when I hit that stage, I made a real impression. Everybody's attention was on me. You could have heard a pin drop. That was the clearest and most articulate presentation I ever gave, and I could see in their eyes, as I gave my forecasts, that they were with me every step of the way. I had them in the palm of my hand.

Of course, halfway through my speech I realized that they weren't in my palm, but in my lap. I had forgotten to zip up my fly, and as it was a Tuesday, I wasn't wearing any underwear. I got a little uncomfortable for a minute, began to lose my cool, but then I remembered that at moments like these, laughter is a healing balm. So I cracked a joke. You know, that one about the pearl diver and the eel? Sure made a rousing closer for my speech.

**When they see how funny we are, they see how precious we are.**

# COMPROMISE/CONVICTIONS

*Two all beef patties, special sauce, lettuce, cheese, pickles,*
*onions, on a sesame seed bun.*

McDonald's slogan

The Big Mac. What a glorious monument to men and meat. I have a friend who prefers The Whopper. We don't see each other much anymore.

Some things a man just can't compromise on. I learned that from Bob. Bob was my pet chameleon, and he was a reptile who knew how to compromise. Whatever he was sitting on, he'd turn that same color. For instance, if he was sitting on a gray rock, he'd turn gray. Bob was flexible, but he had his limits. One time, I bought a fluorescent green bridge. You know, one of those glow-in-the-dark numbers you put in your fish tank, although when you think of it, why would a fish need a bridge, anyway? Anyway, I put Bob on the bridge, but no matter how many ants I fed him, he wouldn't turn chartreuse.

I learned a lot from Bob. He was a chameleon of character who stuck courageously to his own spectrum, and would only eat live ants and McDonald's beef. Bob has since died. Karl, my Gila monster, ate him, along with about two tablespoons of Burger King hamburger that Bob had refused just two hours before.

**I learned three important lessons from Bob that will live with me forever. Never eat dead ants, never turn chartreuse, and never, ever, hang out with Gila monsters who prefer Burger King.**

**Catherine George** was born in Wales and, following her marriage to an engineer, lived in Brazil for eight years at a gold-mine site. It was an experience she would later draw upon for her books, when she and her husband returned to England. Now her husband helps manage their household so that Catherine can devote more time to her writing. They have two children—a daughter and a son—who share their mother's love of language and writing.

## Books by Catherine George

### HARLEQUIN ROMANCE

### HARLEQUIN PRESENTS

# OUT OF THE STORM
## Catherine George

## *Harlequin Books*

TORONTO • NEW YORK • LONDON
AMSTERDAM • PARIS • SYDNEY • HAMBURG
STOCKHOLM • ATHENS • TOKYO • MILAN
MADRID • WARSAW • BUDAPEST • AUCKLAND

Original hardcover edition published in 1991
by Mills & Boon Limited

ISBN 0-373-03261-7

Harlequin Romance first edition April 1993

OUT OF THE STORM

# CHAPTER ONE

THE process of waking up was painful. Both eyelids seemed weighted down. She decided to leave it for a while. Her head was throbbing so vilely that the effort was too much. And the weather outside sounded so bad that it seemed wise to stay as she was a little longer. The howling wind kept firing salvos of rain against the windows, but after a while she stirred reluctantly. Weather or no weather, if she was awake it must be time to get up. Steeling herself against the pain in her head, she forced her eyes open, then stared in horror and shut them quickly, her heart thumping. She lay rigid for a count of ten, eyes tightly closed, then very slowly opened them again.

It was no dream. The room was still there. It was small, with a sloping ceiling and a pair of windows set in deep embrasures. And she'd never seen it before in her life. She stared, teeth chattering, at white-painted walls, a heavy oak chest, the ornate brass-work of the bed. As she heaved herself up against the pillows she discovered she was wearing a man's shirt, extra-large and striped, and she'd never seen that before, either. She thrust back the bright patchwork quilt and levered herself to a sitting position, her feet dangling over the edge of the bed. She sat very still for a moment, the room revolving around her like a carousel as the pain in her head hammered to a crescendo then receded again to a just bearable throb. Slowly the mist in front

5

of her eyes cleared. She breathed in slowly and regularly a few times, then got shakily to her feet.

This last proved more taxing than expected. The floor seemed to be heaving about beneath her feet like the deck of a ship. To reach a window she was obliged to cling to the brass footrail of the bed en route. This was no ordinary headache, she thought grimly. Seeing an upright chair stationed between the windows, she made a lunge for it and collapsed sideways on the rush seat to lean, exhausted, against the cold wall.

It was some time before she could gather her forces sufficiently to stand up and rest her hands on the chill white plaster of the window embrasure. As she peered through the double glass her blood ran cold. Not that there was much to see: only a stretch of close-cropped, undulating turf, broken here and there by protrusions of rock. And beyond that nothing but sullen grey sky and miles of stormy, heaving sea.

Panic surged up inside her, taking her breath away. She fought it, leaning on her clenched fists, her eyes closed until the wave of terror receded, leaving her limp and breathless. Where in heaven's name *was* this place—and what was she doing here?

She tensed, trembling. Heavy footsteps were mounting the stairs. She turned wildly, then staggered, her hands groping for the brass footrail of the bed. Her breath quickened painfully. She stared, hypnotised, as the heavy iron latch lifted, the door opened and a very tall man backed into the room, ducking his head to clear the lintel, his attention on the tray he was carrying. She received a fleeting impression of shaggy black hair and massive shoulders, then the tray was dumped down on the bedside table and she herself dumped in turn on the bed.

'You shouldn't be up.' The man tucked the quilt around her then straightened, eyeing her petrified face irritably. 'For heaven's sake! I don't bite.'

She shrank away in undisguised terror as he sat on the edge of the bed, reaching for her hand. She snatched it away, burrowing deeper beneath the covers.

His eyes glittered coldly. 'You're in no danger from me, I assure you.'

The voice was musical, with a slight cadence it was hard to pin down. And even in her present state of turmoil she could appreciate that he was a very handsome man, in a sombre, brooding sort of way. The cold eyes scrutinising her so impersonally were deep set beneath heavy black brows, and shadowed with fatigue. His mouth was wide and well cut, with a deeply indented upper lip, and a decidedly grim set to it, and there was something about him which kept her rigid with tension beneath the covers.

She cleared her throat experimentally. 'Where is this place, please?' She grimaced as her voice, unused for some time by the sound of it, came out in hoarse, rusty spurts. 'And who are you?'

'I was just about to ask the same of you,' he countered promptly. 'But before we go into all that tell me how you're feeling.' He leaned forward. 'Give me your hand, please.'

Her eyes narrowed in alarm. 'Why?'

'So I can feel your pulse,' he said impatiently. 'I'm a doctor, not a fortune-teller.'

Flushing, she extended her hand.

He held her wrist loosely between long, slim fingers, his eyes on his watch. 'How's your head?'

'It's aching. Badly.'

'Not surprising. You've had a nasty knock.' He looked up. 'Your pulse is racing—don't tell me you're *still* scared of me!'

She nodded dumbly. The movement lanced pain through her head and she gasped, her face contorted.

His hand tightened on hers for a moment.

'Your head will probably improve if I tell you where you are—and who I am,' he began conversationally. 'Answer one, we're on an island called Gullholm, just off the west coast of Wales. Answer two, my name is Penry Meredith Vaughan, by profession I'm a consultant physician, and I own the island.' He looked at her commandingly. 'Now return the compliment, please. Tell me who you are, young lady, and why the devil you're trespassing on my property.'

She gazed at him in horror. 'But that's *why* I'm so frightened, Dr Vaughan.' Her teeth caught in her trembling lower lip for a moment. 'I don't know. My mind's a blank.'

He rose to his feet, tall as a giant in the small room. 'You expect me to believe you have no idea how you got here?'

'I'm afraid I do.' She eyed him despairingly. 'I know it sounds far-fetched, but I—I don't know who I am, either. Not even my own name!'

Penry Vaughan studied her in brooding silence for a moment, then glanced at the forgotten tray on the bedside table. 'I've brought you some soup——'

'I couldn't eat anything,' she said with a shudder.

'If you don't eat,' he said grimly, 'you get no medication for that head, nor an account of how I found you.'

She struggled to sit up. 'Please——' she began, then clenched her teeth, perspiration standing out on her

forehead as the vice-like pain gripped her skull. She subsided against the pillows, breathing shallowly until the spasm began to subside. 'All right,' she muttered at last.

Dr Penry Vaughan nodded in approval as he poured hot, fragrant liquid from an insulated flask into a mug. 'While you drink this I'll go downstairs and make tea and toast——'

'No toast!' she said hastily as she took the mug.

'As a house-guest you leave a lot to be desired, young woman,' he said cuttingly. 'The presence of a semi-invalid is something I neither invited nor desired, so please make it easier for both of us by giving as little trouble as possible.' He looked down his formidable nose. 'Drink that soup by the time I get back and possibly, just possibly, I'll give you a mild pain-killer. If not I'll leave you to your own devices until you see sense.'

She stared after him mutinously as he went from the room, willing him to bump his head as he went through the door, but to her disappointment Dr Penry Vaughan ducked his tall head with the grace and dexterity of long practice.

Alone again, she eyed the soup in her mug malevolently, convinced it would act as an emetic. For a moment she thought of staggering to the window again to throw the soup out, but decided against it. Not only was she too shaky on her feet, but by the sound of the storm raging outside anything thrown from the window would be hurled back in her face, courtesy of the wind. Gingerly she took a sip of the soup, surprised to find it was not only delicious but nothing to do with any can or packet. Dr Vaughan, it seemed, liked cooking. And instead of rebelling her stomach gave an appreciative

little rumble. She sipped absently, so desperate to remember who she was and how she came to be here that the mug was empty before she realised it.

'Good,' said Penry Vaughan when he returned. He took the mug with an approving nod. 'I'm glad you decided to be sensible.'

'Thank you, Dr Vaughan. I'm sorry to be such a nuisance. I feel better already. I can be on my way soon. . .' She trailed away at his sardonic expression.

'On your way where?' He turned back to the tray to fill two cups. 'How do you like your tea?'

'Milk, no sugar, please——' Her eyes lit up as she took the cup from him. 'If I know that—which I do, somehow—surely I'll remember the rest pretty soon?'

'Quite possibly.' He handed her a plate containing four small triangles of toasted wholemeal bread, sparsely buttered. 'Now eat this while I tell you how I found you.'

Dr Penry Vaughan, she learned, had come to Gullholm for peace and solitude to get on with a series of articles. 'I needed a break from routine rather badly,' he said as he drew up a chair and sat down. 'A colleague advised a couple of weeks in the sun, away from it all.'

The girl in the bed glanced towards the windows involuntarily, as a vicious gust of wind drove rain against the windows like a fusillade of shot.

Penry Vaughan shrugged. 'Not much sun on Gullholm at this time of the year, I admit, but you can't beat it for peace and privacy. As a rule, anyway,' he added morosely.

She stiffened. 'My intrusion was involuntary, Dr Vaughan. I can't have meant to come here if it's private property.'

'I found you at first light this morning,' he said, getting up to take her half-empty plate. 'Good girl, I'll let you off the rest. Now drink some of the tea.'

She obeyed, then thanked Penry Vaughan gratefully as he handed her two tablets and a glass of water.

'These are pretty mild,' he said as she swallowed them down. 'But they should take the edge off the pain. Drink as much as you can, please.'

Once she was propped comfortably against the pillows Penry Vaughan sat down again and went on with his story. It was his habit to go for a run round his island every day before breakfast, and that morning, because rain was forecast for the rest of the day, he'd taken advantage of the brief spell of fine weather early on to gather up driftwood from the beach after his run. The shape of the island, he told her, was a rough figure-of-eight, with a narrow neck of land joining the two halves of landmass. The two inlets either side of the Neck were called Seal Haven to the westward, Atlantic side, and Lee Haven facing the Pembrokeshire coast.

'On Lee Beach there's a safe anchorage where I keep my old fishing boat,' said her host. 'But Seal Haven is a mass of rocks, with fierce currents boiling round them most of the time. And that, Madame X, is where I found you.'

As the promised rain swept in from the sea Penry had climbed the cliff path from Lee Haven with his bundle of driftwood, but as he reached the Neck a small patch of bright colour had caught his eye far below.

'Your scarf,' he told her. 'I jettisoned the wood, climbed down the path and there, neatly stashed away in a narrow inlet between the rocks, was my castaway,

complete with gash on temple, soaked through, ice-cold to the touch and so deeply unconscious I thought at first you were dead.'

She shivered. 'But how on earth had I got there?'

'No idea. I was hoping you'd be able to tell *me* that.'

She slumped against the pillows, depressed. 'Well, I can't. I mean, it's not exactly swimming weather, is it?'

'Far from it. Nor, presumably, would you go swimming fully dressed with a small weekend bag slung over your shoulder.'

She stared at him. 'I came complete with luggage? Wasn't there something in the bag to say who I am?'

'I'm afraid not. It's a small nylon affair with some underwear and a spare sweater and that's about it. But you should be grateful to it,' he added. 'The bag may well have saved your life, first by doubling as a lifebelt, then by getting caught on a needle of rock in the inlet. Otherwise you'd have been swept away again.'

She hugged her arms across her chest convulsively under the bright patchwork quilt. 'Do you think I fell out of a boat?'

'It seems the most likely explanation.' He lounged back in the chair, a commanding figure, despite his ancient white fisherman's sweater and salt-stained jeans. 'But *what* boat? And where was it heading?'

She shook her head helplessly. 'I wish I knew!'

'I've contacted the coastguard and police by radio telephone. They should shed some light on the mystery once you're reported missing. As,' he assured her, 'you most certainly will be when you fail to turn up at whatever destination you were bound for.' He leaned forward to take her hand. 'No rings. Not that I expected any. You don't look old enough to be married.'

She pulled her hand away. 'How old is that?'

His face hardened. 'It depends. Marriage calls for a certain degree of maturity. Some people never achieve it.'

Ouch, she thought. A sore subject. 'I don't feel all that young,' she said tentatively. 'But you're a doctor. Can't you tell by my teeth, or something?'

His sudden smile transformed him to an astonishing degree, revealing the man behind the remote consultant. One who'd probably mowed the nurses down in his student days, too, she thought with a flash of insight. But the change was fleeting, the brooding mask in place again almost at once.

'Don't worry about it,' he advised, then searched in his pocket for a moment before holding out something which glittered in the palm of his hand. 'This was pinned to your sweater. Does it ring any bells?'

She examined the silver brooch eagerly. It was unusual. And, she knew beyond any doubt, it was hers. The workmanship was very fine, depicting a lioness and a vixen at ease together on what looked like a sleigh.

'Strange combination,' she said slowly, turning the brooch over in her hands. 'And why a sleigh, I wonder?'

'I don't think it's a sleigh. Turn it up on end.'

She did as he said, her eyes lighting up. 'Of course— it's a capital L!' She smiled for the first time, wincing as the pull of facial muscles reminded her she'd had a crack on the head. She reached up a hand to find a dressing near her hair-line. 'Was it much of a gash?'

'Too much to leave as it was. I put a couple of stitches in it while you were unconscious,' he said

casually. 'You came to in the middle of it, unfortunately for you, but it gave me the opportunity to make a superficial examination.'

She frowned. 'You shone a light in my eyes!'

His eyes were suddenly intent. 'You remember?'

'Only vaguely.' Her mouth dropped. 'It's so frustrating—like having someone twitch a curtain aside then let it fall back again before I can see properly.' She swallowed. 'I felt a sharp pain and—and the light, blinding me. Like a fragment of a dream.' She sighed heavily. 'What a nuisance for you, having to stitch me up. I'm deeply indebted to you, one way and another, Dr Vaughan.'

'Nonsense,' he said briskly. 'I could hardly leave you in the condition I found you. Your clothes, by the way, are all drying on a rack in the kitchen.'

'Thank you,' she said politely, her sense of obligation increasing by the minute. She turned the brooch over in her hand. 'Since I was wearing this I assume it's mine. "L" for what, I wonder?'

'There's a lioness on the brooch,' he pointed out. 'It could stand for Leonie, or Leonora, perhaps. Ring any bells?'

She shook her head. 'Not really.'

'Nevertheless, my child, you must answer to something, if only for the time being.' He gave her a wry look. 'Not that you look remotely like a lioness—more like a half-drowned kitten.'

'I'll answer to anything you like,' she snapped, her eyes flashing, 'other than "my child"!'

One of his black brows rose tauntingly. 'Ah—the kitten has claws! Very well. If you're leaving the choice to me I vote for Leonora. Perhaps your father shared my taste for Beethoven.'

She shrugged. 'I don't, that's for sure.' Her eyes filled with sudden, angry tears. 'How in heaven's name do I know I don't like Beethoven, when I can't remember my own name?'

'Because you're suffering from amnesia, Leonora,' he said brusquely. 'A temporary loss of memory due to the blow on your head. You could wake up tomorrow with total recall. In the meantime, don't try to force it.' He got to his feet. 'I'm going to cook myself some lunch. Try to sleep. This afternoon, if you feel better, you can come downstairs.'

She felt a sudden violent disinclination for solitude. 'Can't I come now?'

'No.' He turned in the doorway. 'You've had a bad experience, Leonora. You're lucky to be alive. And because I took the trouble to save this life of yours I insist on seeing you recover properly and make full use of it. I'm a doctor, remember. So please follow my instructions. They're meant for the best.'

Leonora bit her lip in remorse. 'I'm sorry, Dr Vaughan. It must be a terrible drag having a patient foisted on you like this—a real busman's holiday.' She smiled diffidently. 'I haven't thanked you properly, either, for rescuing me from—from a watery grave. I'm very grateful. Truly.'

Penry Vaughan shrugged his formidable shoulders indifferently. 'Don't mention it. Now, if there's nothing more I can do for you for a while, I'll leave you to rest.'

'There is something,' she muttered, embarrassed. 'Could you point me in the direction of a bathroom please?'

'Of course. Sorry—I should have thought of that

before.' He returned to the bed, holding out his hands. 'Up you come.'

'If you'll just tell me where it is I can manage by myself, thank you.'

He frowned irritably. 'My dear child, is it possible you're embarrassed? Who do you think stripped your clothes off and put you to bed?'

Her face flamed. 'Nevertheless, Dr Vaughan, if it's all the same to you I'd still prefer to get to the bathroom under my own steam.'

'Oh, for——' He checked himself. 'All right. Have it your own way. The bathroom's just across the passage. But be careful. It's an old house, and the floor's uneven in places, so don't try exploring on your own just yet, please.'

'I wouldn't dream of trespassing,' she assured him stiffly.

'Don't talk nonsense,' he said impatiently. 'When you get back to bed try to sleep for a bit. I'll be up to see you later.'

Leonora watched him go with mixed feelings, not really sure she could make it to the bathroom alone, despite her fine words. If a visit there had been less pressing she'd have been very willing to cuddle down into the comfortable bed and let sleep blank out her problems for a while. It took her a long time to negotiate the journey to the small, functional bathroom across the passage, but in the end she accomplished it without incident. Then before she resumed her snail-slow progress back to bed she steeled herself to look in the mirror above the washbasin.

Her face was a great disappointment in more ways than one. Not only was it unremarkable and rather battered, it did nothing at all to jog her errant memory.

She had a lot of hair, but it was so tangled and matted it was impossible to determine the colour. And she was skinny. The shirt hung straight to her knees unimpeded much by feminine curves. No wonder Dr Vaughan had jeered at her maidenly modesty. She eyed herself with gloom. One of her eyes was passable; dark, and a rather pleasing almond shape. But the other was swollen and half closed, with a Technicolor bruise below it right down to her razor-sharp cheekbone. By some miracle her nose had escaped a battering. It was short and straight, which was more than could be said for her mouth, which was curvy and rather wider than it should have been for her ashen, wedge-shaped face.

Leonora shook her head sorrowfully at her reflection. 'What a scarecrow! All in all, my girl, you're lucky Dr Penry Meredith Vaughan didn't throw you back in the sea.'

# CHAPTER TWO

WHEN Leonora woke again it was dark. Physically she felt much better. The pain in her head had dulled to a quite bearable ache, but her mind, she realised in panic, was still a blank. Her identity, her home, her family were still lost in the terrifying mist in her mind. And if she was missing from home why weren't her family moving heaven and earth to get her back? She beat down a gush of self-pity, knuckling away tears as she slid gingerly from the bed to make for the bathroom again. As she reached the door a tall, dark shape blocked out the light.

'You're awake,' said Penry Vaughan, and snapped on a switch, dazzling her.

Leonora blinked at him owlishly. 'You've got electricity?'

'My own generator.' He took a dressing-gown from the back of the door and held it for her. 'Put this on if you must wander about the house.'

'I was only venturing as far as the bathroom,' she said with dignity.

'I've put a spare toothbrush in there for you, but otherwise I can't offer you much in the way of beauty aids.'

'Pity. I could use some—badly.' She smiled ruefully. 'I plucked up enough courage to look in the mirror. But the toothbrush is welcome,' she added, then hesitated awkwardly. 'What would you like me to do

18

afterwards? I can go back to bed and keep out of your way, if you prefer.'

'Don't talk nonsense!'

'Don't keep saying that!' she snapped, then flushed, embarrassed.

'I apologise.' He bowed slightly. 'I should be honoured to have your company at dinner, Miss Leonora X. Whenever you're ready to come downstairs give me a shout and I'll come and collect you. The staircase is a bit steep. The last thing you need is another concussion.'

'Is that what I had? Does concussion put the memory out of action?'

'Sometimes.' He opened the bathroom door for her. 'Now get a move on. No more questions until you're downstairs.'

Leonora eyed the bath longingly as she brushed her teeth. If there was a generator it seemed likely there was hot water. A sudden need for a bath overwhelmed her. As the bath filled she inspected the sparse supply of male toiletries, interested to find Penry Vaughan was not a man for sexy French fragrances. The only things on offer were a flask of shower-gel, a roll-on deodorant and a cake of soap, all from a chain of shops famous for herbal products.

The bath water was brownish, but wonderfully soothing to her quite remarkable display of bruises. She eyed her body wryly. Not a sight to inspire any man to raging lust, let alone a doctor. She had breasts after all, she noted; smallish, but quite respectable, but the rest of her was narrow, with angles outnumbering the curves. Her bruises stung badly as she anointed herself with gel, but the discomfort was a small price to pay for feeling clean again. After a moment's

hesitation she lay back, plunging her head deep in the water before shampooing her hair with the gel, gasping as her wound smarted horribly. She sat up quickly, her head reeling for a moment. When it steadied she pulled out the bath plug and knelt to hold her protesting head under the running water from the tap. She endured the renewed pain stoically until the water ran clear, then turned off the taps and clambered from the bath, feeling very shaky, but wonderfully, blissfully clean.

Leonora wrapped herself in one of the large white bathtowels piled on a wicker stand, then, afraid to rub her hair, she swathed a towel turban-wise round her head and subsided on the chair, exhausted but triumphant. A few minutes later, when she'd got as far as wrapping herself in her host's dressing-gown, Penry Vaughan knocked loudly on the door.

'Are you all right in there, Leonora?' he called. 'You're taking a hell of a time.'

She opened the door, smiling guiltily. 'I'm fine. I hope you don't mind—I couldn't resist having a bath.'

Penry glared at her wet head. 'You weren't stupid enough to wash your hair?'

'I used some of your bath-gel——'

'Never mind the bloody bath-gel, it's your wound I'm worried about!' He cursed beneath his breath as he pushed her down, none too gently, on the chair. 'Let me take a look at it.'

He yanked open the bathroom cabinet and took out antiseptic and fresh dressings. She submitted meekly to his expert ministrations as he re-dressed the wound, giving her terse instructions to keep it dry from then on until the stitches were removed.

'I hope I haven't undone all your good work,' she

said repentantly, 'but I just couldn't exist a second longer without washing myself all over.'

'I sponged you down this morning, child. You weren't dirty!'

'I *felt* dirty.'

Penry gave her a fulminating glance, then shrugged. 'All right. But since you were silly enough to wash that mop I suggest you put a dry towel round your shoulders while we eat. No hairdryer.'

Leonora complied in smouldering silence, then followed the large figure of her host from the room. He paused as they reached the head of the stairs, eyeing her bare feet.

'I can't offer you anything in the way of shoes. Your own are still sodden. How about some socks?'

'Fine. Thank you.'

He led her back into the bedroom and sat her on the chair while he rummaged in the chest.

Leonora watched him in dismay. This was his bedroom, then. Which was pretty obvious, really. The bed was very large, which was only to be expected for someone of Dr Vaughan's heroic proportions. It had probably been the only one aired and ready for the unexpected guest this morning. She thanked him, subdued, as he handed her a pair of stretch-towelling socks.

'What's the matter?' he demanded. 'Not glamorous enough for you?'

'It's not that—I just realised I've put you out of your bedroom,' she muttered, pulling on the socks.

'It's not the only one in the house. There are three others, plus a sofa-bed downstairs. Mine happened to be the only one made up.'

'You're very kind.'

He put a finger under her chin and turned her face

up to his. 'You're wrong. Get that through your head right now, Leonora. You were a human being in desperate need of medical care. I'm a doctor. I supplied it. End of story. Don't invest me with qualities I don't possess.'

'Right.' She got to her feet, then tripped over the flapping toe of one of the socks.

Penry sighed, picked her up, and walked with her to the door.

'Please put me down, Dr Vaughan,' Leonora said with dignity. 'I can manage.'

'Oh, shut up and stop fussing,' he said forcibly, ducking neatly through the doorway. 'Tomorrow you can get around on your own once your clothes are dry.'

Leonora lay rigid in his arms, resentful of being carried about like a bundle of laundry. 'Tomorrow,' she said tartly, 'I hope to be away from here and on my way back to wherever I came from.'

Penry carried her carefully down a staircase which led straight into a large sitting-room. 'I doubt it. Even if your memory starts functioning by then the forecast is diabolical. March wind doth blow for some time to come, according to the coastguard, and believe me it blows hellish hard round Gullholm.'

Leonora digested this peace of news with mixed feelings as he set her on her feet. If he was right she had no alternative but to stay put. And since she had no idea where to go yet, even if she could get off the island, the only course possible was to take things a step at a time and try not to rail against a spiteful fate. Besides, she didn't feel so wonderful that she wanted a boat ride to the mainland just yet, even if it did mean staying shut up here with only this moody man for company. At least she now knew it was March.

She turned her attention to the room, which had obviously been three smaller rooms at one time. A wood-burning iron stove occupied the hearth of a big stone fireplace at one end. The rest of the room was crowded with shabby, comfortable chairs and sofas piled with cushions, small tables littered with electric table-lamps, oil lamps, candles in holders. There were shelves full of books and cassettes, a few water-colours on the walls, a model sailing-ship in a big glass bottle on a side-table.

'This is lovely,' she said sincerely, and turned to smile up at Penry Vaughan.

'You like it?' he asked, surprised.

'I do. It's such a friendly room.'

'Unlike its owner, you mean.'

Leonora looked at him levelly. 'You said that, Dr Vaughan. Not me.'

He acknowledged the hit with a small bow. 'Right. Sit on the sofa nearest the stove. I'll bring in your dinner in a moment.'

'I'd offer to help,' she said apologetically, 'but I still feel a bit wobbly.'

'For pity's sake just sit there and try not to do anything silly for the time it takes me to fill two bowls with *cawl*.'

Leonora eyed him coldly. 'I didn't ask to get hit on the head—*or* to intrude on your private property, Dr Vaughan.'

'I'm referring to the shampooing session,' he said curtly, and strode towards a door at the far end.

The kitchen, I assume, thought Leonora, and swung her feet up on the sofa, chuckling at the ludicrously large socks. She spread her towel over a cushion so that she could lean her damp, aching head against it,

then shivered as she listened to the howl of the wind outside. The rain had stopped, but the gale seemed to be gathering strength. The thought of crossing to the mainland, however near it was, brought a return of the panic she'd felt earlier. She clamped down on it hard, wishing passionately she could tear away the veil in her mind, see behind it to find out who she was and why she was cast away on Penry Vaughan's island. Someone, somewhere, must be worried to death about her. If only she could remember who it was. Who *she* was!

It was a relief when Penry returned with a tray containing two steaming bowls. He set it down on one of the small tables, then handed her a paper napkin, a spoon and a fork before giving her one of the bowls.

'*Cawl*,' he announced, then sat down with his own.

Leonora eyed her bowl warily. 'What is *cawl*?'

'A main dish soup made with lamb and root vegetables and leeks. Dumplings, too, when my mother's doing the cooking.' One eyebrow shout up. 'You look surprised. Is that because I can cook, or because I possess a mother, like other men?'

She smiled. 'Neither. You're so efficient it seems strange you haven't mastered the art of the dumpling. Even *I* know how to make those——' She stared at him, arrested. 'There I go again. My stupid mind knows I can make dumplings, so why on earth can't it tell me who I am?'

Penry continued with his meal, unmoved. 'It will, in time. Just be thankful your skull wasn't fractured. I can't X-ray it, of course, but I'm pretty sure you've suffered no more than a bad concussion. Once the wind drops I'll get you over to the mainland and get an X-ray done at St Mary's.'

'St Mary's?'

'It's a nursing home. I do a clinic there once a week.' He looked up from his bowl. 'What do you think of my cooking?'

'Wonderful!' She smiled. 'When I woke up this morning I felt like death. I never dreamed I'd actually be sitting up and taking nourishment so soon—*and* enjoying it.'

'The human body has amazing powers of recuperation.' His eyes travelled over her impersonally. 'There's not very much of you, but you're wiry, and you're young. You should be fine in a day or two.'

Leonora went on with her meal in silence until the bowl was half empty, then laid down her spoon. She looked across at her companion, whose gesture at dressing for dinner had been a newer, cleaner white sweater, and slightly less disreputable denims.

'But what will happen to me if I still can't remember who I am?' she asked forlornly. 'Or if no one reports me missing?'

Penry continued with his dinner with unimpaired appetite. 'You'll just have to stay with me, I suppose. I'm here for three weeks, barring accidents or terminal boredom. Until this weather changes you're marooned with me here, anyway. So let your mind rest. You'll regain your memory all the sooner. For the time being you've got bed, board, and a resident physician on hand. How many castaways can say that?'

She tried to smile. 'True. I just wish I didn't feel I was playing albatross to your Ancient Mariner.'

'Ah! The lady likes poetry.'

She thought for a moment. 'I don't know that I *like* it exactly. But I seem to remember the poem about the Ancient Mariner quite well.'

'You probably learned it at school, as I did.' He got

up to put their dishes on the tray. 'I draw the line at
puddings, I'm afraid. There's plenty of cheese but at
this time of night, with that headache, I don't advise it.
You can't have coffee, either. Too much caffeine.'

'I'd like *something* to drink,' she said wistfully.

'Weak tea, then.'

Leonora lay listening to the wind while Penry
Vaughan was in the kitchen. After a time she heard
him talking to someone on the telephone, but, when
he didn't reappear immediately, gathered that he had
no news for her. Dejectedly she ran careful fingers
through her hair, resigned to learn its colour was a
light ash-brown.

'Why so down in the mouth?' asked her host, returning with a tea-tray. 'I thought I told you to stop
worrying.'

'It's the colour of my hair.' She smiled crookedly. 'I
was hoping for platinum-blonde, or red, but now it's
dry I find it's plain old mouse.'

Penry cast an eye over her hair judicially. 'I wouldn't
have said mouse, precisely. I told the police just now
that you have very dark eyes and golden-brown hair.'

Leonora sat up, swinging her feet to the floor, biting
her lip against the inevitable throb from her temple.
'What did they say?' she asked eagerly. 'Has anyone
reported me missing yet?'

'Afraid not.' He handed her a cup. 'But it's early
days. I only found you this morning, and reckoning by
the tide you couldn't have been there long. Perhaps no
one's missing from the Irish ferry, which rules out one
line of inquiry.'

'Perhaps I fell out of a plane,' she said despondently.

'Out of the everywhere into the here!' He shook his
head. 'I don't think so.'

Leonora sipped her tea in silence, watching him dispose of a large slice of cheese and several whole-wheat biscuits. There was, she conceded, a great deal of him to fill up. A large machine like Penry Vaughan's body must need a fair amount of fuel to keep it running efficiently.

He looked up to meet her eyes. 'I feel I should point out one other possibility, Leonora.'

Something in his tone put her on her guard. 'What's that?'

'There are quite a few islands around here. You could have been making for any one of them in a boat. And in all probability you weren't alone, which means that either you fell, or were swept, out of a boat someone else has landed safely somewhere.'

Her eyes lit up. 'Then they'll contact the police and the coastguard as you did, Dr Vaughan!'

He rubbed his chin. 'Possibly. But not everyone owns a radio telephone, or a way of contacting the shore. Which means this wind will have to die down a bit before they can return to the mainland.'

'So all I have to do is wait, then.'

'Don't get your hopes too high. Your companion might not have made it at all.'

Leonora paled. 'Did you have to say that?'

'I believe in facing facts.'

She digested the last, unwelcome fact in silence for some time. 'Will my own things be ready tomorrow?' she asked after a while.

'I'll bring them up in the morning after breakfast.'

'Dr Vaughan——'

'Let's dispense with the formalities, shall we? Since I can't address you as Miss Whatsit I don't see why you should keep to the "Doctor" bit—Penry will do.'

'It's an unusual name.'

'Not in Wales—means son of Henry. Until the English clamped down on the custom my forefathers all used the prefix "ap" in front of their names—the last king of South Wales, for instance, was Rhys ap Tewdwr. Needless to say, my father's name was Henry.' He smiled sardonically. 'Here endeth the history lesson.'

'Fascinating. Just like the Russian patronymics— though to me it sounds like a sort of spoken misprint— what's the matter?' she added, as he eyed her speculatively.

'I was just wondering what you do for a living.'

She shrugged. 'Who knows?' She thought for a moment, looking at her outspread hands. 'Perhaps I'm a chocolate moulder, or a poodle-clipper, or maybe I paint water-colours like those on the wall over there.'

'Lord, I hope not. They were perpetrated by my great-aunt Olwen, an eccentric lady with more enthusiasm than talent!'

She giggled, and he nodded approvingly.

'That's better. You're beginning to lighten up a bit. Is your head better?'

'Somewhat. It makes its presence felt now and then.' She smiled at him cajolingly. 'Could I have some more tablets before I go to bed?'

He shook his head. 'I'd rather you didn't, Leonora. Try to stick it out until tomorrow.'

She sighed. 'All right. Can I have a book to read, then?'

'I'm afraid it's no to that, too. Give your head a chance—count sheep if you can't get to sleep.'

She decided not to argue. 'Are there any sheep on Gullholm?'

'There used to be. This was a farmhouse once. A trawler-owning ancestor of mine bought the island, apparently convinced he could make a go of farming in a place surround by his beloved sea.'

'Was he Penry, too?'

He stretched his long frame comfortably in the deep leather chair as he explained that the gentleman in question was his mother's grandfather, a roistering old sea-dog by the name of Joshua Probert, more inclined to raising Cain than crops. The small-holding had failed to prosper due to the owner's propensity for fishing off Lee Haven, or drinking in the pub across the sound in Brides Haven.

'Since old Josh's time it's been used as a holiday retreat by various Proberts down the years,' he added, 'with some of the land let out for summer grazing to mainland farmers.'

'What happened in winter?'

'Ferreters used it in the past. These days I pay someone from Brides Haven to come over here at regular intervals to keep an eye on the place.'

Leonora was impressed. 'The island's your sole property?'

He nodded. 'My mother was an only child, so my grandfather Probert entailed Gullholm on me, which means I couldn't sell the place, even if I wanted to. He meant me to pass it on to my son.'

'How feudal!' She looked at him hesitantly. 'Do you *have* a son?'

His eyes went blank. 'No. I don't.'

'Sorry—didn't mean to be nosy.'

'Not at all,' he said politely. 'It's not classified information. I confess I did have a wife until recently, but, alas, no son—or daughter.'

Leonora felt a sharp pang of sympathy. The melancholy was explained. The poor man was here to get over a bereavement. 'I'm so sorry.'

A cynical gleam lit his eyes. 'Now what, I wonder, are you sorry for, Leonora?'

'Why—because you've lost your wife.'

'I didn't *lose* her, exactly. That smacks of carelessness, wouldn't you say?' His smile set her teeth on edge. 'Melanie merely lost interest in marriage to a busy consultant. She required a consort with more time—and money—to spend on her. The divorce became absolute not long ago,' he added abruptly, and got up. 'Would you like more tea?'

Leonora nodded dumbly, wishing the subject had never come up, as Penry Vaughan strode off to the kitchen. She gazed across the room at the door he kicked shut behind him, biting her lip. He must have loved the faithless Melanie very deeply to be so bitter over losing her. Tears welled in her eyes as she wondered about her loved ones. She must have a family, maybe even a boyfriend, all of them frantic, imagining her missing, even drowned. She slammed a mental door shut on the harrowing thought. What she must do was concentrate on getting her memory back so that she could get home to them as soon as humanly possible. The prospect of being marooned on Gullholm for days with a Heathcliff bereft of his Cathy gave her the creeps.

When Penry returned with her tea, looking withdrawn, as though he deeply regretted the mention of his wife, he put a plate of biscuits on the small table beside her. 'Eat a couple of those with the tea. You'll feel better.'

Leonora doubted that biscuits were much of a cure

for what ailed her, but she bit into one meekly, deciding that the best policy was to fall in with Penry Vaughan's wishes whenever possible, to keep the peace. He poured tea for her then retreated to his chair again with a glass of whisky.

'The weather forecast's pretty grim,' he said moodily. 'Gale-force ten in these parts soon, I'm afraid.'

'Pretty noisy already, isn't it?' She glanced nervously at the windows, wondering how they'd hold out against fiercer gusts than those already battering the house.

'Don't worry. There's secondary glazing everywhere. Keeps out the worst of it, and blankets the noise a bit too.' He smiled faintly. 'It's a good few decibels higher out of doors.'

Leonora shivered. 'Then I don't think I'll venture out for a stroll before bedtime.' She swallowed some tea hurriedly, then dropped the cup with a scream as the room was plunged into darkness.

'Are you all right?' demanded Penry urgently, shining a torch beam in her eyes.

'Yes—only I've broken your cup and spilled tea on your dressing-gown,' she said breathlessly, running a hand down over the dampness on her chest. 'What's happened?'

'The confounded generator's on the blink again.' Penry struck a match and lit the oil lamp nearest Leonora, his face Mephistophelean over the flame as he replaced the glass chimney.

Leonora felt better instantly once there was light. She watched Penry moving round the room to light the other lamps, realising now why there was such a plentiful supply of non-electrical light sources everywhere.

'This happens a lot, I take it?' she asked. She bent

to pick up broken shards of china, gritting her teeth as her head protested.

'Too damned often for comfort,' he said irritably. 'The generator's old. I should replace it, but usually it only takes a bit of tinkering to get it going again. And to be honest I'm rather attached to it. I'm afraid I'll have to leave you to your own devices for a while.' He went to the shelves lining one wall and selected a handful of cassettes, then picked up a transistor radio. 'Would you like some music or a story for company while I wrestle with my old adversary? I keep a supply of batteries to save the blasted generator, so you might as well make use of them.'

Leonora received the offering with delight. 'Why, thank you, that's wonderful.' She scanned the selection of cassettes eagerly, then smiled up at him. 'No Beethoven?'

He shook his head. 'I remembered! And if you don't like any of those look for something else on the shelf, but try to move about as little as possible, please.'

'Yes, Doctor.'

'Are you being cheeky, by any chance?'

'I wouldn't dream of it,' she said demurely. 'I'll be good as gold, I promise. Besides, I've got Prunella Scales here, reading Jane Austen's *Emma*. I won't move a muscle until you're back.'

'My mother left that last time she was here. You share her taste in reading, obviously.'

Leonora looked up at him. 'Apparently so. It's like little bits of a jigsaw, isn't it?' Her mouth drooped. 'I just wish the complete picture would fall into place.'

'Now stop that!' he ordered. 'And mind you don't move until I get back.'

It was no hardship to obey. Lying on the sofa to

listen to her favourite story read with such consummate skill, Leonora shut out her worries and closed her ears to the howling wind while Penry went off to apply his healing skills to the rebellious generator.

Leonora lay with her eyes closed, so absorbed that Penry was obliged to turn off the radio to gain her attention. She sat up with a start, blinking, to find the room full of electric light again, and her host occupied in turning off the lamps, his face streaked with oil and his black hair wildly untidy, but with an air of triumph about him which she registered with some amusement.

'The patient recovered, I gather?'

He nodded with satisfaction. 'This time, at least. Every time it goes on the blink I wonder who'll win. So far I've come out on top, but one day the damn thing will expire just to spite me.'

'It didn't take you long!'

One eyebrow rose quizzically. 'It's an hour and ten minutes since I left you here with Jane Austen. A mere flash to you, but a long, hard grind out there in a freezing outhouse, young lady.'

She bit her lip. 'Was it really that long? I was so deep in the story I never noticed.'

'While I, on the other hand, was sweating blood to get the contraption going again in case you were frightened on your own in here!'

Leonora looked sceptical. 'Come off it, Dr Vaughan. I fancy you've been enjoying yourself just as much as I have.'

Penry smiled, shrugging, then looked down at his filthy sweater in distaste. 'I need a bath. Will you and Jane wait there for a while until I'm respectable again?'

Leonora, afraid he'd been about to order her to bed,

assented so rapturously that Penry eyed her in amusement as he crossed to the stairs.

'You're obviously feeling very much better tonight, Leonora.'

She thought about it. 'Yes—yes, I am. My head aches a bit, and I still feel battered, but if only my wretched memory would behave I'd soon be good as new.'

'Be thankful you're as good as you are, Leonora. You could have been drowned, remember.'

'Yes, Dr Vaughan,' she said, subdued. 'If it weren't for you I'd have been fish-food by now.'

'Stop that!' he ordered. 'Switch the tape on now, please, before I go upstairs.'

This time Leonora was allowed only a short session with *Emma* before Penry returned, damp about the head, but clean again in navy guernsey and tracksuit trousers, his bare feet in ancient espadrilles.

'Right, Leonora,' he said briskly. 'Time you were in bed.'

She switched off the tape, looking glum. 'Couldn't I stay down a bit longer, please?'

'You happen to be occupying the only sofa-bed in the room, young lady, and I need it——'

'Oh, but *I* could sleep down here,' she said instantly. 'You could have your bed back, and——'

'Nonsense.' He held out his hand. 'Come along. I want you safely upstairs in bed, not free to wander about down here, keeping me awake.'

Leonora eyed him resentfully, ignoring his hand as she took off the large borrowed socks. She stood up gingerly, relieved that the room stayed still. Her head gave a warning thump, but subsided almost at once to

the now bearable ache. 'Very well,' she said grandly. 'But this time I go up under my own steam.'

'It really doesn't matter to me how you get upstairs,' he said indifferently as he followed behind her. 'Just as long as you get up there in one piece and stay put all night you can crawl up on your hands and knees for all I care.'

She preserved a dignified silence as she gathered up the trailing dressing-gown in one hand and kept the other on the rail attached to the wall on one side of the staircase. She mounted the uneven stairs with immense care, determined not to trip or fall, then turned as she reached the top. 'I shall be perfectly all right now, Dr Vaughan. Thank you for my dinner. Goodnight.'

He scrutinised her clinically. 'Right then, Leonora. Goodnight. If you need anything else in the night just call.'

She gave him a gracious little nod, determined to die first rather than do any such thing. Tomorrow, she assured herself, as she brushed her teeth, she would wake up with total recall of who she was and where she came from. All she had to do was get a good night's sleep. By morning perhaps the storm would have blown itself out, and the fog in her mind along with it.

When Leonora returned to the bedroom she found the bed turned down invitingly. A glass of water stood on the table beside the rose-shaded lamp, along with a torch and a candle and a box of matches in a pretty pottery holder. If the generator broke down in the middle of the night Penry had seen to it that she'd still be able to lighten her darkness. Unable to resist a look in the mirror, she gave a despairing sigh. Her hair, left to its own devices to dry, looked like the business end of a witch's broom. Hoping Penry Vaughan wouldn't

mind if she borrowed his hairbrush, she set to work. It took some time, and no little resolution, before the tightly curling mass hung round her face tangle-free at last, and she could crawl wearily into bed.

Leonora leaned back thankfully against the piled pillows, listening to the wind, which howled around the house like a hundred banshees demanding entry. She lay motionless, utterly worn out by her exertions, yet at the same time ominously wide awake. She would put out the lamp in a little while, she promised herself. As soon as she felt actually drowsy she would turn it off. Drowsiness, however, was not forthcoming. She shifted a little against the pillows, wishing now she'd left her hair alone. Her head throbbed in rhythm with her bruises, yet she'd hardly noticed any of it downstairs. She sighed, feeling resentful towards Penry Vaughan for making her come up here. Which was unjust, she told herself firmly. If it weren't for Dr Penry Vaughan she might well be dead.

A tap on the door sounded above the wind. Leonora's eyebrows rose. Talk of the devil!

'Come in,' she called, surprised.

Penry Vaughan ducked his tall head through the doorway and moved to stand at the foot of the bed in the shadows beyond the arc of light from the small lamp. 'I saw the light under the door, and wondered if you'd like some company for the night.'

# CHAPTER THREE

LEONORA gazed at him, heart hammering. She cleared her throat drily. 'I'm sure I'll drop off soon, Dr Vaughan. I must have slept too long this afternoon.'

He eyed her narrowly. 'What's the matter? You look petrified again.'

'Your knock startled me.'

'I'm surprised you heard it above this wind.' He bent to pick something up, then came round the side of the bed holding out the transistor. 'If you're wakeful I thought you might like company in the shape of *Emma*——' He stopped, his eyes narrowing as he saw the expression on her face. '*Now* what's the matter?'

Praying he couldn't see her agonised blush, Leonora smiled shakily. 'Nothing. It's very kind of you.'

Penry Vaughan's eyes lit with sudden, derisive comprehension. 'My dear little castaway,' he drawled, 'surely you didn't imagine I was offering *myself* as companion for the night? Ah—I can see you did.'

Burning with mortification, Leonora looked away, sliding lower beneath the quilt like an animal burrowing for cover as Penry sat on the edge of the bed.

'Leonora,' he commanded, 'look at me.'

Unwillingly she raised her eyes to his.

'How can I succeed in convincing you?' he demanded. 'When I said you had nothing to fear from me I meant it, young lady. I don't know just what kind of monster you imagine I am, but having my wicked

way with a girl in your state of health is not precisely my style.'

'I'm sorry,' she got out after a painful silence. 'I misunderstood—which was very stupid. After all, I've seen myself in the mirror. You'd have to be pretty desperate to want—anything like that with someone who looks like me.'

'I wouldn't say that, exactly.' There was an unsettling gleam in his eye as he got up. 'You're very appealing, Leonora, black eye or not. Which doesn't mean I intend to leap into bed with you just because fate washed you up on my beach. And if you're imagining I pine for the delights of the conjugal bed now my wife's left me, you're a bit off-beam there, too. I was accustomed to a lonely bed long before she left me for someone else.' He checked himself, his face suddenly harsh. 'And why the hell I told you that I don't know. It's not something I want broadcast to the world.'

Indignation cancelled out any stray pang of compassion. Leonora eyed him angrily. 'Your marital problems don't interest me in the slightest, Dr Vaughan. Why would I want to talk about them to anyone else?' She sighed despairingly. 'At the moment I don't even *know* anyone else!'

Penry's harsh face softened a little. 'Be positive, Leonora. In the morning you'll probably wake to full recall. In the meantime listen to Jane Austen for a while, then try to sleep.'

She shifted her head restlessly against the pillows. 'I'll try. Thank you very much for bringing me the transistor—and I'm sorry, Dr Vaughan. For getting the wrong end of the stick, I mean. It was pretty far-fetched, really.'

He smiled slowly. 'Not that much, you know! But

you needn't lose any sleep over it, I promise—scout's honour.'

Leonora smiled faintly. 'Were you a boy scout?'

'No—too busy playing rugby. Were you a girl guide?' he countered swiftly.

'Oh, no, not my scene at all. . .' She halted, then blew out her cheeks. 'There I go again. Perhaps I'll do it by process of elimination; find out what I'm not bit by bit until I know who I am.'

'Go to sleep, child——' He checked himself, shrugging. 'Sorry, Leonora, but you look about twelve or so in this light.'

'Which is pretty clever of me, considering I feel so aged and infirm.' She smiled. 'Goodnight, Doctor.'

'Goodnight, Leonora.' He paused before ducking through the doorway. 'But remember, if you want anything just shout.'

She smiled non-comittally, then turned to the transistor, grateful for the wit and irony of Jane Austen. After an hour or so her eyes grew heavy and her yawns more frequent, and at last she stopped the tape at a suitable break. Hoping the generator could cope with one small lamp left on all night, she wriggled lower in the bed, pulled the covers over her ears, and fell asleep to the howl of the wind and the pounding of the waves on the rocks below.

Leonora woke in the night, gasping, her body drenched with perspiration. Still rigid with the horror of her nightmare, she heaved herself up in bed as the door flew open and Penry charged into the room at a run, his hair on end and his chest bare.

He took her by the shoulders, his eyes urgent. 'What's wrong? You were screaming your head off. Good lord, you're drenched, girl.' He went over to the

chest, rummaging through it until he found a large white sweatshirt. 'I'll get a towel. Get back under the covers.'

Leonora fought for calm, her breath ripping through her chest as she clenched her teeth together to stop them chattering. Penry returned quickly with a warm, dry towel, which he draped round her shoulders as he took her wrist in his.

'I had—a nightmare,' she said jerkily.

'I gathered that! Quietly now, please.' He looked at his watch as he took her pulse. 'Hm. A bit rapid, but not unduly so under the circumstances.' He smiled encouragingly. 'Come on—off with that sodden thing. This sweatshirt will drown you, but it's warm and dry.'

Leonora's mouth set stubbornly.

'Did you hear?' he said impatiently. 'Get the damn thing off.'

'Turn your back, please.'

He stared at her in exasperation. 'Leonora, I'm a *doctor*——'

'I don't care. Turn your back. Please!'

Penry threw up his hands in surrender. 'I'll do better than that. I'll go downstairs and make you a hot drink.'

Leonora shuddered at the memory of her dream as she peeled the damp shirt over her throbbing head. She struggled into Penry's thick white sweatshirt, rolled the ludicrously long sleeves back, then began tidying the bed.

'Don't bother,' said Penry, coming in with an armful of bedding. He tossed her a blanket. 'Wrap yourself in that while I change the sheets.'

Leonora watched numbly as Penry, who had now added the navy guernsey to his tracksuit trousers, made the bed with a swiftness and dexterity any ward sister

would have approved. When it was ready she got up, handing him the blanket as she slid wearily beneath the covers. Penry propped up the pillows behind her, then opened the bag he'd brought with him and took out a small torch.

'Right. Hold still now.' He held up his left forefinger in front of her. 'Keep watching that while I take a look.' He shone the slender beam into each eye in turn, then nodded. 'Pupil reaction satisfactory. How's the head?'

'Thumping,' she admitted. 'Not surprising after all that commotion.'

'Lie perfectly still for a while. I'll get these damp sheets out of the way then fetch that drink.' He paused in the doorway. 'Better now?'

'Yes.' It was the truth, Leonora realised, when she was alone. Her desperate, unreasoning terror had left her the moment Penry Vaughan hurtled through the door. She smiled faintly, wondering what he was like with his patients. Probably they got better rather than risk his wrath by doing otherwise.

'You're very clever not to bump your head just once now and then,' said Leonora hoarsely as Penry ducked through the doorway with a laden tray. She coughed drily. 'Listen to me! I'm croaking like a frog.'

'You've screamed yourself hoarse.' Penry handed Leonora a steaming mug, then hooked a large wicker chair near the bed and sat down. 'Right. Tell me what you were dreaming about,' he commanded.

She shuddered, then took a sip from her mug. 'This is nice,' she said evasively. 'What's in the milk?'

'Just sugar and a pinch of cinnamon.'

Leonora took a few more sips of the hot milk, then met his eyes. 'It didn't seem like a dream.'

'It sounded like a full-scale nightmare from downstairs.'

She breathed in deeply. 'I think my subconscious found a way of telling me a bit of what happened, Dr Vaughan.'

Penry leaned forward to take the mug from her. He put it down on the tray then captured her hand, suddenly very much the professional consultant. 'All right, Leonora, take your time. Was anyone else in the dream?'

'No. Only me.' She swallowed. 'I was in a dinghy—the kind you can use with an outboard engine.'

'Go on,' he said gently.

Her breathing quickened, her eyes dilating as they stared into his. 'The sea was very rough. I was soaked to the skin, my hands so cold I could hardly keep hold of the tiller. The wind rose and the dinghy was bucketing about like mad, then—then——'

Penry caught both her hands in his. 'Steady. What happened next?'

'The engine stopped. The dinghy spun like a top, a huge wave came at me, sweeping me overboard, and—and then I woke up.' She swallowed a sob of pure terror at the memory and Penry jumped up to sit beside her on the bed. He took her in his arms, holding her close in silence, the sheer size and warmth of him calming her very quickly.

'Sorry,' she muttered, pulling away. 'I didn't mean to fall apart like that.'

Penry stacked the pillows more comfortably behind her. 'You'll probably feel all the better for it. Drink up.' He returned to the chair, looking thoughtful. 'I think you're right. It's too relevant to be merely a dream. I think your subconscious decided to provide

you with a sort of extract from the main story. It would certainly explain how you came to be washed up in Seal Haven.' He looked up. 'A good thing you were near Gullholm when the engine failed or you'd never have survived.'

Leonora nodded, shivering. 'I can't have been making for Gullholm, though, can I?'

'True. Only a fool would try to get here in a dinghy. I've got a chunky old fishing-boat myself, the type locals use for crabbing.'

She pulled the covers higher, feeling drained but oddly relaxed, as though the dream had relieved some of the pressure on her brain. 'If the dream is accurate——' She pulled a face. 'Something so realistic just has to be accurate! Anyway, it's a hint as to how I got here, if nothing else.' She eyed him apprehensively. 'Do you suppose I'll have a nightmare like that every night?'

'I've no idea. Try not to think about it,' he ordered, then added casually, 'Can you swim, Leonora?'

'Yes,' she said without thinking, then stared at him, shaking her head. 'I don't know how I know. But I do.'

He nodded. 'It probably saved your life.' He got up, stretching, his head endangering the overhead light. 'Right, Leonora. Do you think you can sleep now?'

She nodded, secretly doubting it very much. 'Yes, Dr Vaughan. Thank you. I'm sorry to be so much trouble.'

He smiled wryly. 'It relieves the monotony of my own company, if nothing else.' He paused in the doorway. 'By the way, was it daylight in your dream?'

Leonora thought for a moment. 'Yes. Yes, it was.' She looked at him questioningly. 'Why do you ask?'

'It means you couldn't have arrived in Seal Haven all that long before I found you. If you'd been there overnight it's unlikely you'd be alive to tell the tale.' He gave her a kindly nod. 'Now for heaven's sake get some sleep—and let me do the same!'

Leonora stared at the closed door forlornly, certain she'd lie awake for what was left of the night. After what seemed like only a doze she woke to daylight, the wind driving hail against the window with a force which threatened to break it. She reached over and turned out the light, sick with disappointment to find she was no wiser about her identity than the night before. She climbed wearily out of bed, consoling herself that her physical injuries, at least, were healing fast. She pulled on the red wool dressing-gown hastily, glad of its warmth as she tiptoed to the bathroom, doing her best not to wake Penry.

The confrontation with her reflection was encouraging. Both eyes were now wide open and reasonably bright. One, it was true, still sported a bruise which gave her a rather raffish air, but it was already fading. She was no raving beauty, she thought wryly, but at least she now looked human. Back in the bedroom, she brushed her hair gently, then got back into bed, uncertain what else to do until she knew Penry was up and about. She turned on the transistor very quietly, found a local radio station, and discovered, surprised, that it was nearly nine. Outside it looked more like twilight than early morning. She waited until the news summary at nine o'clock, but, when there was no mention of a missing female person, eyes dark, hair mouse, she returned to Jane Austen's *Emma* for consolation.

Shortly afterwards there was a perfunctory tap on

the door heralding Penry's practised juggling act with a laden tray as he ducked into the room. He eyed her closely as he set the tray down. 'Good morning, Leonora. I heard you up and about. How do you feel?'

'Better.' She smiled ruefully. 'At least my body does. My memory, wretched thing, is still playing truant. After my dream last night I had such hopes, too.'

Penry handed her a plate of steaming porridge. 'It'll come. Try not to worry. In the meantime eat that while it's hot. I've put a sprinkling of brown sugar and a dash of milk on it. OK?'

'Wonderful,' she said, tasting it. 'It's years since I had porridge—I think. I'd forgotten how good it is——' She stopped, grimacing. 'I wish that was all I'd forgotten!'

'Now then!' He checked the contents of the tray. 'Toast, butter, tea, milk. Anything else you'd like?'

'Absolutely not!' She smiled shyly. 'It's very good of you to bring me breakfast, Dr Vaughan——'

'Penry.'

'All right. Penry. But you shouldn't be waiting on me like this.'

'From now on I won't,' he assured her, on his way to the door. 'I'll bring your clothes up in a minute, then you can come downstairs. Not,' he added, with a wave at the rain-lashed window, 'that either of us is going anywhere in this. The shipping forecast said it should moderate later, so with luck I'll get you X-rayed tomorrow. We'll see.'

Leonora settled down to her breakfast in a better frame of mind than she would have believed possible the day before. Breakfast in bed was a luxury, that much was certain. In fact, she thought, crunching on a piece of toast, she was pretty sure breakfast didn't

feature much at all in this unknown life of hers. She frowned as she remembered her dream. It had been so vivid it *seemed* real, yet had she really been idiot enough to set out on a rough sea in a mere dinghy?

'That's a very black frown,' commented Penry. He deposited a small pile of clothes on the end of the bed, then took her empty plate. 'Shall I pour some tea for you while you take a look through your things?'

'Yes, please.' Leonora examined the clothes eagerly. There were two pairs of jeans, one newish, one elderly, two chambray shirts, one pink and checked, the other plain light blue, plus a heavy navy wool sweater from the same chain store as the pretty cotton underwear. There was also, she saw with a slight flush, a peach silk camisole and French knickers. Three pairs of navy wool socks and a white-spotted red cotton scarf made up the total.

'Your shoes are downstairs, stuffed with paper— navy leather moccasin type. And you were wearing a ski-jacket, puffy navy thing. Probably supported you for a bit once you were in the water.' Penry handed her a cup of tea. 'Any of it ring a bell?'

'All of it.' She shrugged helplessly. 'I'm not sure about the silk things but the rest of it is mine, I know. But that's all I know. It's so frustrating!'

Penry collected the tray, looking thoughtful. 'In this dream of yours, did the dinghy have a name, by any chance?'

She shook her head, and winced sharply. 'I must remember not to do that!' She thought hard. 'It's all a bit blurred now anyway, but I was inside the boat during the dream. The name would be on the outside.'

'Merely a thought before I contact the coastguard and the police again.'

Leonora eyed him over her cup. 'Are you really going to tell them about the dream?'

'Yes. Any lead is worth following up.'

The moment Penry was through the door Leonora got out of bed, eager to see if the familiarity of the clothes would jog her memory. The cotton bra and briefs were a perfect fit, as were the pink shirt and the rather worn jeans, but there was no blinding flash of enlightenment once she had them on. Sighing, she pulled on socks and sweater, then knotted the scarf at her throat and secured one of the ends to her sweater with the silver lioness brooch so automatically that she paused, eyeing herself in the mirror. The little routine was second nature to her, evidently. She went on looking at herself, willing her reflection to start up some reaction in her brain, but with no success. She sighed as she tidied her hair, which hung to her shoulder-blades, curling tightly. Surely she didn't wear it loose like this?

Leonora made her bed then collected her cup and started downstairs, deeply thankful that she felt so much better than the day before. As she reached the foot of the narrow stair Penry emerged from the kitchen, his black eyebrows knitting together in a daunting frown at the sight of her.

'Hello.' She smiled at him warily. 'Have you got an old shoelace?'

His eyes dropped to the socks on her feet. 'Why do you need one?' he asked shortly.

She gestured at her hair. 'To tie this lot back. Whoever I am I'm in crying need of a haircut.'

'I'll see what I can do.'

Leonora stared at him blankly as he went into the

kitchen, wondering what she'd done to incur his displeasure again. Dr Penry Vaughan's brooding Celtic moods were a bit hard to take at times, to say the least. Scowling at his broad, white-sweatered back, she followed him into a room as neat and orderly as an operating theatre. Cupboards, surfaces, refrigerator, cooker, everything shone with pristine cleanliness, no clutter of any kind in sight beyond an electric kettle, a large cast-iron cookpot on the back of the wood-burning Aga. The only blots on the landscape were a pair of small shoes beside the Aga and a nylon ski-jacket airing on the back of a chair. Wondering if she dared risk sullying the gleaming sink, Leonora rinsed out her cup, then eyed the cupboards, wondering where to put it.

'In the cupboard on the right,' said Penry curtly as he searched through a drawer.

Leonora opened the cupboard and added the cup to a row of others, rather awed by the perfect symmetry of plates in orderly stacks according to size and function. When she turned round Penry was holding out a pair of unused white shoelaces.

'Will these do?'

'Perfectly. Thank you.' Leonora gave him a polite smile as she tied her hair securely at the nape of her neck. 'I don't suppose you were able to go for a run this morning in this weather?'

'No. I wasn't.'

She gestured to a half-open door beyond him. 'Is that a pantry?'

'It used to be. I've converted it into a study. The radio telephone's in there. And,' he added brusquely, 'I want it understood from the start that the study's off-limits to visitors.'

Leonora's chin lifted. 'Certainly, Dr Vaughan.'

'I should explain that I've got a deadline for the series of articles I'm writing. I fondly hoped the isolation of Gullholm would give me the requisite peace and quiet to meet it.'

'Instead of which you're landed with a nuisance like me!'

Penry Vaughan made no attempt to deny it. 'Since the situation is unavoidable I suggest that now you're better you make yourself as useful as possible, preparing meals and so on while I get on with my work. The moment the weather improves I'll take you over to the mainland and get that X-ray done. The sooner you recover your memory the better.'

Her mouth tightened. Anyone would think the loss was due to her own carelessness!

'I live for the moment,' she assured him coldly. 'In the meantime I'll earn my keep, don't worry.'

'Can you cook?'

'I believe so.'

He nodded briskly. 'Right. For lunch use the soup left in that pot. With a sandwich of some kind, that will do. While I go up for a bath you can take stock of the supplies I brought.'

'If I weren't here what would you have had for dinner?'

'Something easy. You needn't put yourself out too much.' He paused. 'But if you feel ill in any way, please say so. It's not my intention to jeopardise your recovery in any way.'

Leonora felt utterly flattened as he left her to go upstairs. What on earth was wrong? When he'd appeared with her breakfast Penry Vaughan had been reasonably friendly—and in the middle of the night

he'd been kindness itself after her nightmare. But from the moment she'd come downstairs he'd been a different man. She cast a malevolent eye at the window as a squall of rain battered the glass, then began an inspection of supplies. It was no surprise to find enough food for a siege. The cupboards held tins and packages of every kind, even a box of fresh vegetables. The fridge was stocked with salad greens, several kinds of cheese, bacon, eggs, the remains of a cooked ham. A large porcelain crock contained several loaves of bread. Whether she could cook or not, thought Leonora drily, they were unlikely to starve.

Abandoning the kitchen, she wandered across the large living-room to the windows. A driving curtain of rain blotted out everything other than the sodden turf nearest the house, the view so depressing that she turned away with a shiver, drawn like a magnet to the books on the shelves. Penry Vaughan's family had diverse tastes, she found. There was something to suit everyone; Tolstoy, Hemingway and Hardy, thrillers and spy stories, historical novels, light romances. All tastes were catered for admirably. Leonora chose a brightly coloured paperback novel about the Crusades, and went over to the fireplace to curl up on the sofa. By the time Penry Vaughan came downstairs again she was deep in the adventures of a lady who had decided to dress as a boy to search for her lost crusading husband. She looked up with an absent smile.

'Shall I make some coffee?'

He nodded. 'Thank you. There's only instant, I'm afraid. I'll take it in when I make a start. I'll top up the stove here while you're in the kitchen.'

Couldn't he bear to stay in the same room? Huffily Leonora filled the kettle, made coffee, then took hers

into the other room. 'I've left yours in the kitchen,' she said quietly, resuming her seat.

Penry straightened from his inspection of the stove. 'Thank you. This should be all right for hours now.'

She looked up at him diffidently. 'I don't suppose you've had time to ring the police for any news yet?'

'Of course. I'm just as eager as you to establish your identity,' he assured her with irony. 'I rang them first thing, but no one fitting your description has been reported missing anywhere in the entire country as yet. There were no reports of a dinghy washed up anywhere, either.'

Leonora turned away, her lips tight. 'I see. Thank you.' From the corner of her eye she saw him walk away, pause for a moment, then give an indifferent shrug as he went through the kitchen to his study. The door slammed shut behind him with a 'keep out' message she received with resentment. Penry Vaughan's irritation at being saddled with an unwelcome guest was understandable enough, but surely he could have let her know he'd spoken to the police!

Her animosity did her throbbing head no good at all. She laid her head back against a cushion, breathing in deeply and regularly to relax the tension in the back of her neck, but it was no use. Her mind kept wrestling with the problem of her identity, her imagination running riot as she pictured loved ones mad with anxiety about her. A particularly ferocious gust brought Leonora to her feet to roam about the room wishing passionately that the weather would improve. Not even her fear of setting foot in a boat again would keep her from making the crossing to the mainland the moment the trip to Brides Haven was feasible. Someone, somewhere out there just had to be searching for her.

Leonora pulled herself together after a while. This just wouldn't do, she told herself sternly. Then she paused, her attention caught by a canvas bag of knitting on one of the armchairs. The bag contained wool, needles and a pattern for a sweater obviously intended for Penry, by the measurements ringed in red. The design was complicated, with a serpentine pattern of dark blue and white with touches of black, and whoever was knitting it had completed only a few inches of ribbed welt.

*I* can knit, thought Leonora with a sudden flash of self-knowledge. One look at the intricate pattern was enough to tell her she could follow it with no trouble at all. She looked at the clock, frustrated to find it was only a little after eleven. Bearding the lion in his den just to ask about some knitting was a bad idea. She'd have to be patient until lunchtime, then soften up Penry Vaughan with a snack before she made her request.

Ten minutes before midday Leonora retired to the kitchen, tiptoeing past the closed study door. At first she tried to be as quiet as possible as she began preparations for lunch, but after a few minutes gave up and worked normally, deciding to impress the moody Dr Vaughan by making dumplings to top the soup. While they were steaming on top of the savoury liquid she whipped up a small quantity of French dressing, sprinkled it on shredded lettuce and tomato slices, then added grated cheese and made some sandwiches.

When two trays were ready she tapped on the study door.

'Yes?' barked her host.

'Your lunch, Dr Vaughan. Shall I bring it in?'

'I'll fetch it.' He emerged, closing the door firmly

behind him as he looked from Leonora to the kitchen counter. 'Thank you. I'll eat mine at my desk.'

Leonora bristled as she marched into the other room, realising she'd expected murmurs of appreciation to greet her offering. She had no objection to working for her keep, but if Penry Vaughan went on treating her as if she were some kind of serf she'd stick to plain, basic cooking from now on, she thought resentfully. As she began on her soup she tried to think of what possible sin she could have committed to change his attitude towards her. He hadn't been exactly jumping for joy to have her here in the first place, as she knew very well. But he'd shown definite signs of resigning himself to the situation—until her arrival downstairs after breakfast. She shrugged. There was nothing she could do about it, other than keep a low profile and stay well out of his way.

Leonora took her time over her lunch. When she went back to the kitchen Penry's tray stood on the counter, the plates satisfactorily empty. She cleared away, made coffee, then tapped on Penry's door, opening it warily as he called her in. He sat at a large desk covered with papers, journals, medical books, a portable typewriter pushed to one end. The radio transmitter, a surprisingly small, modern affair, occupied its own bracket on one wall, which was foot-thick whitewashed stone like the others, the chill only a little alleviated by the portable bottled-gas heater alongside the desk. Penry thrust his black hair back from his forehead, frowning as he looked up.

'Well?'

'Your coffee. Shall I bring it in?'

'Yes—please.'

Leonora collected the steaming mug and went into

the study, placing it carefully on the only unoccupied space on the desk.

'Thank you,' muttered her host, leafing impatiently through some notes.

Leonora braced herself. 'Dr Vaughan, would it disturb you if I listened to the transistor this afternoon?'

He looked up. 'No. If you keep the doors closed it won't make any difference to me.' He leaned back in his chair, looking at her. 'How's your head? Does reading make it ache?'

'A little. It would be easier to listen to a story for a while. But I feel much better today.' As she met the clinical look in Penry Vaughan's eyes she stiffened, the reason for his change of mood suddenly, mortifyingly, obvious. She drew herself up to her full height. 'Tell me the truth, please, Dr Vaughan. Do you by any chance think I'm faking?'

One eyebrow rose. 'Faking?'

'The amnesia. Ever since I came downstairs this morning you've been different, hostile. I've been racking my brains for what I could have done, then it struck me. You think my loss of memory is put on!'

'It had better not be,' he said cuttingly, then shrugged. 'I suppose you merit an explanation.' He swallowed some of the coffee, then eyed her moodily. 'I had no choice when it came to rescuing the helpless victim of an unknown accident. When I found you all my energies were directed towards mending, healing, reviving. You were the patient, I was the doctor. But today things are different. You look much better, less of a victim. To put it in basic terms, Leonora, you're no longer merely a patient in my eyes. You're a

woman. Young and over-thin, it's true, but a woman just the same.'

Leonora stepped back involuntarily, her cheeks burning. 'I can't help that, Dr Vaughan!'

'True. But the fact remains that I retreated to Gullholm because it's the one place in my world *free* of the entire sex.' His eyes gleamed suddenly. 'Not that I'm a misogynist, Leonora. Far from it. Given time I'll no doubt revert to normal. But for the moment,' he added significantly, 'the fact remains that you're female, I'm male, and we're marooned here alone together—a dangerous situation, though none of my seeking.'

'Nor,' she said passionately, 'of mine! Oddly enough I didn't set out from wherever I come from to trespass on your island, or to lose my wretched memory. If I could leave right now I would!' Then she remembered her request, and forced herself to calm down. 'Dr Vaughan, who does the knitting belong to?'

He stared at her blankly. 'Knitting?'

'I found a bag with wool and a pattern for a sweater,' she explained.

'My mother must have left it here.'

'Do you think she'd mind if I went on with it?'

Penry Vaughan gave her a smile of genuine amusement. 'On the contrary, she'd probably be delighted. The pattern infuriated her, now I come to think of it. She abandoned it in disgust.'

Leonora made no attempt at an answering smile. 'Then may I carry on, please? I can knit while I listen.'

'If you're certain your head is up to it.'

'If it starts protesting I'll stop.'

As she went through the door he called her back,

eyeing her speculatively. 'You know you can knit, then, Leonora?'

'Yes. It's utterly maddening. Some things are crystal-clear, yet the rest keep lurking in the fog. By the way,' she added, 'what time would you like dinner?'

Penry Vaughan turned back to his work dismissively. 'I generally work until six-thirty. Give me an hour or so to unwind.'

'As you wish.'

He looked up. 'I forgot. It may cheer you up to learn that the weather forecast is promising. Tomorrow we should be able to get over to the mainland. Make a list of any supplies we need.'

Despite the disquieting exchange with her host Leonora felt rather more cheerful when she settled down with her knitting. Less apprehensive of the weather now she knew it was due to improve, she was glad of permission to use the transistor. Concentrating on *Emma* would help to keep her worries at bay for a little while. Then, just as she was about to press the switch to 'Play', it occurred to Leonora that Penry Vaughan's eyes weren't dark like her own, after all. At close quarters, meeting them across his desk just now, she'd discovered they were blue. A dark, smoky sort of colour, it was true, but very definitely blue.

# CHAPTER FOUR

LEONORA found no difficulty in following the pattern which had defeated Mrs Vaughan. The design, the cover informed her, was inspired by ancient Viking jewellery, which explained the serpentine interweaving of the colours, and her brain and fingers co-ordinated over the task with such dexterity that Leonora had no doubt this was something she'd done often before.

It proved soothing. With her fingers busy and her mind occupied with the story it was late afternoon before the end of a tape brought Leonora back to earth with a start. Several inches of intricately patterned knitting hung from her needles, she saw with satisfaction, almost as if her fingers had worked independently while she listened. She went quietly into the kitchen to make tea, then knocked on the study door.

'Come in,' said Penry absently, looking up, yawning, as Leonora popped her head round the door.

'I thought you might like some tea, and a slice of the fruit-cake I found in a tin.'

He eased his shoulders. 'Sounds good.'

She deposited the tray on the desk, then took her own tea and a small piece of cake back to her former post, slotted a new tape into the machine for the next instalment of the story and settled down to enjoy the rest of the afternoon in peace.

'Isn't it time you had a rest?' enquired Penry Vaughan, startling her. At some stage Leonora had

switched on the lamp beside her to see her knitting, but otherwise the room was in darkness.

Leonora stopped the tape. 'What time is it?'

'After six.' He went round the room drawing curtains and turning on lamps. 'Time you called it a day.' He stooped to replenish the stove then came to look at what she was doing as she finished off a row. 'Have you done all that this afternoon?' he asked, astonished.

'Oh, no. Your mother did the ribbing. I've only done the patterned bit.'

'Only!' As she finished he took the needle from her. 'This is extremely well done. You're obviously an expert.'

'I think I must be,' she agreed. 'The pattern seemed easy to me, anyway.'

He shook his head in surprise. 'My mother's knitted for all of us as far back as I can remember, but she acknowledged defeat on this one.'

Leonora stowed the knitting away carefully, then got up. 'Right. I'll go and make the sauce, then I'll have a bath while it's simmering if the generator's up to it.'

'Are you sure *you're* up to it?' he asked sharply. 'You look very pale.'

'My head's aching a bit, now you come to mention it, but I expect that's all the concentration,' she said cheerfully. 'I'll be fine after a bath.'

'Hang on a moment! I'll take a look at you first.' He went off to fetch his medical bag.

Once again Leonora was obliged to submit to light directed in her eyes, after which Penry Vaughan took her pulse and her blood-pressure before he was satisfied. 'I suppose you'll do,' he said grudgingly. 'But don't attempt anything too complicated for the meal. Bacon and eggs will do.'

'You can have that for breakfast. It's tagliatelle for supper. You've got some in the cupboard so I assume you like it,' she said, making for the kitchen.

Penry came to lean in the doorway, his eyes following her about as she took packets and tins from the cupboard, making her decidedly uneasy.

Leonora frowned over her shoulder. 'Your kitchen's small and so am I, Dr Vaughan, whereas you most definitely are not. I'll get on faster on my own.'

His eyes lit with an unsettling gleam as he brushed past her. 'I'll get some wood in for the stove, then. But once you've made this sauce of yours I suggest you have a bath and a rest before we eat. I want you fit and well as quickly as possible.'

'So do I!' Leonora snapped, then set to work at top speed while Penry was out chopping driftwood. In minutes she had garlic, onions, carrots and celery cooking together gently in olive oil. As she sieved the contents of two cans of tomatoes, Penry returned, sniffing the air.

'Great smell,' he said, pausing, the basket balanced easily on one hip.

'I forgot to ask if you like garlic, but there was some in with the vegetables so I took a chance,' she said, adding the tomato purée to the pot with care.

'I'm very fond of it, but until recently had to forgo the pleasure. My former wife disliked not only the taste of it herself but refused to come near me if *I* succumbed to its temptation.' Penry raised an eyebrow. 'The smell of your sauce is a two-fold comfort, Leonora. It points out advantages to my divorced state I hadn't thought of before.'

Leonora made no comment, determined to avoid personalities at all cost after his remarks earlier on.

'Dinner will be ready in an hour,' she informed him, and went up to run a bath.

She let herself down gingerly into the hot water, gritting her teeth as various bruises stung as they came in contact with the heat. The water cooled too quickly for her to stay long in the bath, but afterwards she lay fully dressed on the bed for a while, listening, her spirits rising as she realised that the wind had dropped at last. She could still hear the pounding of the waves on the rocks below, but felt lulled rather than threatened by the muffled boom, accepting it as an inescapable sound on an island surrounded by the Atlantic ocean.

When Leonora went downstairs she found Penry lounging in front of the fireplace listening to a newcast on the transistor. He jumped up as she joined him.

'I've rung the police, but nothing yet, I'm afraid. I don't know who you belong to, Leonora, but no one's anxious about you yet, obviously, so you'll just have to be patient.'

The sharp pang of disappointment seared her like a physical pain. 'I must belong to someone,' she said tartly to hide it. 'You'd think someone would have made enquiries about me by now.'

The smoky-blue eyes softened slightly. 'Probably you haven't been missed yet.'

'I suppose so. Thank you for ringing.' Leonora blinked hard as she forced a smile. 'I suppose I'll come to terms eventually with the blank in my mind. They say you get used to anything in time. Perhaps I won't like it when I find out who I am.'

'Of course you will,' he assured her, then looked down at himself in distaste. 'Sit down and listen to the radio for a bit while I go up and wash. I'll make up a

bed in one of the other rooms tonight. This sofa wasn't designed for someone like me.'

· She frowned. 'I wish you'd let me sleep in another bed. I don't need a big bed, and you do.'

He shook his head. 'I prefer not to risk further disorientation for you, Leonora. You stay where you are. The bed in the room next to you is perfectly adequate for me, I promise.'

Leonora wasn't at all sure she fancied the idea of Penry in the next room in the night. Now he'd brought the subject up it was very hard to forget that they were a man and woman isolated together miles from anywhere. Even harder to ignore the fact that her reluctant, brooding host was all male, with an attraction rendered more rather than less dangerous by his current attitude towards the female sex. Dr Penry Vaughan, she realised with deep misgiving, was pro tem the only other person in her entire world, and, like it or not, he was doomed to play Adam to her Eve until her memory deigned to function again.

But what if it never did? Leonora fought down a sudden rush of panic. It was only thirty-six hours since she'd been washed up on the island like a piece of flotsam, she reminded herself; early days to start bewailing her fate. She could hear Penry moving about upstairs as he made up the other bed. She jumped to her feet, suddenly in need of occupation, and went into the kitchen. She put a big pan of water to boil, ready for the pasta, then added canned mushrooms to the tomato sauce, which was giving off such a heavenly aroma that she felt hungry despite her inner turmoil.

Delivering a brief lecture on self-control, Leonora began frying bacon, cutting hunks of crusty bread, grating cheese, determined to keep so occupied that

there was no attention to spare for the worries which seemed to be multiplying by the minute.

'Is it nearly ready?' said Penry, startling her.

Leonora whirled round, flushing as she found him watching her from the doorway. 'More or less. Shall I put the pasta on now?'

'Please do!' He leaned against the door-jamb, his hair brushing the lintel. 'I could eat a horse, Madame Chef.'

'No horse. You'll have to make do with bacon.' Cross to find her fingers transformed into thumbs by the watchful blue eyes, she added a spoonful of olive oil to the boiling water, then threw in the coils of pasta. 'Don't wander off, please,' she said, stirring busily. 'Once this is ready it must get to the plates quickly while it's hot.'

'I'm not going anywhere,' he said lazily. 'I'm perfectly happy where I am. Watching you.'

As a cure for clumsiness his statement was a failure. With such a disturbing audience of one, Leonora took far longer than intended to serve the meal. She was heartily glad when they were installed at last in front of the fire, trays on knees. Silence reigned for some time as they attacked the meal. Penry's plate was half empty before he said a word, other than grunts of pure appreciation.

'This is first-class, Leonora,' he said at last. 'It deserves some wine as an accompaniment, but I advise keeping off alcohol for a bit.'

'I don't drink very much, anyway,' she began, then paused, fork in hand. 'Ah. Another piece of the puzzle. Oh, Penry, I just wish the rest of it would fall into place!'

'It will.' His eyes gleamed. 'In the meantime I see

you've reverted to addressing me as Penry. This morning I was Dr Vaughan.'

'Mr Hyde, you mean,' she said tartly, twirling her fork round in the pasta. 'You were so horrible all of a sudden that formality seemed the order of the day.'

'I explained that.'

She flushed, her eyes falling. 'Let's forget all that—unless——'

'Unless what?'

'Unless you change back to Mr Hyde overnight and lump me in again with the rest of the female sex you're running away from.' The moment the words were out of her mouth Leonora could have kicked herself. His face took on the forbidding, sombre look which made her so uneasy.

'In actual fact I imagine it was myself I was trying to escape.' He shrugged violently, shaking off the thought as a dog shook water from its coat. 'But enough of that. I promise faithfully not to talk about it again. I'm normally quite an equable sort of guy, you know.'

She eyed him with scepticism. 'I'll take your word for it.'

'And when it comes to females I'd have a problem trying to escape them anyway,' he said, determinedly light. 'I've got far too many in my own family for starters. My father's no longer with us, unfortunately. He was a doctor too, a GP, and a damn good one. I miss him badly. But I still have my mother, three sisters, a sort of sister-in-law, and four nieces. Luckily the girls also managed to provide me with some nephews to balance it up a bit.'

Leonora sighed despondently. 'It's not fair! You're knee-deep in relatives, while I haven't a clue whether I possess any at all.'

'You'll soon find out.' Penry got up to take the trays. 'You look tired. *I'll* make coffee. I think I'll have some cheese to round the meal off. How about you? Would you like some cake, or a biscuit or something?'

'No, thanks. No room.'

'You should eat more. You could do with filling out a bit.'

'Ah, but would I fill out in the right places?' she said rashly, then bit her lip as Penry eyed the places in question with a deliberation which brought colour to her face. He went off to the kitchen, leaving Leonora apprehensive about the rest of the evening. To her surprise she enjoyed it very much, despite the fact that the only entertainment came from her host, who seemed bent on atoning for his earlier hostility by keeping her amused. Some of his anecdotes from his student days were hilariously funny, featuring enough females in them to convince his listener that he'd been the object of female adulation all his life until very recently.

This Melanie of his must have been a right madam, thought Leonora when Penry went off to get himself a glass of whisky. Penry Meredith Vaughan was a man of potent physical attraction, an attraction made doubly powerful by the formidable intellect behind it. He had to be brilliant, she thought, to be so well up in his profession at his age. His one big mistake seemed to have been his choice of wife.

'Would you like a soft drink?' he asked when he returned.

Leonora shook her head. 'I'll take a glass of water to bed later, but that's all.'

'An early night would do no harm. Not,' he added

swiftly at her frown, 'that I'm anxious for my own company, I assure you.'

'I only wish I had some anecdotes of my own to compete with yours.'

'I've probably bored you rigid!'

'Far from it—I could listen all night!' She hesitated. 'I'd like to stay down a little while—hear more about your family, too. At the moment it helps to console me for my lack in that direction.'

'All right—but not for long.' He slid down in the chair comfortably, his long legs stretched out in front of him. 'I saw my mother only last week. She stayed with me for a couple of days before going on to Spain to my sister. Charity runs a couple of hotels there with her husband Luiz Santana. Mother generally visits them in March before the season hots up so she can see something of Charity and spoil her grandchildren unmercifully.'

'Lovely,' said Leonora wistfully.

Penry's eyes softened as he went on to describe the rest of his family; Katharine, married to a merchant banker and mother of two teenage sons, and Clemency, Charity's twin, married to a writer and broadcaster and mother of twin girls and a son.

'Are your sisters identical twins?' asked Leonora.

'Unfortunately, yes.'

'Unfortunately?'

'You try walking down the street with two identical, sexy-looking blondes!' He pulled a face. 'Don't get me wrong—I'm very fond of them both, but I prefer them one at a time.'

'What about your other sister? Is she blonde too?'

Penry smiled warmly. 'No. Kit's the same colouring

as me. Not as tall as the other two, and a different personality altogether from the heavenly twins.'

'She's your favourite!'

'I suppose she is. The other two are a set, so to speak—a unit—so I suppose it's only natural I've always gravitated towards Kit.' He paused, eyeing her in the clinical way she'd come to recognise. 'You look very tired, Leonora. Enough chat for tonight. If it's fine tomorrow I'd like to be up to catch the tide. When you're in bed I'll bring up a hot drink.'

Leonora felt a deep reluctance to go upstairs, to face the night alone. She longed to stay where she was, listening to Penry talk in the resonant voice with the attractive trace of Welsh lilt, but she got up promptly, conscious that he probably wanted to get off to bed himself.

'Thank you. You're very kind.' She put the knitting away carefully. 'I feel I should say that if I had to get washed up on a beach minus my memory I was lucky the beach was yours, Dr Vaughan.'

His mouth tightened. 'Your luck was in surviving at all, Leonora. You escaped death by a hair's breadth.'

A shiver ran through her. 'Don't I know it! Instead of whining about my memory I should be thanking my lucky stars I'm alive at all.'

'And since you are, you'll feel a lot better if you get a good night's rest,' he said briskly. 'Don't hang about in the bathroom; it's cold up there.'

Leonora did as she was bidden, shivering as she brushed her teeth. A look in the mirror confirmed that the bruise round her eye was fading rapidly. If she could buy some make-up after the X-ray expedition the discolouration would be hardly noticeable—only she'd have to borrow some money from Penry, she

realised, frowning. Which seemed like colossal cheek on top of everything else.

When Penry arrived with the promised drink he also brought a hot-water bottle.

Leonora received it with rapture. 'Wonderful,' she said, snuggling her feet against the warmth. 'It seems colder than last night.'

'It is. But it's not freezing. We rarely get frost here.' Penry stood over her while she drank the milk, then put a hand to the lamp, but she smiled at him coaxingly.

'Will the generator object if I keep it on? Sorry to be a coward, but I don't want to be left in the dark.'

'Not surprising, under the circumstances. And if the generator gives up the ghost in the night you've got a torch on the table, and a candle. Or you can holler for me. I won't mind.' Penry Vaughan smiled down at her, then yawned hugely. 'Sorry! Goodnight, Leonora. Sleep well.'

'Goodnight.' Her answering smile was thoughtful as she watched him duck gracefully through the doorway. With a sigh she slid down further into the blissfully warm bed, realising she was no longer in the least uneasy at the thought of Penry only feet away beyond the bedroom wall. Disturbingly attractive male though he might be, Dr Penry Vaughan was nevertheless a match for any peril which might threaten in the small hours.

The dream came again in the night. Once again Leonora found herself fighting with the tiller in a dinghy threatening to stand on its head in a mountainous sea, but this time when the engine cut out she was plucked from the boat before she could hit the water.

'All right, all right, Leonora,' said Penry, holding her close. 'It was only a dream. You're safe now.'

She clung to him convulsively, gasping as the wound on her temple struck his collar-bone. She pulled away a little, opening her eyes to find herself cradled on Penry's lap like a child.

'It was the same dream,' she said hoarsely. 'I'm sorry I woke you. What time is it?'

'Just after three.' He set her on her feet, then tidied the bed. 'In you get.'

She climbed into bed, leaning back against the pillows he'd stacked so expertly. 'Three in the morning,' she said sombrely, 'when life's at its lowest ebb.'

'Yours isn't,' he said sternly. 'Enough of the self-pity.'

She sniffed hard. 'Right. Sorry.' She tried to smile. 'Thank you.'

'Nothing to thank me for,' he said on his way to the door. 'I merely shut you up so I could get some sleep!'

She lay rigid and wide-eyed once he'd gone, afraid to sleep in case the nightmare returned, then to her relief Penry came back into the room.

'I thought you'd gone to bed!' Feeling unutterably guilty, she saw he'd brought her another drink and a fresh hot-water bottle. 'Coals of fire,' she said ruefully, as he slid the bottle in the bed.

'No, just a glass of hot milk—half a glass, actually, so we can have some breakfast.' He smiled. 'I wasn't expecting visitors. We'll buy more tomorrow.'

Leonora sipped the milk, frowning, then looked up at him. 'When I thanked you just now, by the way, it was because you got me out of the boat before I hit the water this time.' Her eyes held his. 'And I know the name of it, I think—or part of it. Do the letters SEREN mean anything? Part of *serenade*, perhaps?'

He shrugged, then sat down on the edge of the bed

and took her hand. 'I'll ask the coastguard and the
police tomorrow before we set out. It's certainly a lead.
Take heart, Leonora. It's another piece of the puzzle.
Soon you'll have the complete picture.'

She nodded despondently. 'I suppose so.'

'In the meantime stop fretting yourself to fiddle-
strings!' He leaned closer, his smile teasing, but as their
eyes met the smile faded slowly.

Leonora lay hypnotised, unable to look away. She
forgot her dream as she saw the blue eyes darken
almost to black. She ran the tip of her tongue over her
lips, heard the sharp hiss of Penry's intake of breath,
then his head blotted out the light as his mouth met
hers in a kiss which shot a jolt of electricity through
every vein in her body.

She tore her mouth away, averting her burning face
as Penry got unhurriedly to his feet.

'A mere kiss goodnight,' he said softly. 'It can't have
been your first.'

Leonora forced herself to look at him. 'I—I don't
know. I don't remember.' She blinked back tears
fiercely. 'You may not believe me, but I honestly *don't*
remember. Anything. Lord knows I wish I did. This
blankness terrifies me!'

Penry sat down again on the edge of the bed. He put
a hand under her chin to raise her face to his, so much
the physician again that Leonora wondered if she'd
dreamed the kiss. 'You will remember,' he said with
emphasis. 'Sooner or later something will trigger off
your memory and everything will come flooding back.'

# CHAPTER FIVE

BUT when morning came, bright and clear with only a slight breeze, it arrived alone. Leonora woke up to find her mind as stubbornly blank as before.

'I feel much better otherwise,' she told Penry, trying hard to be cheerful. She held up her face. 'Look, my bruise is fading.'

'You'll soon be good as new,' he agreed. 'I've phoned in the news about the boat, by the way. There's no report of a missing dinghy, but I mentioned the name you saw in your dream and both police and coastguard promise to look into it.'

'They must think you've got a right lunatic on your hands,' she said, grimacing, then brightened. 'But at least I can go outside today. Can we explore the island when we get back? If you're not too busy, of course,' she added guiltily as she put on her jacket.

'We'll see how you feel.' Penry took the paper from her shoes, which felt stiff and hard as she slid her feet into them. He pulled on a bright yellow weatherproof jacket over his thick jersey and moleskin trousers, slid his long feet into rubber boots and collected some keys from the study. 'Right, then. Ready to face the great outdoors?'

Leonora emerged from the house into a bright spring day which belonged to a different world from the gales and rain of before. She held up her face to the pale sunshine, sniffing ecstatically at the salt air. As she followed Penry as quickly as she could she looked

about her at the island with interest, curious to see what had lain behind a veil of sea mist and rain since her dramatic arrival. The house itself, she found, had been erected in a shallow depression in the mound surmounting the central part of the island.

'Old Joshua decided to use the site of an Iron-Age settlement when he built his new home,' said Penry, and pointed out an unhewn standing stone at the edge of the cliff. 'That was probably some cult object for the prehistoric island dwellers.'

'Creepy! Do you make offerings in front of it on Midsummer's Eve?' asked Leonora, impressed.

'Absolutely. We tie a maiden to the stone and dance round it by firelight!' He laughed, taking her hand to hurry her along. 'The maiden arrived a bit early, this year.'

'How do you know I qualify?' she said without thinking, then flushed as he halted in front of her, his eyes mocking and very definitely blue in the bright morning light.

'Informed guess. Now watch your step; the path gets a bit steep further down.'

She had no time to spare for embarrassment, due to shoes totally unsuitable for climbing down a cliff path. With Penry in front of her to see she didn't slip, their progress was slow down the steep path towards the strip of land which formed the waist of the figure-of-eight. She tugged on Penry's hand as the path levelled out.

'This must be the Neck. Show me where you found me, please.'

He looked at her searchingly, then stopped and led the way across the rabbit-nibbled turf to a point where she could look down on the inlet he called Seal Haven.

She stared down at water foaming round a row of rocks which looked horribly like jagged teeth in some monster's half-open mouth.

Penry pointed. 'See that small, needle-like rock at the mouth of the inlet? You were very lucky. You got caught on that. If you'd been tossed around in the eddies down there I wouldn't have given much for your chances.' He looked at her colourless face. 'Come on—we'll be late.'

Leonora felt very subdued as she followed him down to the relatively peaceful little beach of Lee Haven, where years before Joshua Probert had built a safe anchorage for his boats. The *Angharad*, a sturdy fishing-boat with a fair-sized cabin, had weathered the storm safely, well out of harm's way. Penry lifted her aboard, then untied the moorings and leapt on deck after her.

She eyed the distant shoreline with misgiving. 'Is it far?'

'You'll be there before you know it.' He smiled reassuringly as he started up the engine, which obliged first time. 'Good girl!' He patted the bulkhead affectionately, then gave all his attention to manoeuvring the *Angharad* out of Lee Haven and into the fast-flowing sound which separated Gullholm from the Welsh coast.

Leonora gripped a rail with white-knuckled hands when the boat bucked as it met the wilder waters of the sound. Teeth clenched, she held on like grim death, determined not to embarrass Penry Vaughan with a fit of hysterics just because she was in a boat again. Besides, she told herself firmly, this time the sea was merely a bit choppy. The wind was brisk, but it was only a wind, not a gale. And the sun was shining.

Bracing her feet against the *Angharad*'s deck, she fixed her eyes on the grey smudge of land in the distance, willing it to come nearer.

'Are you OK?' shouted Penry above the cabin noise.

'Fine,' she assured him loudly. She'd be even better, too, she thought prayerfully, once she was on dry land. But Penry was right. The trip was mercifully short. All at once the shore was suddenly very close indeed, the grey smudge resolving into green fields and a sandy beach with houses in a grey and white arc behind it. And then they were over the bar into a small, natural harbour and the deck steadied beneath her feet as Penry piloted the boat skilfully into a mooring where the *Angharad* would wait for their return. As a boy raced to take the ropes Penry flung out, Leonora began to breathe more easily again, her pulse-rate calming as she felt the usual shamed reaction to terror once safety was assured.

'You can let go now,' said Penry quietly.

Leonora flushed as he prised her stiff hands from the rail. 'Sorry. I was a bit tense.'

'You were very brave, my lovely.' He smiled down at her with warm approval. 'After your nightmares a boat trip must have been an ordeal.'

Her knees rattled together like castanets as he helped her down on to the jetty. 'I suppose it was like getting straight back on a horse after being thrown.' She breathed in deeply and smiled. 'I'll be fine on the trip back, I promise.'

'Good girl. Come on, then. We've a lot to do before then.'

Penry hurried her off to a row of garages on one side of the road leading from the beach into the village. As they walked along there were smiles on all sides as they

passed. Dr Penry Vaughan, Leonora noted, was popular with everyone in Brides Haven.

Halfway along he unlocked a garage and let the door slide up to reveal a newish Range Rover. He lifted Leonora into the passenger-seat then leapt up to back the vehicle out into the narrow street, waving his thanks as a weather-beaten old man slammed the garage door shut with a wide smile before waving them on their way.

Brides Haven was small. The Range Rover left it behind quickly on a steep road which wound up in hairpin bends for a mile before levelling out on the road to Haverfordwest.

'I know how you felt in my boat,' said Penry, glancing sideways at her. 'How are you in a car?'

'Great,' said Leonora, relaxing. 'How far is it to St Mary's?'

'Sixty miles or so.'

'Goodness—that far!' She bit her lip. 'You'll be glad to see the back of me, Dr Vaughan.'

'Nonsense. If it's any consolation to you I needed to check up on a patient anyway. I'll kill two birds with one stone.'

'Not the happiest of metaphors for a man of healing!'

He laughed, then gestured at the surrounding farmland, which stretched away to the purple rise of the Preseli hills in the distance. 'Any of this ring a bell?'

'No.' She sighed. 'I was hoping Brides Haven would, I must confess, but it didn't. None of this looks remotely familiar. Have you got a comb, by the way?' she added. 'I feel a bit wind-blown—among other things.'

'If you reach over in the back you'll see a suede jacket. There might be a comb in the pocket.'

To Leonora's relief there was. She untied the shoe-lace and did what she could to tame the unruly curls, then took off her red scarf and used it to tie her hair back firmly at the nape of her neck. 'I don't want to disgrace you in front of the nuns.'

'I've already had a word with Sister Concepta. I gave her the bare outline of your problem, Leonora—it was necessary to explain why I wanted an X-ray in a hurry. There'll be a radiologist waiting for us.'

'Won't that cost a lot?'

'Don't worry about that,' he said dismissively, and focused his attention on the traffic of Haverfordwest as he skirted the town to make for the road to Carmarthen.

St Mary's was a modern, purpose-built nursing home erected in the grounds of an older house, once the property of a Member of Parliament in Gladstone's government. The nuns were kindness itself to Leonora. They fussed over her as though she were a sick child, then, once the X-rays were completed, returned her to Penry, who was chatting over coffee with Sister Concepta in her office.

'Take Leonora into the gardens for a stroll round in the sunshine while you wait for the results, Doctor,' advised the serene, smiling nun. 'She's a bit pale, poor child; she could do with some fresh air.'

Penry, who had changed his rubber boots and yellow waterproof for heavy shoes and suede jacket before entering the hospital, ushered Leonora outside, agreeing with Sister Concepta that his charge looked a bit peaky.

'Are you all right, Leonora?' he asked as they strolled along the gravelled paths.

'Yes. I don't think I'm ever the rosy-cheeked type.'

She smiled cheerfully as they passed beds massed with daffodils. 'I can tell we're in Wales. Is there a kitchen garden full of leeks, too?'

He chuckled. 'Probably.'

'How was your patient?'

'I've sent her home. Her tests confirmed my diagnosis, so I prescribed some mild medication, a strict diet and bullied her into taking more exercise.'

'Will she do as you say?'

Penry smiled with supreme confidence. 'Of course. People always do as I say—in the end.'

The X-rays confirmed that Leonora's skull had come off surprisingly scot-free from her adventure.

'Not that I had any doubts on the score,' Penry assured her as they set off towards Haverfordwest. 'But I wanted confirmation.'

Leonora was silent, frowning at the passing countryside in deep preoccupation.

'What's bothering you now?' he asked.

'I'm trying to screw up enough courage to ask you a favour,' she muttered, flushing.

'Ask away.'

'Could I possibly borrow some money?' she asked, turing in her seat to look at him. 'I hate to ask, after all you've done, but there are one or two things I need.'

'How much do you want?'

'A few pounds?' she asked hopefully. 'Once I—I get back to normal I'll repay it immediately, I promise. And I won't spend more than I can help. I just want some shampoo and so on.'

'Of course, child. Buy what you want. We'll get some food, too.' He shook his finger at her. 'Was that so very hard to ask, Leonora? Am I such an ogre?'

'Today no,' she said bluntly. 'Yesterday very much so.'

'Let's draw a veil over yesterday,' he suggested. 'It won't happen again. And to make up for it I'll treat you to a slap-up lunch in Haverfordwest.'

Leonora stared at him in dismay. 'Not the way I look at the moment! I'd much rather go home, please.'

Penry made no answer for a moment as he edged past a cattle-truck on a straight stretch of road. After a while he gave her a sidelong glance under his enviable black lashes. 'Was that a slip of the tongue, Leonora? Do you really think of my island as home?'

She bit hard into her lower lip. 'For the moment I don't have much choice. It's the only home I know.' Tears trickled from the corners of her eyes, and she knuckled them away fiercely. 'Sorry to be so feeble.'

'Don't be. It's bound to get you down.' He put a large hand on her knee, then withdrew it swiftly as she cringed away. 'Hey!' He eyed her askance. 'I was trying to comfort you, not grope you, girl.'

Leonora flushed bright red. 'Sorry,' she muttered.

'You need food,' he said decisively, and began to slow down. 'There's a nice little pub along here. Very quiet; no one will stare at your black eye. Which isn't black now, anyway,' he added. 'It's barely noticeable.'

'I'm not hungry,' she said mutinously.

'Too bad—I am!'

Minutes later they were installed in the bar of the White Lion, where the dish of the day, to Leonora's astonishment, proved to be roast beef and Yorkshire pudding with vegetables from mine host's own garden.

'I thought it would be chips with everything,' she whispered.

'Oh ye of little faith! People come from miles around

for Myra's Yorkshire pudding—not to mention the gravy!'

The substantial lunch sent Leonora to sleep in the car on the next stage of the journey. When she came to with a start she found they were in the car park below the ruins of the castle in Haverfordwest.

'Come on, sleepyhead. Time to get out.' Penry took out his wallet and handed her some notes. 'There's your pocket-money. Where do you want to spend it?'

She rubbed her eyes, frowning when she saw how much he'd given her. 'I don't need all this.'

'You might. You can always give me change!'

Penry was tactful enough to leave her to her own devices once he'd directed her to a chemist. 'I'll be outside in twenty minutes. Will that do?'

Leonora darted into the shop, eager to utilise her time to the full. Determined not to hold Penry up, she made her purchases at such speed that she was outside, waiting, when he came striding down the narrow street to collect her. He walked head and shoulders above the crowd in every way, she thought, with such a sudden, overwhelming rush of pleasure at the sight of him that she was tongue-tied.

'We'll call at the supermarket en route,' he announced on the way back to the car. 'Did you bring a list?'

'Just basics—I wasn't sure what else you'd want.'

The Range Rover was crammed with so much food as they finally set off for Brides Haven that Leonora expressed doubt that the boat would carry it all.

'Nonsense. The *Angharad* can cope with a lot more than this! How do you think I get my oil to the island for the generator and the Aga?'

Leonora confessed she hadn't really given it much

thought, all her attention on the weather as Penry loaded the boat. The sun had disappeared behind swollen grey clouds which threatened a rougher crossing back to the island than the trip earlier on. She was right. But when they cast off Penry seemed reassuringly unconcerned, and sang under his breath as the *Angharad* headed for the turbulent stretch of sea separating Gullholm from the coast.

'OK?' he asked, as the *Angharad* bucked over the harbour bar into the open sea.

Her stiff lips tried to smile. 'Fine,' she gasped.

'Come here.' Penry reached out a long arm and drew her in front of him so that she stood in the shelter of his arms as he held the wheel. 'You're quite safe. The wind won't strengthen until after dark.'

Leonora, aware of Penry's warmth in every fibre, found the security of his arms an effective antidote for her fear as the *Angharad* butted her way across the choppy waters of the sound. By the time Gullholm was in full view she was sorry the crossing was over.

'There,' said Penry, putting her aside gently as he prepared to pilot the *Angharad* into her anchorage. 'That was pretty painless after all, wasn't it?' He killed the engine, then leapt out to secure the boat. He held up his arms to swing Leonora to the jetty. 'Can you manage to get up to the house under your own steam while I bring up the food?'

'Of course.' She became very busy with the packages he was stacking on the jetty. 'I can carry some myself as well. You don't know how grateful I am! Thank you for being so kind. I won't be frightened again.'

His lips twitched as he patted her cheek carelessly. 'My dear girl, it was no hardship to hold you in my arms for a while, I assure you!'

She flushed scarlet, hastily collected as much as she could carry and started off up the cliff path. 'Will I hold you up?' she called over her shoulder as Penry came behind her.

'A bit, but I'd rather you went first. I can catch you if you fall. Stop immediately if you feel giddy.'

'I won't!'

She toiled up the path with her packages, sheer will-power keeping her going until the four-square shape of the house came into view.

'I'm out of condition,' she panted, as Penry opened the door and pushed her inside the kitchen. 'You're not even breathing fast!'

'I'm used to it. Go and collapse on the sofa in there. I'll light the stove as soon as I've stowed everything away.'

Leonora nodded obediently, but the moment he'd gone she drew the kettle over the heat on the Aga before going upstairs with her little hoard of shopping. She hurried back down to put away the food already in the kitchen, and by the time Penry returned with the last couple of boxes she had a tea-tray waiting, complete with a plate of tempting cakes from the small bakery in Brides Haven.

'I thought I told you to rest,' he accused, dumping the boxes on the kitchen counter.

'I fancied some tea.'

'Right.' He stripped off his yellow waterproof. 'I'll take it in there, and you can drink it while you watch me light the stove. I cleared it out and relaid it this morning, fortunately. I thought you might be cold when we got back.'

'After that scramble up the cliff? You're joking!' She followed him into the other room and sat down on the

sofa to pour out while Penry put a match to the kindling in the stove. One cup of tea and half a custard tart later it dawned on her that she felt a remarkable glow of well-being, for someone in her particular dilemma. She looked down on Penry's wind-blown dark head as he knelt in front of the stove to make sure the fire was established. 'Shall I pour a cup for you now?'

'Yes, please.' He got to his feet in one sinuous movement, stretching hugely, his arms above his head, before he sank down in the chair opposite. 'I hope you haven't eaten both those tarts.'

'No. I forced myself to leave one for you.'

He surveyed her at length as he demolished the cake. 'All in all you don't look too bad at all, Leonora, considering the exertions of the day. How's the head?'

'The stitches tweak now and then, but otherwise it's not aching much.' She smiled cheerfully. 'Basically I fancy I'm fairly tough.'

'You've got guts, I grant you that. You faced your ordeal pretty well today, young lady.'

She frowned thoughtfully as she refilled her cup. 'I was frightened, I admit. But only because of the dream. Somehow I don't think I'm nervous of boats and water normally. Otherwise,' she added, looking across at him, 'I would never have been in a boat alone, would I? Unless all that *was* just a dream, after all, and nothing to do with what really happened.'

'I think it happened, right enough.' His blue eyes held a hint of warning. 'It's quite possible you'll dream again tonight, Leonora.'

She shrugged. 'I know. But if that's what it takes to find out what happened—and who I am—I'll just have to put up with it every night until the last piece of the puzzle falls in place. I'm only sorry you have to put up

with it too.' She smiled ruefully. 'You'll be thankful to see the back of me, one way and another.'

'Not at all—I'll lose my cook!'

'Ah, but you've only sampled my pasta. I can't make Yorkshire pudding like Myra's, you know.'

'We all have our crosses to bear,' he said piously. 'And because you were so brave today, Leonora, I bought you a present in Haverfordwest.'

She jumped up, frowning in dismay. 'But you can't give me presents as well. I'll never be out of your debt at this rate.'

'Hey—steady on.' He took her by the elbows, his frown mock-severe. 'I shall not only be deeply wounded if you spurn my offerings, I shan't know what to do with the things. All my womenfolk are at least six inches taller and a few sizes bigger than you.' He went off to the kitchen and returned with a carrier-bag. 'Nothing exciting—just a couple of things to make life easier, since you can't fly away home just yet, ladybird.'

The 'things' were a pair of rubber-soled navy canvas deck-shoes, a miniature version of Penry's rubber boots, and a strawberry-pink lambswool sweater. Leonora looked at the haul, wide-eyed, a lump in her throat.

'Well?' demanded Penry. 'Will they do?'

She cleared her throat noisily. 'Of course they will. Exactly what I need—except for the sweater, which was sheer extravagance!' She blinked hard. 'How will I ever repay you for all you've done for me?' On impulse she stood on tiptoe and kissed his cheek. 'Thank you very much indeed.'

Without warning Penry's arms shot out to pull her on tiptoe against his broad chest, returning the brief

little caress with a kiss which left them both shaken when he finally set her square on her feet again.

'Do you require an apology?' he demanded roughly. 'I warned you this type of thing might arise from our particular situation, Miss Castaway.'

Leonora's chin went up. 'Please don't apologise. I'm to blame. I was stupid to kiss you first. I'll take care never to do it again. Now,' she added, deliberately matter-of-fact, 'what time do you want supper?'

'Later!' he snapped, his face like thunder. 'I've wasted too much bloody time today as it is. I need to put in a couple of hours' work before I can think of eating.' He flung away to his study, slamming the door behind him.

# CHAPTER SIX

IT WAS almost eight that evening before Penry emerged from the study. Leonora eyed him warily as she switched off the transistor.

'Are you ready to eat now?'

He stared at her, sudden heat in his eyes for an instant before the shuttering lashes came down to hide it. 'What the blazes have you done to yourself?' he demanded.

Leonora glared back, incensed. Her motives unclear, even to herself, she'd taken enormous trouble with her face after her bath, disguising the bruise with a cover-up stick, accenting her eyes with a hint of shadow. She'd lavished the new moisturiser on her face, outlined her mouth with a muted pink lipstick, and for the finishing touch gathered her hair into a loose knot on top of her head with a length of black velvet purchased along with the cosmetics. And until now she'd been naïvely pleased with the result. Penry's derision acted like a red-hot needle, pricking the fragile balloon of her vanity.

'I thought it was time I began looking like a human being,' she snapped.

'Exactly like every other female, you mean!'

Leonora gave him a look of active dislike. 'Ah! Return of Heathcliff, I see.'

'You've got your casting wrong. Not Heathcliff. Pygmalion, perhaps, or Dr Frankenstein.'

Her eyes flashed angrily. 'And I'm the monster, I suppose!'

'Don't be childish.' He looked mortifyingly bored. 'Since you've gone to so much trouble I suppose I'd better change into something more in keeping with your splendour.'

'Don't be so damn patronising! I'm wearing jeans and a jumper and a spot of make-up—big deal!' She turned back to the salad, chopping herbs for the dressing as if she had Penry Vaughan's neck under the blade.

'You're angry. I'm sorry, Leonora.' He reached out to touch a hand to the elaborate topknot, but she dodged away, retreating in haste along the counter, her face flaming at the scathing glitter in his eyes.

'My dear young woman,' he drawled, 'must you shy away like a startled horse every time I get within yards of you? It's bad for my nerves—*and* unnecessary. I'm sorry I kissed you earlier, but I swear on the Bible I've no intention of ravishing you on the kitchen floor before supper—or any other time.'

She hugged her arms across her chest, hot all over. 'I know that! It's just that I—well, I don't seem to like being touched.'

'I'll remember that next time you start screaming in the night!'

Her chin lifted. 'That's different. Then you're just a doctor, not a man.'

'The two are not incompatible!' Penry eyed her flushed face with rancour for a moment, then shrugged. 'Come on—pax! Put the knife away, you're making me nervous.'

The rest of the evening passed without further reference to Leonora's attempt to gild the lily. After the

meal she went on knitting the complicated sweater while Penry immersed himself in the newspapers he'd bought earlier in the day. At first there was an uneasy silence, but after a while he thawed enough to read odd items of news aloud to her. When he put down the papers at last he looked abstracted.

'I didn't expect anything in the nationals, of course,' he said, frowning, 'but I thought one of the local rags might have had something about a missing boat.'

'Or even a missing person. Would you stand up, please?' she added.

'Are you sure that's meant for me?' he asked, as she went on tiptoe to measure her knitting against his back.

'Don't you like it?'

'Yes. It's very striking, but not my usual sort of thing. I'm not convinced Mother intended it for me.'

'From the measurements she must have,' she assured him, as her needles resumed their swift, effortless rhythm. 'Surely no one else in your family is built to the same scale?'

'No,' he admitted. 'Something for which, I imagine, the girls are profoundly grateful. I'm a throw-back to old Josh Probert, according to my lady mother. Only *he* was six and a half feet in his socks, apparently, which tops me by an inch or two.'

'I pity his wife if she knitted much for him!'

Penry laughed as he went over to the stereo to put on a compact disc. 'They ran sheep here in those days, so I imagine she did, if only to keep him in socks.'

As the ethereal strains of Ravel stole through the room, Penry let himself down on the sofa, eyes closed. Leonora looked at him, unobserved, as she worked. His mood seemed to have lightened now, she noted with some relief, and pondered, frowning, over his

unexpected reaction to what must certainly be her normal other-life guise.

Unaware of her scrutiny, Penry lay full length, guernsey and shoes discarded, his long, bare feet crossed at the ankles as they hung over the arm of the sofa. He was, thought Leonora with detachment, well worth looking at. His face, less hollowed and drawn already than her first impression of it, possessed a quality in repose she could only describe as beauty, of a very virile, masculine variety. Where the skin stretched taut along his cheekbones it held a faint flush of colour after the day out, the disfiguring bitterness in the blue eyes hidden for the moment behind closed, black-fringed lids. Leonora counted stitches for a moment, then let her eyes stray over Penry Vaughan's magnificent physique. He was all muscle and sinew, with no spare flesh as far as she could tell, the aura of strength very marked even in repose as he lay relaxed, his hands clasped behind his head, his face shuttered and dreaming as he listened to the music.

'You like Ravel?' he asked without opening his eyes.

Leonora applied herself to her knitting hastily. 'Not the piano music, nor the hackneyed old *Bolero*, but Ravel in this mood I find irresistible.'

'Know the piece?' he asked idly.

'*Daphnis and Chloe*. . .' She turned to find him watching her. 'Ah! There I go again.'

He smiled. 'So you do.'

'But why is my memory so selective?' she demanded, and thrust the knitting in its bag, suddenly tired of it.

'For the moment it's simply refusing to remember anything other than the pleasant things, Leonora.' He sat up, thrusting his feet into his shoes. 'Mind you, I'm a mere physician, not a psychiatrist——'

'You could never be a "mere" anything!'

'Ah, but you don't know me very well, Leonora.' His face set in harsh, familiar lines. 'I'm as subject to the frailties of human nature as the next man—or woman.'

She looked at him consideringly. 'It's hard to be believe. You seem like a man who gives frailties of any kind short shrift.'

'I said I was subject to them, not that I let them rule me!' He stood up, holding out his hand. 'Come on, young lady. Time for bed.'

Leonora contemplated argument, abandoned it, and, without taking the hand, got up and started for the stairs on leaden feet, full of foreboding about the night ahead.

'Don't worry, child,' he said kindly. 'If you dream, I'll come running, I promise.'

She gave him a melancholy little smile. 'At the risk of sounding ungrateful, I sincerely hope you won't have to.'

Penry stood at the foot of the stairs, looking up at her. 'Get some sleep. You look exhausted.'

'The constant battle to remember's a bit draining.'

'Then stop it. Make your mind a complete blank.'

'You mean more of a blank that it is!'

He frowned impatiently. 'Look, Leonora, trying to force yourself to remember will do a lot more harm than good. Things could be a hell of a sight worse for you, remember. You've got shelter, food, and although I'm not the easiest of companions at least you're not facing your problem alone.'

Leonora felt a sharp pang of remorse. 'I know, and I'm sorry to sound ungrateful. Goodnight.'

She prepared for bed in haste, then got into bed

without turning off the bedside lamp, willing the friendly glow to hold off the dreams which came with the night. It was something of an anticlimax to wake next morning to pale dawn light after a night of sleep unbroken by nightmares or dreams of any kind. Leonora sat up, rubbing her eyes as she switched off the lamp, so exhilarated to find she'd slept the night through that she was less cast down than expected to find her identity was still a mystery. Today, she decided, she would forget that she couldn't remember. Her body was healing rapidly. No doubt her mind would do the same if she stopped chivvying it. She snuggled back down under the covers, deciding it was too early to get up yet. If she kept quiet Penry might sleep longer, and wake in a better mood.

When Leonora surfaced next she found Penry, fully dressed, standing at the edge of the bed. She sat bolt upright, pushing her hair back from her face guiltily. 'Goodness, what time is it?'

'Only a little after eight.' He smiled. 'How did you sleep, Leonora? If you had any nightmares there was no soundtrack last night.'

She smiled radiantly. 'There weren't any! Just wonderful, wonderful sleep—twice, too! I woke earlier on, but I thought I'd disturb you if I got up so I had another nap.'

'You look very much better.' He took her wrist between impersonal fingers and consulted his watch. 'Good. Pulse normal.' He bent slightly to examine her face. 'The swelling's down, and the bruise almost gone, but I'd better change the dressing on your wound after you come downstairs.'

'Right. I'll only be a few minutes, then I'll cook you some breakfast,' she said briskly.

Penry smiled faintly as he made for the door. 'When you finally go back to wherever you belong, Leonora, what shall I do without you?'

She looked sceptical. 'Enjoy the solitude you came here for, I imagine. And in any case,' she added, 'if you are lonely I'm sure there must be any number of—of people you can ask here to keep you company.'

'You mean women,' he said swiftly, his eyes icing over. 'For the past three years I've been a respectable married man, young lady. I never had enough time to spare for my wife, let alone other women—even if I'd been so inclined, which I was not.'

'Oh, come on! In your position you must know a gorgeous nurse or two, or a pretty lady medico, Dr Vaughan.'

His black brows flew together forbiddingly. 'If I do,' he said cuttingly, 'that's my business.'

As he ducked through the door Leonora stared at him in astonishment, then stuck out her tongue irreverently as she slid out of bed, refusing to let Penry's snub spoil her new well-being. She washed hurriedly, then pulled on her old jeans and jersey and tied her hair back with the shoelace. If Dr Penry Vaughan preferred scruffy, she thought resentfully, scruffy was what he'd get. When she went downstairs Penry was feeding wood into the stove in the living-room. She went past him without speaking on her way to the kitchen, and soon had breakfast under way. She began frying bacon and eggs, then filled the kettle and sliced bread for toast. She put cutlery and napkins on two trays, then went to the door.

'It's nearly ready.'

He got up, dusting off his hands. 'Thank you. It smells marvellous. Have I time to wash?'

Leonora nodded silently then returned to her labours. While Penry went upstairs she took his tray into the study, then went into the other room with her own. When he reappeared she gestured through the open door. 'Yours is on your desk.'

Penry stood at the foot of the stairs, frowning as she plugged in the transistor to listen to Radio Four while she ate. 'Are diplomatic relations severed?' he enquired drily.

Leonora buttered toast with a steady hand. 'I don't know how much longer you'll be forced to put up with me, but until the happy day I can bid you farewell I'll try to keep out of your hair as much as I can. To be honest,' she added, 'I find your swings of mood rather a pain. Just when I think you're the kindest man in the world you suddenly get the glooms again. Since I'm obviously the cause of them I'll do my best to keep out of your way.'

Penry looked as though he was about to burst into speech for a moment, then his face set in the familiar harsh lines, and without another word he turned on his heel and made for his sanctum, slamming the door behind him.

Leonora lost interest in her breakfast. Penry's displeasure gave her a sudden, desperate longing to get back to wherever—and more importantly whoever—she belonged. Swallowing her tears, she went back to the kitchen to clear up. She knocked on the study door and put her head round it.

'May I take the tray?'

Penry looked up. 'I'll look at your forehead first.'

Leonora sat in the kitchen chair alongside the desk while Penry removed the old dressing. She sat very still, eyes closed, as he examined the wound, willing

herself to remain immune to his nearness, to think of him only as a doctor.

'There,' he said at last, standing back. 'That should do now until I take out the stitches.'

Leonora got up. 'Thank you. How long will that be?'

'A day or two.' He picked up the tray and followed her from the room. 'I'm sorry, Leonora. You happened to hit on a sore subject.'

'As you said, it's none of my business,' she said flatly, and began washing up, her back to him.

'Unlike you I couldn't sleep. Which is an explanation for my bloody-mindedness, I know, but no excuse.' He leaned against the counter, eyeing her withdrawn face. 'Being a Celt, I'm prone to moods. A broken marriage hasn't done much to lighten them, either.'

She maintained a stony silence until she'd finished, then turned briskly. 'Right. Since it's such a lovely day I think I'll go exploring.'

'Not on your own!' he said quickly.

Leonora thrust out a foot clad in one of the new rubber-soled shoes he'd bought her. 'I'll be fine in these. I'll keep to the paths, I promise. I shan't climb down cliffs, or do anything stupid.' Her eyes flashed. 'I may be missing in the memory department, but I do have a brain. Of sorts.'

He eyed the small foot, unimpressed. 'Brain or no brain, I'd rather you didn't go out alone, at least not the first time, please.'

Their eyes clashed for a moment, then Leonora shrugged. 'Oh, very well. Will the generator expire if I use the vacuum cleaner, then?'

'There's no need——'

'I must do something, or I'll go mad!'

Grudgingly Penry agreed to a little housework, after

which, he said firmly, she must rest. Leonora set to with a will. An hour later every room was spick and span except for the bedroom Penry was using. A large suitcase lay on the bed, still full of the clothes he'd taken from the other room. Leonora took out sweaters and shirts and underwear, putting them away with a vague feeling of trespass which failed to keep her from peeping into a folding leather picture frame lying at the bottom of the suitcase.

One half was crammed with snapshots of various adults and children, presumably all members of the Vaughan clan. But it was the single large photograph in the other half of the frame that caught Leonora's attention. Melanie was dark and very lovely, with an aura of warmth and tenderness which filled Leonora with unexpected dismay. But then, Leonora reminded herself sternly, what little she knew was Penry Vaughan's side of the story. Melanie might have a different tale to tell.

Suddenly Leonora felt restless, penned in. She leaned on the wide sill, looking out with longing at the part of Gullholm visible from the window. A path wound away from the house, leading through the ridges and furrows of fields long left to nature. There wasn't a tree in sight, but nearer the cliff edge she could make out carpets of thrift and sea-campion, and yearned to explore.

She turned away, frustrated, and went downstairs to make lunch. After handing over a tray to the absorbed, absent man behind the desk, Leonora ate her own sandwich at the kitchen counter, staring mutinously at the sunshine pouring through the window. The booming surf far below called to her like the beat of a jungle drum. With sudden resolve she began to prepare a beef

goulash for dinner. When it was simmering slowly in the Aga she went into Penry, who was searching distractedly through piles of medical tomes.

'If you don't need anything else,' she said distinctly, 'I thought I might take the transistor up to my room for company and have a rest on my bed.'

'Sensible girl. I'm fine—run along.' He plunged back into his work, forgetting about her before she was through the door.

Leonora hurried upstairs gleefully, inserted a new set of batteries in the transistor, turned up the volume and left her bedroom door open a crack. She collected her jacket then crept downstairs on noiseless, rubber-soled feet, taking extra care as she skirted the study on her way out. Exulting in her escape, she closed the outer door behind her and made for the great outdoors like a child let out of school.

Leonora restricted herself to the main tableland of the island, knowing perfectly well that Penry had her safety in mind in his veto of exploration on her own. She kept well away from the edge of the cliffs, perfectly happy to stay in the fields which displayed such fascinating evidence of Iron Age occupation. Excited to find she could just make out traces of narrow fields with dividing banks and walls, she ventured further towards a rounded mound which could well have been an Iron Age barrow, and just beyond it she found the standing stone, where she shivered pleasurably, her imagination running riot about the monolith's precise function in the days when the settlement had been a live, thriving community.

Leonora turned her back on the past, bracing herself against the wind as she walked briskly towards the spot where the cliff path began its decent to Seal Haven.

Shading her eyes with a hand against the bright sunlight, she paused to watch the acrobatics of a troupe of black-backed screaming gulls, but the wind blew suddenly colder, tearing at her hair. Reluctantly she made her way back to the house, then gave a gasp of dismay as Penry erupted from it like a rocket. He tore towards her, menace in every line of him as he caught up with her and grabbed her by the shoulders, his eyes blazing.

'What the hell do you think you're doing?' he shouted.

'I came out for a walk,' she said, shrugging off his hands. 'I'm coming back now.'

'You bet your life you are!' He glared at her as he dragged her along by the hand at top speed. 'When I went up to your room I found Goldilocks wasn't sleeping in my bed after all. The transistor was a nice touch! Planned your escape well, didn't you?'

'Let me go,' she said breathlessly, trying to break free. 'I can't—run as—fast as—you.'

Penry slowed down, his eyes on her face. 'Are you giddy?' he demanded.

'No. Not that it's any thanks to you!'

'Sorry.' Penry ushered her into the kitchen, unzipping her jacket as though she were a child. He lifted her up and perched her on one of the kitchen stools, then filled the kettle. 'Stay there,' he ordered. 'I'll make you some tea.'

Leonora kept her temper with difficulty, feeling ridiculous with her legs dangling from the high stool. 'Dr Vaughan, I crept from the house like a thief to avoid the very fuss you're making right now. I am perfectly all *right*! A gentle stroll in the spring sunshine is hardly a capital offence.' As a blast of hail hit the window she shrugged. 'It was sunny when I went out.'

Penry handed her a mug of tea. 'I know.' He thrust a hand through his hair. 'Sorry I blew my top, but I had visions of finding you down there on the rocks like the first time.'

'I wasn't anywhere near the edge!'

'How was I to know that? I imagined you getting vertigo, even falling!'

'I never dreamed you'd look in my room,' she muttered.

'My sole reason for invading your maiden privacy,' he said with sarcasm, 'was because I'd heard from the police. I assumed you'd want to know that wreckage of a dinghy was washed up a few miles north of here on the Welsh coast last night. There was enough of it to identify her as the *Seren*—or "star" to you barbarians across Offa's Dyke.'

# CHAPTER SEVEN

THE police had traced the dinghy to Londoners who owned a weekend cottage a few miles away up the Welsh coast. Because several locals had permission to borrow the boat for a spot of fishing, its absence had gone unremarked.

Penry took Leonora by the shoulders. 'Does any of it ring a bell? Could you be one of the owners of this cottage they're talking about?'

She shook her head wildly. 'I don't know, I don't know.' Tears of frustration and disappointment welled up in her eyes. 'I wish I did. I just want to go home, wherever it is.'

Penry put his arms around her very carefully. When she leaned against him without flinching away he stroked her hair as she buried her face against his chest, and at the delicate caress she sobbed into the thick navy wool without inhibition. It was a long time before she drew away, knuckling the tears away from her reddened eyes.

'Hey—come on,' he said softly, and smiled at her as he reached over to tear off a sheet of kitchen-towel.

Leonora mopped herself up drearily. 'Sorry. Only I was happy out there for a while. For a few minutes I was free of this terrible worry about who I am, about my family. I can't stop thinking about them. They must be going out of their minds with worry.' She blew her nose forcibly. 'Not only that, you could be sheltering a

97

criminal of some kind. What was I doing with someone else's boat, for a start?'

'Stop worrying—that's an order!' He patted her good cheek lightly. 'Now, off you go. Have your bath. By the wonderful smell I assume dinner is already under way, so just tell me what else you intend us to eat and I'll see to it.'

'No, I'll do it,' she insisted, and slithered down off the stool. She bent to transfer the casserole from the oven to the top of the Aga, too depressed to note the lack of protest from her head.

Penry sniffed appreciatively. 'Frankly, if you can cook like this I don't care if you're the greatest lady criminal of all time.'

She gave him a wry smile as she added seasoning to the pot. 'It obviously takes food to keep you in a good mood, Dr Vaughan.'

'I'm sorry if I was a bear this morning. I haven't had much chance to run in the mornings since you arrived. Makes me introspective about certain things missing from my life these days.'

Leonora frowned. 'You mean women, and—and so on? I find it hard to believe that an attractive man like you lacks feminine company.'

'Why, thank you, Madame X.' He gave her a mocking bow. 'And of course your former remarks about lady doctors were quite right. I know several. The trouble was that Melanie believed I was in bed with one of them every time I was half an hour late.'

'Were you?'

'No, I damn well wasn't! I'm a consultant,' he added. 'Part of my function is to supervise and instruct those junior to me, male *or* female. After a hard day it wasn't unusual to gather for coffee with a bunch of registrars

of both sexes, and sometimes I was late home.' His mouth tightened. 'Melanie refused to believe the truth. I wish now her suspicions had been correct. I might as well have had the game as well as the name.'

Leonora restored the pot to the oven and straightened. 'There. I'll leave the rest until after my bath.' She eyed him diffidently. 'I tidied the bedrooms today. When I did yours I couldn't help looking at the photographs in the leather frame.'

'My rogues' gallery! Handsome lot on the whole, we Vaughans, don't you think?' he said smugly.

'Very.' Leonora felt a sudden pang to learn he still thought of the fair Melanie as a Vaughan. 'Your wife—your ex-wife, I mean, is very lovely.'

Penry frowned. 'How do you know?'

'Isn't she the dark lady in the studio portrait?'

His face cleared. 'No, that's Kit, my sister—taken years ago when she got engaged. She's been Mrs Reid Livesey for a fair time now. The demon sailing duo opposite her are Rick and Harry, her sons.'

Leonora went off for her bath, feeling oddly pleased by this information, but otherwise very depressed. The news of the *Seren* had ignited a bright flame of hope which left her cold and utterly despondent when it shed no light at all on the mystery of her identity. To warm herself up she lay in hot water up to her chin, her hair tied up on top of her head, consoling herself with the fact that physically she was almost back to normal. She could, she told herself stringently, be a lot worse off.

After dinner Leonora returned to her knitting, glad of its soothing monotony, when Penry began musing about her background.

'I wonder what you do for a living?' he asked

thoughtfully. 'Maybe you haven't started working yet—you could be a student.'

She shook her head. 'I'm sure I'm not, somehow.'

'Well, don't fret about it.'

Leonora, doing her best to obey, changed the subject firmly. 'What do *you* do?' she asked. 'Apart from treating patients, I mean. Do you play golf?'

He sat back in his chair, staring into his glass. 'No. When I was young rugby was the love of my life, but these days I just manage a game of squash now and then. Lately these blasted articles have taken up all my spare time. I've just got to get them out of the way before I get back to work.'

'Where are you based?'

'In a hospital which serves a large area of Wales. I also have a fairly flourishing private practice.' He raised his eyebrows. 'You look surprised.'

She nodded. 'Only about the location. Somehow I just took it for granted you worked in London.'

'I did until last year. I'd spent all my post-Oxford life in London hospitals. I decided it was time for a change.'

'To get away from painful memories?'

He smiled mirthlessly. 'What a romantic you are! Actually it was the change of job which finally decided Melanie to divorce me. She was appalled at the idea of living in the "wilds", as she put it. To expect her to bury herself in the back of beyond, away from all her friends with just Penry Vaughan for company, constituted adequate grounds for divorce in her view.'

'How on earth did you come to marry her?' asked Leonora before she could stop herself, then pulled a face. 'Sorry!'

'Don't be. Lord knows it's a question I've asked

myself often enough. Melanie's beautiful, wilful, and she's been spoiled rotten all her life.' He smiled wryly. 'I was a challenge to her. When I was a young houseman I—well, enjoyed a hectic love-life. Lord knows how I managed it. A working week of over a hundred hours should have been ruinous for the libido, looking back. But I was young, then. And I came in contact with a lot of pretty nurses. Melanie already knew I was popular with the fair sex, but when she discovered I was tipped for the top in my career as well she decided it might be a good idea to marry me.'

'Yet after all that she wanted a divorce. Did you agree to it?'

'Gladly. By that stage I was as keen on it as she was. What I wasn't prepared for was my reaction to her rejection. My ego suffered. To be honest I'm still smarting from the various wounds she inflicted. But there'd been precious little joy in our marriage for some time. Besides,' he added grimly, 'by then Melanie had found husband number two. Pots of money and willing at first to squire her to the latest "in" restaurants and nightspots, charity balls, Henley, Ascot, the whole shebang.' He jumped up, looking restless. 'Right. Enough soul-baring for tonight, Leonora. Time you went to bed.'

To Leonora's relief there was no nightmare that night, nor in the nights that followed. Life on Gullholm settled into an uneasy, hard-won routine. After Leonora's stitches were removed, painlessly, to her relief, Penry pronounced her well enough to help with his articles, since typing proved to be another of her accomplishments. Her help proved less of a boon than expected. Once the work was finished, much sooner

than he'd ever dared hope, Penry was left without
occupation. While the weather was fine he worked off
his surplus energies by a twice-daily run, sandwiching
an outing of exploration with Leonora in between. But
when the gales returned and rain swept the island,
penning them both indoors, Penry's mood worsened,
darkening, it seemed to Leonora, like the weather. His
restlessness permeated the entire house, and she felt
guilty, certain that her presence was tying him to
Gullholm, that if it weren't for her he would go home,
or visit one or other of his sisters or his mother, all of
whom made regular telephone calls.

'Do they know about me?' asked Leonora, after a
day of sheeting rain.

'No,' said Penry shortly.

'Why not?'

'If they knew they'd never leave me in peace. One
or the other of them would insist on having you to stay.
But in my opinion the best way to recover your memory
is to stay close to the place where you lost it.'

She stared at him, resentment flaring suddenly. 'And
you, of course, Dr Vaughan, are never wrong!'

Suddenly the atmosphere in the comfortable room
thickened with hostility.

'Of course I can be wrong,' said Penry, a pulse
throbbing at the corner of his mouth. 'And the moment
I feel you need proper psychiatric help I shall enlist it
for you, believe me. But for the time being I happen
to think it best to wait a little, in the hope that
something triggers your memory into returning of its
own accord.' He looked at his watch. 'It's time you
went to bed.'

'I suppose I might as well,' she said bitterly. 'Goodness knows you're not much company. In fact you've

been downright unbearable ever since we finished your articles for the journal.' She stabbed her needles through her knitting, and stuffed it into its bag. 'May I have some more batteries for the transistor, please?'

'I'd rather you tried to get to sleep,' he said dismissively.

She jumped to her feet and stood over him, her eyes flashing. 'And of course I must obey your slightest wish as if you were God. I'd heard that consultants suffered from delusions about their own deity—you're the living proof of it.'

Penry got to his feet very slowly, standing over her in a way which made Leonora long to back away, but she stood her ground, refusing to let him intimidate her.

'What's the matter with you these days?' she damanded. 'Is it me? Are you regretting that you ever brought me back to life, Pygmalion? Would you rather Galatea had remained a cold block of marble after all?'

'What a lot of questions,' he said coldly, and put her out of his path rather less gently than he intended.

Leonora jumped away, rubbing her forearms resentfully. 'All right, I'm going—no need to use force.'

Penry closed his eyes tightly as though praying for patience. When he opened them again they fastened on hers, blue and cold as tempered steel. 'If you must know, Leonora, I am irritable these days for a very simple reason.'

'You mean you're itching to be rid of me so you can get off this island!'

'Not quite. Something more basic than that.'

She frowned. 'What do you mean?'

'To put it in words of one syllable,' he said, each word encased in ice, 'we are a man and a woman shut

up together alone in a house, separated from all other humans by a stretch of Atlantic. Ah,' he added as she backed away. 'Comprehension at last.'

'I'd better go to bed,' said Leonora hastily, moving further away, but he held up his hand.

'Not yet. You started this. You can stay to hear me out.'

She stayed where she was. Penry Vaughan in this mood looked too dangerous to cross.

'Sensible girl,' he said silkily. 'To proceed with the lecture, I'm aware that my somewhat variable moods disturb you. But surely you're not so naïve that you can't understand that for any normal man to be in close contact with a girl for days on end without wanting her is damned impossible?' His eyes lit with a gleam which frightened her badly. 'And this man, Leonora, has been celibate for a long time. Not from choice, you understand, but because Melanie withdrew her favours as a punishment when I wouldn't relent about the move to Wales. Bloody fool that I am, my pride wouldn't let me accept other consolation, even when offered, neither before the divorce, nor since.'

Leonora gazed at him in silence, her heart beating against the blue chambray shirt like a tom-tom.

'Don't be nervous,' he said lightly. 'I've no taste for rape. And I assume that's what it would amount to, since you flinch at the slightest touch of my hand.' Abruptly his face set in bitter, angry lines. 'Oh, go to bed, child. You're in no danger. If it makes you feel better I'll sleep down here tonight.'

It was an effort for Leonora to wish him goodnight, an even greater effort to walk upstairs slowly, instead of running headlong to her room, where she lay

sleepless for hours, unable to get Penry Vaughan's handsome, cynical face out of her mind.

She slept at last, but in the small hours the nightmare returned. This time it spared her nothing. She relived the agony of trying to control the boat, the moment of horror when the engine cut out, the desperate struggle to keep the dinghy from capsizing, and the ultimate horror as a giant wave swept her into the sea. For a while she managed to swim, but eventually she grew tired and her mouth filled with water, and she sank choking beneath the waves. . .

# CHAPTER EIGHT

'ALL right, all *right*, Leonora, I've got you.'

She opened desperate eyes on Penry's face and collapsed against his bare chest in relief, shuddering. 'I was drowning,' she gasped. 'I was drowning.'

He held her tightly as violent tremors ran through her slender body. 'It was only a dream, child. It's all over. You're safe.'

Leonora clutched at him, terrified he'd leave her. As she quietened Penry heaved himself upright against the head of the bed, taking her with him as he pulled the bright quilt up over her shoulders. She clung to him as he smoothed her hair in wordless comfort, reassured by the sheer size and solidity of him, but at last Penry stirred, and she panicked.

'Don't go!'

'I'm going to tuck you in, then go downstairs and make you a hot drink.'

Leonora scrambled inelegantly to the floor, barring his way. 'I'll come with you. I don't want to be alone.'

Penry slid to his feet, the hollows and planes of his face in sharp relief in the shadows above the lamplight. 'You'll get cold.'

'Then stay with me. I don't want a drink.'

He frowned, then swiftly remade the bed, shaking up the pillows. 'In you get.'

'Bathroom first,' she muttered.

'Right. While you're in the bathroom I insist on making that drink. Two drinks. Then I'll come back

with them and stay with you until you fall asleep. Agreed?'

Leonora nodded, eyeing the dark hall nervously. 'Will you put the light on for me, please?'

'Afraid of the dark?' he said gently, as he shepherded her to the door.

'Right now I'm afraid of everything.'

'Not me included, I hope!'

Leonora gave him a wavering smile as he switched on the hall light. 'No, not you. There's a black, uncharted place at the back of my mind labelled "here be dragons". You're my only defence against them, Dr Vaughan!'

'Fanciful child!' His smile was wry as he turned away. 'Go on, get a move on. I want you tucked up in bed, stat.'

Leonora flew to do his bidding, feeling better once she was back in bed, her face sponged and the tangles brushed from her hair. When Penry returned he smiled in approval to find her propped tidily against the pillows, covers drawn up to her chin.

'Good girl.' He smiled as he poured hot chocolate from a vacuum flask for her, then drew a chair up near the bed. 'Now then, Leonora. I know it's harrowing for you, but think hard. Was there anything different in the dream this time? Some other clue we can go on?'

Leonora forced herself to go back over the dream sequence in every terrifying detail. 'It went on longer, that's all. This time I—I began to drown.'

'Since we know perfectly well you didn't, let's forget that bit,' he said crisply. 'Now think. Did you see the name of the dinghy again?'

Leonora nodded. 'Yes. I did. And I had to struggle to start the engine. It took several pulls of the cord

before it caught. There was a strong smell of fuel, and the water was like ice round my feet as I pushed the boat out before jumping in. . .' She stared at him, breathing faster. 'Penry! That part wasn't in the dream.'

He leapt up to take the mug from her shaking hand. 'All right, my lovely. Gently now.' He sat on the bed and slid his arm round her shoulders.

She twisted round to look up at him. 'I was actually *remembering* the first part! Clearly, too. But from then on it's all mixed up. I can't tell where the real bits and the dream overlap.'

Penry's arms tightened. 'Don't worry about it. It's probably an indication that your memory's about to return.'

Leonora tried to smile back, shocked to find herself suddenly unsure about wanting her memory to return. Gullholm had been her entire world for almost a fortnight, except for the trip to the nursing home. Suddenly she was deeply afraid of what awaited her in the other world beyond it.

Penry put a finger under her chin to raise her face to his. 'What is it?' he asked softly. 'Got cold feet about meeting yourself face to face?'

She nodded dumbly. As their eyes held Penry's changed, narrowing to a sudden glitter between his lashes.

'I'd better go,' he said huskily, and removed his arm, but Leonora shook her head violently, catching his hand.

'Don't leave me. Please!'

'Leonora, stop that! You know I can't stay.'

She took her hand away, turning her back to him. 'Go, then.' She buried her face against the pillows,

biting hard into her lower lip to keep from begging. At the touch of his hand on her hair she twisted round, her eyes alight with hope, and Penry breathed in deeply, his face set.

'All right,' he said grimly. 'You win!' He threw himself down in the chair, like a man beset by demons. 'Now for pity's sake go to sleep.'

Leonora turned to face him. 'I'm afraid to go to sleep. Couldn't we just talk?'

'No, we could not,' he snapped, and drew his chair nearer the lamp. Ignoring her, he looked through a small pile of paperbacks on the bedside table then settled down with the latest Ken Follett.

'You'll get cold sitting there,' ventured Leonora.

'That's the least of my problems!'

Afraid to be alone, Leonora nevertheless found it impossible to sleep with the large figure of Penry Vaughan beside her bed. She lay watching his face as he tried to concentrate on the complexities of the novel. It was no hardship to look at him, she thought dreamily. This Melanie of his had to be a complete idiot to prefer someone else.

'If you keep looking at me,' said Penry, without raising his eyes from the page, 'I shall go back to my room.'

'Sorry.' Leonora turned on her back and stared at the ceiling. The wind was rising again, mocking the arrival of spring as it lashed rain against the windows. 'You must be tired. I'll be fine on my own now.'

Penry shot to his feet with unflattering alacrity. He stood at the edge of the bed, looking down at her. 'Are you sure, Leonora?'

'Quite sure.' She smiled up at him valiantly, the smile fading as his eyes began to darken in a way she

recognised. Afraid to move, even to breathe, she stared, mesmerised, as Pentry leaned down slowly until his lips met her cheek. Leonora tensed, colour rushing to the spot he kissed. Her mouth turned blindly to meet his, and Penry's breath caught in his throat, his arms closing round her like steel bands. She reached up to lock her hands behind his neck, her mouth parting beneath his. As Penry's breathing quickened she pushed herself closer without shame, desperate to keep him with her, fired with triumph at getting her own way rather than with sexual response when he laid her flat on the bed. He let himself down beside her and took her in his arms, and Leonora yielded to him without a qualm. If letting him make love to her was the price for keeping him with her all night she would pay it gladly. Not that Penry Vaughan's lovemaking was a hardship. For a while she even forgot why she was letting him make love to her in her surprise at the pleasure of it.

But inevitably the quality of kisses changed, his hands became urgent, and she tensed as with sudden impatience he pulled her nightshirt over her head. The moment his body covered hers she felt a great tide of revulsion and panic surge upwards until it threatened to choke her, and she threshed her head from side to side in blind, unreasoning panic, thrusting him away with frantic hands. Penry shot upright and Leonora slid from beneath him, scrambling from the bed towards the door. Hands at her mouth, she bolted to the bathroom, slamming the door behind her to shut out the sounds of her vomiting as her stomach relieved itself of its contents with such violence that she was left retching drily long afterwards until the spasms died away.

She dragged herself to her feet as Penry came into the room, wearing a dressing-gown. His face set grimly, he wrapped her in a warm, dry bathsheet, then sat her on a stool and sponged her face, smoothing the tangled curls from her pallid face.

'Did my lovemaking revolt you so much, then?' he demanded roughly at last.

She shook her head, her teeth chattering. 'No. I'm sorry. It wasn't my intention to—to tease.' She shut her eyes tightly, a dry sob catching in her throat.

Penry bent to hold her wrist between his fingers, his mouth tightening as he took her pulse. 'Don't say any more for a moment. Back to bed for you, young lady.' He swung her up in his arms, tense for a moment before she burrowed her face into his neck like a tired child.

Back in the bedroom, he handed her the discarded nightshirt, his face carefully blank as Leonora scrambled into it, so unsteady on her feet that it was a relief to get back beneath the covers.

Penry's face wore a forbidding look as he propped the pillows behind her. 'Will you be all right now?'

'No! Don't leave me alone,' she said hoarsely.

He raised an eyebrow. 'I thought you'd want me to get out of your sight—and stay out.'

She shook her head violently. 'No, no! That's the last thing I want.'

His eyes searched her face, impersonal and assessing now, the man replaced by the physician. 'You've regained your memory, I assume.'

She shuddered. 'Yes. Totally.'

His mouth took on a sardonic twist. 'I've had varying success with the women I've made love to in the past, but I've never made one throw up before!'

'*You* didn't make me sick, Penry! You see, when you——' She halted, swallowing hard, then started again. 'When we came together like that, at the last, it all came back, complete in every nauseating detail.' She tried to smile. 'Perhaps you could write an article on it—new shock treatment for amnesia.'

Penry took her hand in his and squeezed it. 'A fascinating thought! But before you tell me about it, frankly I'm in need of a stiff drink. How about you?'

'Just a glass of mineral water, please.' She eyed him remorsefully. 'I'm desperately sorry, Penry.'

'I'll survive. Shan't be long.'

Left alone, Leonora found her newly restored memory an unwelcome bedfellow. Clenching her teeth in disgust, she burrowed her face into the pillow to shut it out until Penry returned.

'Right,' he said as he settled himself in the chair. 'Get it off your chest. I'm sitting comfortably, so begin.'

Leonora sipped some water to easy her dry throat, at a loss to know how to start.

Penry leaned forward. 'Look, if you don't want to tell me who you are, or what gave you the horrors, then don't. My role in life is to alleviate pain, not cause it.'

'I *want* to tell you. It's just that I wish I'd got my wretched memory back some other way.' She flushed painfully.

'Frankly, so do I!' Penry shrugged, then swallowed some of his whisky. 'But this is the point where you stop thinking of me as a frustrated lover, or even as just a man. For the moment I'm a doctor, one you can talk to in complete confidence. So relax, Leonora. By

the way, before you get to the bad part, was I right about your name?'

'Yes. I'm Leonora right enough, just as you worked out,' she said, feeling rather better. 'The brooch gave us the right clue—in fact it gave us two. My other name is Fox. I live in a town called Chastlecombe, where I create expensive hand-knitted sweaters to sell to tourists. No wonder I can cope with the pattern which beat your mother. It's the way I earn my bread and butter.'

'And is Leonora Miss or Mrs Fox?' asked Penry quietly.

She smiled shyly. 'Miss Fox, Dr Vaughan.'

'And are you attached in any way?'

Leonora turned away, a shadow crossing her face. 'I thought I was. Which turned out to be a rather spectacular mistake. It's a silly story, really.'

Leonora Fox was the youngest of three children born rather late to parents who had died when their last-born was still a child. Left in the care of Jonathan and Elise——

'Your father *was* a Beethoven fan!' interrupted Penry.

'Not my father, my mother. First-born Fox sons are always named Jonathan, but my mother, who was quite a gifted pianist, insisted on her own choice for Elise and me.'

Jonathan Fox, the eldest, was a highly successful systems analyst in the City, and, though newly married, exerted himself constantly with professional advice for his sisters, who ran a shop in an arcade recently built to blend with the architecture of the Cotswold town of their birth.

'We sell my hand-knitted sweaters—at a very steep

price—some very high-class clothes of the classic, tailored type, and pieces of silver and jewellery and wood carvings made by local craftsmen,' said Leonora.

'Hence the brooch,' remarked Penry.

'Right. Want to guess the name of our shop?'

'Surprise me.'

'Elise insisted we call it "Fox's Lair". Eye-catching, she said, and Jon agreed. I loathe it.'

Penry eyed her speculatively. 'If you live *and* work with your sister, why on earth hasn't she missed you?'

'I'm coming to that.'

Elise, ten years older than her sister, was the brains of the business. It was Elise who saw to the accounts and the buying, who had a flair for salesmanship. Leonora, the creative one, was perfectly happy to get on with her knitting in her little nook in the shop, help with the customers when trade was brisk, type what correspondence was necessary and otherwise leave Elise to the hard sell. Leonora also did the cooking when the two of them were at home, but Elise was often out dining with someone, or in Stratford at the theatre with someone else. Elise Fox, happily unmarried at thirty-two, was rarely without an escort, but never showed the least sign of tying herself to one man for good.

The love of Leonora's life was sailing, and during the summer months she spent her Sundays on the water at the local reservoir, weeknights at the tennis club or the cinema, and in the winter she took part in as many activities as possible in the small town where she'd lived all her life.

'Sounds horribly humdrum, doesn't it?' She smiled ruefully. 'My parents left enough money to make sure I went to the same school as Elise, but I was never the

academic type—too fond of games. My career was shaped, I suppose, when I sold my first sweater to a smart shop in Stratford at the tender age of sixteen. When I left school I automatically went into the shop with Elise, and began to knit full time.'

Penry eyed her searchingly. 'Have you never wanted wider horizons than that?'

Leonora shrugged. 'Of course, now and then. But never enough to desert Elise. She was only twenty when she was saddled with me, yet she never made me feel I was a drag, and heaven knows a kid sister must have been at times.'

Penry waited patiently as Leonora paused. When she resumed her story her voice was different, flat and uninflected, as she told him that one day a journalist and a photographer had come to Chastlecombe to do a feature on the shopping arcade for the colour magazine of one of the Sunday papers. Much was made of the sympathetic architecture, and the fact that the arcade brought trade to both new and old shops from the tourists who thronged the town summer and winter.

The Fox sisters attracted a lot of attention. Despite competition from shops offering antiques and locally crafted furniture, Fox's Lair came in for the bulk of the publicity. Elise, tall, red-haired and elegant, occupied pole position on the centre-page shot, wearing one of Leonora's sweaters, a silver fox-head brooch pinned to the scarf thrown carelessly over one shoulder, the interior of the shop in the background.

'Where were you?' asked Penry.

'Hiding. I'm hideously unphotogenic. My hair comes out like a bird's nest and my eyes look slitty. Guy. . .' She faltered for a moment. 'Guy Ferris, the photographer, gave up trying to get a good shot of me in the

end. Whereas you can't take a bad picture of my sister. Her bones are so good.'

Penry's eyes lit with a deliberate gleam. 'So are yours—you could do with a trifle more meat on them, but otherwise they compare very favourably with other bone-structures I've met.'

Leonora chuckled. 'Why, thank you, Doctor.'

'So what happened next?'

'I fell in love.'

'With Guy?'

'With Guy.'

Guy Ferris, already making a name for himself in the right circles, made a surprisingly determined play for the younger Miss Fox. Elise, oddly unenamoured of him, became worried when he took to coming down from London quite often at weekends. But Leonora was in seventh heaven. And to crown her joy Guy Ferris was an expert sailor. He would collect her in his Morgan two-seater with the original strap round the bonnet, then take her off to the sailing club to commandeer the helm of her Enterprise dinghy, dressed in the latest sailing gear. Leonora, bedazzled, crewing for him with devotion, was the envy of her friends.

'What a dope,' said Leonora bitterly.

Penry frowned. 'Didn't he want more than just sailing?'

'What do you mean?'

'Don't play the innocent, my child. You know perfectly well our enforced intimacy was a great strain on *me* after only a day or so.'

Leonora looked sceptical. 'Even though I looked as though I'd gone ten rounds with Mike Tyson?'

'You improved at a very disturbing rate, *cariad*!' He

smiled encouragingly. 'Go on with the story. I want to know what caused the amnesia.'

Leonora took a deep breath and informed Penry that Guy had, indeed, made love to her to a certain extent. Lots of kissing and stroking, but nothing more. She'd been convinced he respected her so much that he had intentions of a more permanent nature.

'I read too many fairy-tales when I was young,' she said bitterly.

The romance continued through the autumn and over Christmas, with intimate dinners and spins in the glamorous car in place of sailing once the season was over.

Then Guy told Leonora he was going away for three weeks to Wales, to take photographs for a travel book, and suggested she went with him. It would do her good, he said persuasively. Elise, however, opposed the idea with surprising violence. And, because Elise hardly ever came the heavy older sister, Leonora, with infinite regret, told Guy she couldn't go. He made quite a fuss about it, saying it was time she left the nest, stood up to the forceful Elise and lived her own life. One day, he hinted, he would insist she did, and for more than just a holiday.

'I was so sure he meant marriage,' said Leonora quietly. 'I pined after he'd gone. I was such a misery that by the end of the first week Elise asked a friend to help out in the shop, and packed me off to join him.'

There'd been no word from Guy after he went away, but, knowing his friend's house was isolated, with no telephone, Leonora was unconcerned. Full of excited anticipation, she caught an overnight train, managed to get a taxi to turn out at the crack of dawn to take

her to Morfa, then set out along the causeway to Brynteg.

'Brynteg!' Penry turned her face up to his. 'Was Ferris staying in the house of that artist chap there?'

She nodded. 'You know him?'

'Of him—and the company he keeps. Go on.'

It had been a wonderful, exciting adventure to Leonora that morning. Undaunted by the rain, she set out along the causeway, feeling like a princess in a fairy-tale about to join her prince. Not even the rising wind had any power to damp her ardour as she flew along the causeway. The house stood at the summit of a rocky mound at the end of it, like a miniature St Michael's Mount, but to Leonora it was Mecca to a believer as she began the steep climb from the beach towards journey's end, and Guy.

'The house is a bungalow, with a studio built on the back of it, facing out to sea. I knocked on the front door, but there was no answer.' Leonora paused for a moment, then steeled herself to go on. 'I was cold and wet by this time, but after a tour of inspection I found the house was deserted. So I went round the back to the studio and looked through one of the windows. There was a raised dais at one end underneath a skylight, with a sort of bed on it. Guy was in the bed——' Her voice cracked, and Penry got up to take her in his arms.

'With a woman?' he said harshly.

'No. With another man.'

# CHAPTER NINE

PENRY held her in a loose, impersonal embrace as her tears fell thick and fast, bitter and scalding enough to cauterise the wound in her memory. At first Leonora's body convulsed with shudders as she wept, but little by little she grew quieter. In the warmth of Penry's arms she came face to face with the truth, survived it, and after a while she detached herself from the comforting embrace, accepting the box of tissues Penry passed to her before resuming his chair. She mopped herself up, then eyed him uncertainly as she saw the set, cold expression on his face.

'You're disgusted,' she said.

His eyes glittered like steel. 'I wish I had this Guy of yours here in my hands. I'd like to wring his bloody neck.'

'Thank you. Oddly enough that's rather comforting.' She blinked her swollen eyes, and tried to smile. 'Not, of course, that Guy can help being—being what he is. And he wasn't expecting me. He didn't know I'd changed my mind about joining him.'

'Making excuses for him?'

'No,' she said wearily. 'Just facing the truth.'

Penry looked grim. 'Did he see you?'

Leonora shuddered. 'No!'

With every nerve straining to turn tail and run, she'd backed away as quietly as possible and once she was out of earshot raced back down to the beach to find the tide had turned.

'Picture my feelings when I found the causeway was under water! I tore along the beach like a maniac, looking for some kind of boat I could borrow to get away. I was lucky. There was an old Heron dinghy drawn up on the beach, with an outboard motor ready attached. I commandeered it without a second thought.'

'Ah. Enter the *Seren*.'

'Yes. I dragged it down to the water on the launching trailer, and pushed off. For a few horrible moments I thought the motor wouldn't fire, but after several pulls it caught, then I just hooked my overnight bag over one shoulder, took the tiller and made for the shore, which looked so close that I felt I could have swum across.'

'At which point, I assume, the engine cut out and the notorious cross-currents of the sound hurled you all over the place until you were swept overboard.' Penry shook his head. 'Miraculously they swept you round to Gullholm, where I must have found you minutes after you got caught in that inlet.' His eyes met hers. 'Have you any *idea* how lucky you were?'

She nodded dumbly, the reality of her escape hitting her suddenly like a body-blow.

Penry frowned. 'When are you expected back, by the way?'

Leonora's eyes opened wide in horror. 'Oh, good heavens, what date is it?'

'The fourteenth.'

She sagged with relief. 'I'm due back tomorrow, then. And I've got to get there on time, too, or Elise will go up the wall.'

He nodded briskly as he jumped up. 'I'll drive you.'

'But I'll be spoiling your holiday. And it's miles out

of your way. If you could just get me to the nearest
station——'

'Don't be silly. Like you, it's high time I returned to
the real world.' He paused on his way to the door,
smiling. 'Besides, without my castaway life on
Gullholm will lose its charm.'

Leonora barely heard him, suddenly stricken with
dread at the thought of long night hours ahead alone.
After a pause she said in a stifled voice, 'Must you go
back to your room? Couldn't you stay with me tonight?
Please?'

Penry's face darkened. 'No, Leonora. We've been
through this once. You know perfectly well I can't.
You'll be fine now. You've slain the dragons. They
can't hurt you any more.'

He turned, their eyes met and held for a long, tense
moment, then suddenly Penry flung away, so precipi-
tate in his hurry to leave that he forgot to duck.
Leonora flinched as his head cracked painfully against
the lintel. She leapt out of bed as he rubbed his head,
cursing.

She caught him by the hand. 'Does it hurt?'

'Of course it bloody well hurts!' Penry glared down
at her, trying to yank his hand away, but Leonora hung
on to it in desperation.

'Please stay. *Please*. Penry, listen to me. I want you
to make love to me. I need you to!' Colour flared in
her cheeks as she met his blazing eyes head on.

'You don't know what you're saying,' he said
through clenched teeth.

'On the contrary. I know exactly what I'm saying.
Look on it from a medical angle if you like, as a cure
for an ailment.' She moved closer. 'Penry, don't you
understand? What I saw that morning could spoil me

for a sexual relationship forever. I need another picture in place of it. If you make love to me I'll have something to look back on with pleasure and gratitude for the rest of my life.'

'That's blackmail!' he said harshly.

'No—just a cry for help.' Leonora flushed painfully. 'Unless the last time put you off completely, of course.'

He stood very still. 'In as much as I cringe at the thought of making you sick a second time, yes. It does. I may be a doctor, but I'm also a man with the usual vanity. I won't deny I find you damn near irresistible when you plead like that, but I don't think my ego could take a repeat of last time.'

Her dark eyes lit with sudden hope. 'There's no danger of that. I just want you to blot out everything about that morning. Just by making love to me. Is it so much to ask?' Suddenly she dropped his hand and slid her arms about his waist, knowing she'd won when she felt the thunder of his heart against her cheek as she burrowed her face against his chest. She wriggled closer, and suddenly Penry's arms crushed her cruelly tight against him.

'Leonora,' he said harshly, his voice muffled against her hair, 'have you any idea what you're doing to me?'

She tipped back her head, exulting as she met the blaze in his eyes. 'No. Not really. I was hoping you'd show me.' She stood back and peeled off the shirt with a nonchalance only a trifle marred when a button caught in her hair.

The air left Penry's lungs with an audible hiss as he helped disentangle her, his square white teeth biting into his lower lip when she stood naked in front of him, hands behind her back as she eyed him diffidently. 'I

suppose bodies are pretty everyday things to a doctor——'

He caught her in his arms, swinging her high against his chest, his mouth seeking hers. 'But this isn't every day,' he muttered against her parted lips. 'It's night. And you've won. I know I'll regret this in the morning, but I want you so badly it's a risk I'll just have to take. Are you sure about this?' He set her on her feet suddenly, his eyes like blue flames in his taut face. 'Because this time, *cariad*, I warn you, I shan't let you go.'

'Of course I'm sure,' she said crossly. 'Do you want me or not?'

For answer Penry picked her up and tossed her into the bed, stripped off his dressing-gown and turned out the light. Then his warm, naked body was against hers beneath the covers and this time everything was magically different. Leonora forgot Guy and everything else in her rediscovered world as Penry's presence transformed the darkness into an exciting, intimate microcosm inhabited by two people oblivious of everything but the sheer physical pleasure of being together.

Leonora, expecting to be taken by storm after she'd flung down the gauntlet, found Penry in no hurry at all. She felt a warm rush of gratitude for his sensitivity as he kissed and played with her in a teasing, light-hearted way which both excited and disarmed her at first.

But gradually the tempo of Penry's caresses changed, became more urgent. Skilfully he tuned every nerve in her narrow body to such a concert pitch of response that she began to initiate caresses of her own, delighting in her power as rippling muscles tightened beneath her questing hands. His mouth crushed and coaxed in

turns, his tongue subtle and importunate, before he moved lower, sliding his mouth down her throat until it reached her breasts. Leonora quivered, her teeth caught in her lower lip as he kissed each breast in turn, his lips lingering over their slight curves. Then abruptly he took one pointing nipple between his lips, pulling on it, and she gasped as a streak of fire ran through her, and his hands grew urgent, the thrusting caresses of his long fingers so expert that fulfilment soon came flooding in shock-waves which surged through her entire body.

Leonora lay gasping, arms outflung, eyes closed, her hair a tangled mass of damp curls against the pillow. Penry reached over her to turn on the lamp, and she opened her eyes to find him looking down into her face, a triumphant, indulgent smile curving his mouth as he slid his arms around her, throwing one long leg over hers in careless intimacy.

Colour rushed into her face and she moved restlessly, her eyes sliding away from the gleam in his. 'What— what happens now?'

'What would you like to happen?'

'I don't know. But surely what—what just happened to me couldn't have done much for you, could it?'

He laughed softly. 'On the contrary, my lovely, it did a great deal for me. Would you care to find out just how much?' He slid her hand lower until it rested on the irrefutable proof of his desire for her.

Leonora blinked, her hand closing over him involuntarily, and she smiled in triumph as he groaned, his eyes dilating as they stared down into hers.

'How do you feel?' he asked raggedly, astonishing her.

'You know exactly how I feel!'

Penry bent his head and kissed her deeply, and Leonora slid her arms round his neck, responding with a fervour which answered his question without words. A long time later he raised his head and said huskily, 'Are you sure?'

'Yes. Oh, yes—now. *Please!*'

Yet even now he took his time to stroke and caress her until she was drugged and dazed with longing. He parted her knees, bending his dark head to kiss both in turn, sliding his mouth in a series of kisses along each smooth inner thigh until Leonora began to plead hoarsely. At last, slowly, victoriously, his eyes never leaving hers, he granted her wish. Leonora clenched her teeth for an instant as her body yielded to his with a fleeting moment of pain, then she relaxed as they lay still for an instant in the very eye of the storm.

'Did I hurt you much?' he said against her lips.

'Not much. And not now, which is strange. Why aren't you crushing the life out of me?'

'Because I'm very, very clever.'

'And practised!'

'Not lately.'

'I'd never have known.'

'It's like riding a bike—you never forget.'

'I can ride a bike. But I've never done this before.'

'Ah, *cariad*, I know, I know! Let me teach you how it's done.' And he began to move, slowly at first, his forbearance rewarded by the wonder in her eyes as they stared, delighted, into his. With every move she gave a little gasp, as her body, previous experience or not, proved an apt pupil. Without consulting her it began to move faster, inciting her lover to a rhythm which he responded to triumphantly, accelerating in time with their heartbeats, taking her with him towards

the culmination she'd been given a foretaste of, which
paled in comparison to the flooding rapture which
overtook her seconds before Penry gasped, stiffened,
then crushed her in his arms as their breathing slowed
in the shared diminuendo of the aftermath.

When Leonora opened her eyes again it was morning
and she was alone. She stretched experimentally, wincing as various parts of her ached in a way which brought
the experiences of the night flooding back in full force.
Heat swept over her as she remembered every little
detail of Penry's lovemaking, and she closed her eyes,
breathless at the memory. But at last, as a tongue
probed an aching tooth, she forced herself to think
back to the scene at Brynteg, and found the exercise
distasteful and painful, but reassuring. It was possible
to think of the episode in a detached sort of way, she
found with relief, as though it had happened in another
time and place to someone else.

From now on, she realised, her life would be forever
divided into two separate halves—the time before her
loss of memory and whatever was to come after
recovering it. This interlude with Penry Vaughan on
Gullholm would be something to remember with gratitude as a sort of enchanted no man's land in between.
At the thought of Penry she stretched, cat-like, her
mouth curving in a dreamy smile. As an experience to
blot out the horror of her discovery on Brynteg it had
been blissfully successful. Penry's wonderful, gratifying
desire for her had been a healing fire which had cured
her forever of the wounds dealt by Guy. Then she
shivered, as though someone had walked over her
grave.

Ah, but who, she asked herself with sudden foreboding, is going to cure you of Penry Meredith Vaughan?

Leonora got up quickly, and took a speedy bath, then dressed at top speed in jeans and jersey, securing the red scarf at her throat with the silver brooch. As she brushed her hair she examined her face in the mirror, amazed when no trace of the experience of the night showed on it. She turned away to strip the rumpled bed, then straightened the room and packed her few belongings in her bag, feeling more reluctant by the minute to face Penry in the cold light of day. At last, unable to delay confrontation any longer, she went downstairs to find Penry emerging from the study as she reached the kitchen.

'Good morning,' he said, no trace of a smile on his face. 'I've informed the police about your recovery.'

'Thank you.' Leonora filled the kettle, utterly shattered to find no trace of last night's lover in the Penry Vaughan of this morning. 'I'd forgotten that. Shouldn't I be compensating someone for the loss of the *Seren*?'

'If you want the episode kept quiet I don't advise it. The owners will claim on the insurance.'

Leonora began frying bacon and eggs, slicing bread for toast, spooning coffee in the pot to cover her secret dismay. 'What will you do with the food in the fridge?' she asked, not looking at him.

'Bryn Pritchard can collect it after I leave the keys with him.' Penry leaned against the counter, his eyes on her face. 'How are you this morning, Leonora?'

'Fine,' she said brightly, flipping the eggs over. 'It feels rather strange now I've got my other world back again, I admit. But it's good to be all in one piece again.'

'Not quite,' he said deliberately, and caught her chin in his hand so she was forced to look at him. 'Memory

or no memory, I wouldn't describe you as all in one piece, exactly, after last night.'

Leonora flushed scarlet as she jerked her head away. 'If I'm not it was entirely my own idea, so I can hardly complain.' She handed him a plate. 'Where do you want to eat this? Here or in the other room?'

Penry looked at the food without enthusiasm. 'I don't know that I want it anywhere.'

'Then throw it in the bin,' said Leonora, incensed.

'All right, all right, I'll eat it.' He put the plate down on the counter in front of him then lifted her on to a stool. 'How about eating something yourself while we talk?'

'Talk?' She eyed him askance as she buttered a slice of toast.

Penry ate some of the meal in thoughtful silence, then laid down his fork. 'We need to talk, Leonora. After last night——'

'Let's forget last night.'

'How can we?' His eyebrows shot together in a black bar. 'It may be something you can dismiss easily. I can't.'

Leonora abandoned any pretence of eating. 'Look, Penry. Last night I asked—begged—you to make love to me. You supplied a deep-seated need in me to blot out what I'd seen. You showed me how beautiful love between a man and woman can be, and afterwards I felt healed and whole and normal again.'

Penry refilled their cups with a steady hand. 'Which puts me on a par with a dose of medicine. Thank you.'

'You know that's not what I meant,' she said impatiently. 'What I'm trying to say is how grateful I am, and how miraculous it was, but that's it. I'm off

your hands. You needn't feel responsible for me from now on in the slightest.'

'How extraordinarily civil of you,' he said cuttingly, 'but aren't you missing a rather important point?'

She frowned. 'What point?'

'Think, Leonora! Surely you don't need a lecture on the birds and bees?'

She stared at him for a moment, then flushed. 'Oh. I never thought——'

'*I* did—fleetingly.' His jaw set. 'But by then it was too late. The basic urge for gratification blotted everything else from my mind.'

'Gratification!' Leonora eyed him with dislike as she slid from the stool and began clearing away. 'What a ghastly word.'

'What else would you call it?' he demanded.

'A service? You provided it. I'm grateful. Now forget about it. It's entirely my own fault if there are consequences.'

Penry grabbed her by the shoulders and turned her to face him. 'Forget about it? What kind of monster do you think I am?'

'I don't think you're a monster at all.' She looked up at him defiantly. 'But one way and another I've been quite enough trouble to you already. If there should be a—a problem, I'll deal with it myself.'

Penry's fingers bit into her flesh cruelly for a moment, then his face drained of expression as he released her. 'As you wish.'

Leonora stared after him, stricken, as he went upstairs to pack his belongings. Her fine words had been so much whistling in the dark. She had fully expected Penry to dismiss them as nonsense, and felt so shattered that he hadn't that it took her longer than

usual to clear away and leave the kitchen immaculate. While Penry was outside seeing to the generator she fetched her belongings, then collected the knitting, stuffing it inside her bag guiltily.

'Are you ready?' asked Penry a little later.

'Yes.' She took a last look round the room which had been her world, then hurried quickly out of the house.

Their progress down to the *Angharad* was slow. There was a fair wind spattering them with rain as they made their descent to the beach. As they reached the little anchorage she looked at the sea with resignation. It would be a rough crossing. Once the luggage was stowed away on board Penry lifted her on the deck of the *Angharad* and cast off. At once the crabber began to bounce about on the waves, as though the *Angharad* was dancing a jig over the water in her pleasure at taking a trip.

Leonora watched the grey smudge of shoreline growing closer, knowing that once she was there this part of her life would be over, and she might never see Penry Vaughan again. Her eyes flew to him, trying to imprint his tall, commanding figure on her memory as he stood with legs braced, his hands on the wheel.

'Are you frightened?' he asked. 'No need to be—it's just a stiffish breeze.' He extended an arm. 'Come here.'

Leonora, depressed rather than frightened, moved to the shelter of his arms for the remainder of the journey. It was a bitter-sweet experience. Through the layers of their clothing she could feel Penry's heart beating steadily against her back, and dreaded the moment of parting which would come all too soon when they reached journey's end in Chastlecombe.

'You're very quiet,' he said into the back of her neck.

She kept her eyes on the heaving sea. 'I was busy composing a graceful speech of thanks for all you've done for me.'

'Unnecessary. You typed the articles, relieved me of the household chores and fed me royally. The debt is on my side.'

She felt glad her face was hidden from him. 'Ah, but you saved my life, remember!'

He moved closer as Brides Haven came into focus in the distance. 'In some cultures that has great significance. Is it the Chinese who would now consider you my responsibility?'

'It's a good thing we're British, then,' she said lightly, and ducked from under his arm. 'We're nearly there.'

The process of visiting Bryn Pritchard to leave keys and instructions took longer than anticipated, since Mrs Pritchard insisted on making coffee and feeding them newly baked scones before they went on their way.

'Is your sister expecting you at a specific time?' asked Penry when they were on the way to Haverfordwest at last.

'I think I said I'd be back this evening some time. Could I ring her en route to say I'm on my way?'

'Of course. We'll stop off somewhere for lunch.'

Leonora thanked him quietly, not quite sure how she felt about this idea. Half of her wanted to get the journey and the parting over, to make a quick, clean break. But the other half wanted the day to go on forever, for Penry to drive at a snail's pace on the way back to prolong their time together to the last possible minute.

As if he'd read her mind Penry took a cross-country route instead of the motorway, driving her through Carmarthen and Llandeilo, then on past Brecon to head for Leominster. When he turned into the car park of an attractive roadside pub Leonora went off to ring her sister while Penry gave their orders.

'Is all well?' he asked when she joined him at a small table in a corner of the crowded bar.

Leonora pulled a face. 'Elise was delighted I rang, but gave me a terrible dressing down for not ringing before or sending a postcard. I told her there were extenuating circumstances and would tell all when I got home.' She gulped down some orange juice hastily.

'What's the matter, Leonora?' asked Penry, his voice so unusually gentle that it brought a sheen of tears to her eyes.

'It suddenly struck me how difficult it's going to be to explain everything to Elise.'

'Surely she'll understand?'

'Of course she will. I just loathe the thought of telling my nasty little tale a second time.'

'It probably won't be as bad as you think,' said Penry briskly, and launched into a description of the house he'd bought on the banks of the River Wye near Builth Wells. Leonora listened wistfully as she toyed with her sandwich, thinking it sounded idyllic, and a great waste for one man on his own. She said appropriate things in the right places, and hardly knew whether she was glad or sorry when it was time to go.

After a leisurely drive through the spring sunshine they arrived in the broad main street of Chastlecombe just after four. Penry parked the Range Rover in the open space behind the arches of the ancient market

hall, then reached over into the back for Leonora's bag.

She smiled at him brightly. 'Thank you for the lift. I'll be fine now. Don't get out.'

Penry's brows drew together. 'Don't be silly. I'll see you home,' he said shortly and got out of the car, striding round to lift her down.

Leonora's heart sank, but she knew better by this time than to argue with Penry Vaughan. She led the way along the pavement of the wide main street typical of most Cotswold towns, smiling at familiar faces as they passed. The new arcade looked very attractive in the spring sunshine. Tubs of daffodils stood outside every shop, except for Fox's Lair, where a pair of bay trees flourished in ceramic pots.

'We live in a flat over the shop,' said Leonora, her feet dragging now they were nearly there.

'Come on,' said Penry firmly. 'Let's get it over with.'

And right on cue there was Elise at the door of the shop, elegant as always in slim skirt and silk shirt, her face alight with welcome which changed quickly to surprise as she realised the man with her sister was a stranger.

'Hello, love,' said Leonora, hugging her. 'This is Dr Penry Vaughan. He was kind enough to give me a lift home.'

Penry held out his hand, smiling courteously. 'How do you do, Miss Fox? Could you possibly spare me a few moments in private? Leonora's had rather a disturbing adventure. Don't be alarmed. I just want to make certain she tells you exactly what happened.'

# CHAPTER TEN

ELISE FOX was a woman who prided herself on her ability to deal with crisis, but at eleven o'clock that Saturday night she still lay limp on the sofa in the flat, looking utterly shattered when her young sister came in from the kitchen with yet another pot of strong black coffee.

'I'm sorry, Elise,' said Leonora for the hundredth time. 'None of it would have happened if I hadn't gone chasing after Guy.'

'You mean if Guy hadn't come chasing after you!' said Elise hotly. 'I was against it from the first. I couldn't put my finger on what it was I disliked about him, yet now it seems plain as the nose on your face. What a ghastly thing to happen to you. I could kill him!'

'Penry felt like that, too.'

Elise looked across at her searchingly. 'Ah, yes. The impressive Dr Vaughan. Full marks to him, anyway.' Her eyes narrowed. 'Was I imagining things, or was there a definite hint of electricity in the air between you and the dashing doctor?'

'Certainly not.'

'Liar!'

Leonora shook back her hair, looking fierce. 'If you don't mind I'd like to drop the subject now. As far as I'm concerned I'd like to forget that the last couple of weeks ever happened.'

Elise jumped up, looking contrite. 'Poor darling,

you've had such a time and I keep rabbiting on and on about it. I'm sorry. I should be the one dispensing coffee and condolences, not you.'

Glad to be alone in her familiar little room later, Leonora forced herself to face the indigestible truth. Forgetting Guy Ferris would be child's play compared to her other problem. Two weeks ago she had never heard of Penry Meredith Vaughan. Now she couldn't imagine life without him. The conclusion kept her tossing and turning in despair for hours, the sound of traffic in the High Street a poor substitute for the lulling boom of the sea round Gullholm. She had never imagined she would miss Penry so much. The memory of their night together haunted her so relentlessly that it was daylight before she fell into an uneasy, exhausted sleep.

Leonora found the next day very long. Normally she loved Sundays. In the summer it was her sailing day, but in the winter she spent it at home, cooking lunch, reading the papers, and generally lazing around. Sometimes Elise was at home all day, sometimes not. This particular Sunday she had an invitation to a dinner party, and was all for cancelling, but Leonora wouldn't hear of it.

'I ruined your Saturday night, so please go off and enjoy yourself. I'll be fine. Besides, Priscilla's probably got some man lined up for you as dinner partner.' Leonora summoned up a grin. 'Think of her anguish if you upset her seating plan!'

Secretly Leonora was relieved to be on her own. Overnight the full force of what might have happened had finally come home to Elise, and she'd spent most of the day clucking round her young sister like a hen

with one chick. Leonora was heartily glad to wave her off to her party. But once she was alone with her knitting depression crept up on Leonora like an incoming tide. Only a short time before she'd had Penry for company while she knitted. Now her sole companion was the television, which was intrusive after two weeks without it.

When the telephone rang Leonora got up listlessly, so certain it would be one of Elise's friends that she slid down on the floor in a heap, heart thumping, at the sound of Penry's voice.

'Leonora? Are you there?'

'Yes. I'm here.' She breathed in deeply. 'Did you get home safely?'

'I did. How are you today?'

'I'm fine.'

'Are you? Honestly?' There was silence for a moment, then he said huskily, 'Leonora—look, there's no easy way to say this, but I hope you're not full of some quixotic notion about keeping it from me if you find out you're pregnant.'

Leonora's hackles rose. 'Why? So you can arrange for an abortion as soon as possible?' she blurted. 'It must be easy enough for someone like you.'

She heard a sharp intake of breath, then an earsplitting crack as Penry Vaughan slammed down his receiver without another word.

Leonora had a good cry, made herself some tea, then settled down to knit furiously. Before long the sweater was finished and the various parts stitched together with her usual professional finish, ready to post off to Penry next day to make certain he had a keepsake to remind him of his castaway.

The following evening Penry rang again, but this

time he spoke to Elise, who was rather mystified when he politely declined to speak to Leonora.

'He just asked how you were, made me promise to keep an eye on you, then rang off,' she said, frowning.

'He rang last night. I was a teensy bit rude,' said Leonora, trying to look unconcerned.

'Oh, I see.' Elise eyed her thoughtfully. 'Never mind. Perhaps he'll look on that amazing jersey you sent off as an olive branch.'

Instead of ringing again Penry sent Leonora a very formal letter of thanks for the sweater. The sight of his indecipherable scrawl gave her a sharp pang of nostalgia for the strange, lost time spent on his island, underlining her dissatisfaction with life in Chastlecombe very heavily now her adventure was over.

When Leonora learned there would be no sequel to her adventure after all, she was totally unprepared for the desolation which swamped her. She hid it away behind a bright, brittle insouciance which plainly worried Elise to death, but for several nights wept silently into her pillow, utterly shattered to find she'd wanted Penry's child quite desperately without even realising it. Now there would be no reason for further contact between them of any kind, a prospect which painted dark shadows beneath Leonora's eyes, and bleached the colour from her face to the point where Elise began muttering darkly about anaemia.

Leonora pooh-poohed this. Her problem had been amnesia, not anaemia, she told Elise flippantly. Nevertheless she agreed to the luxury of a lie-in the following Sunday morning, even allowing her sister to fuss over her a little.

'I should stay there for a while,' said Elise, when she

brought in a breakfast tray. 'You look like something the cat's dragged in.'

But after an hour Leonora grew bored and irritable with herself and went off to have a bath. Afterwards she spent more time than usual on her appearance, determined that from now on she would stop behaving like some Victorian miss with the vapours. She even put on sheer stockings and a brief pleated skirt instead of her usual jeans, then, as final proof of her new outlook on life, she put on the new pink sweater and danced out into the sitting-room, calling. 'How do I look——' She stopped dead, her heart flipping over under the sweater as Penry Vaughan leapt to his feet at the sight of her, the height and breadth of him overpowering the entire room.

'Good enough to eat, *cariad*!' He held out his hand, and Leonora took it, dumbfounded.

'Well?' he demanded, 'aren't you even going to say hello?'

She pulled herself together. 'Hello, indeed. What a surprise. Where's Elise?'

'She had to go out for a moment.'

Storing up a ticking-off for her sister, Leonora managed a rather stiff smile to hide the joy bubbling inside her. 'Do sit down.'

Incensed at being taken by surprise despite her pleasure at seeing him, Leonora was somewhat mollified to see that Penry was wearing the sweater she'd knitted. The complex, serpentine weaving of colours emphasised his impressive shoulders, and in faded old Levis and scuffed desert boots he looked so wonderful as he lounged on the sofa that she could have thrown herself in his arms there and then. Instead she blurted the first thing that came into her head.

'You've had a wasted journey. I'm not pregnant after all.'

He nodded. 'I see. I wondered.'

'About what?'

'Elise rang me to say you were crying your eyes out every night.'

Leonora eyed him in horror. 'She heard me?'

'Yes.' Penry leaned forward peremptorily. 'And I want to know why you cried, please.'

Her eyes flickered. 'You're a doctor. You know perfectly well that women get depressed at—at certain times. I'm no exception.'

'Is that the real reason?' His eyes held hers inexorably. 'Or is it just possible you wanted to be pregnant?'

But Leonora had herself well in hand by this time. She gave him a scornful little smile. 'Oh, come *on*— I'm not a complete idiot!'

He looked unconvinced. 'No, just unhappy. Elise can't have been mistaken about the tears.'

'I can't say I care for the idea of you two discussing me behind my back, but if you must know I was suffering from reaction,' said Leonora with dignity. 'After my recent adventures it's not really surprising, is it?'

Penry's eyes held a sceptical gleam. 'All right, Leonora, if that's the way you want it. Let's talk about why I'm here instead.' He paused deliberately. 'To come straight to the point, I drove down here to make a suggestion. Are you prepared to listen?'

'Since you came so far I can hardly say no.'

'Very well, then. I propose we carry on where we left off, unless you never want to lay eyes on me again, of course.'

Leonora sat very still, her eyes locked with his. 'I'm—sorry—*what* did you say?'

'You know exactly what I said. Now that the spectre of pregnancy is out of the way, is there any reason why we can't just continue with the relationship begun on Gullholm?'

She stared at him uncertainly. 'Are you serious?'

'Why not?' Penry leaned forward to take her hands. 'I'm not asking to be your lover, Leonora. Yet. Ravishing experience though that was, we came to it too precipitately, and for all the wrong reasons. But is there any reason why we can't be friends?' He smiled, a gleam in his eyes she recognised with a sharp pang. 'I've missed my castaway rather a lot, you know.'

She frowned. 'You were pretty fed up with me the other night—on the phone.'

'Are you surprised? It was a bloody awful thing to say. I thought you knew me better than that.'

She shrugged. 'My recent brush with the seamier side of life has made me cynical. Tell me,' she added, determined to put things straight between them, 'purely as a matter of interest, what would you have done if I had been pregnant?'

'I'd have asked you to marry me.' He raised an eyebrow. 'Old-fashioned, I suppose, but none of the other options seemed remotely possible for you—or for me.'

Leonora withdrew her hands and got up. 'I see.' She looked down at him consideringly for some time. At last she nodded. 'All right. In that case I don't see why not.'

Penry rose slowly, his eyes narrowed. 'Why do I have the feeling I've passed some kind of test?'

'Because you have.' She smiled at him, feeling very much better. 'I wonder what's happened to Elise.'

'She said something about tidying the shop.'

'Poor darling, I'd better go and put her out of her misery.'

Penry reached for her, barring her way to the door. 'Wait a moment. Convince me that all's well between us now—one friendly little kiss would do.'

Leonora hesitated, then held up her mouth. At the first touch of his lips she trembled, and Penry took her in his arms, his kiss suddenly fierce until a tactful little cough from the doorway brought an untimely end to the embrace.

'Can I come in now?' asked Elise apologetically. 'I can't think of another thing to do down there.'

Penry relinquished Leonora without embarrassment, smiling at the relief on Elise's face.

'I gather diplomatic relations have now been resumed,' she remarked with satisfaction.

'I suppose they have.' Leonora smiled happily at Penry. 'Are you in a hurry to be off, or would you like some lunch?'

That Sunday marked the beginning of a new phase in Leonora's life. The mere fact that Penry Vaughan wished to go on seeing her, however few and far between their meetings, did wonders for her self-esteem. It also compensated very thoroughly for the disaster of her relationship with Guy, who received short shrift when he telephoned on his return to London from Wales. She made no mention of her disastrous trip to Brynteg, told him she'd met someone else, and wished him good luck with deliberate finality when she said goodbye.

At first Leonora wasn't sure precisely what Penry had in mind regarding their relationship, and lived in a state of tension between his phone calls. But after a while he augmented the phone calls with occasional visits, and as the summer wore on came to see her with increasing regularity, eventually as often as his professional commitments allowed. On free weekends he drove to Chastlecombe on a Saturday afternoon, took Leonora out for a meal somewhere, stayed the night at the Kings Arms in the town, and spent most of Sunday with Leonora before driving home to face his Monday morning clinic next day. To her delight he even took to discussing his work with her, and Leonora listened, rapt, utterly fascinated by glimpses of the other, professional Penry Vaughan she secretly found so impressive.

Their relationship was an oddly comfortable one, with nothing more demonstrative about it than a swift goodnight kiss, or hands joined on a walk in the beautiful countryside around Chastlecombe. At first Leonora felt strangely happy. It was enough for a while just to have this clever, charming man as a friend, flattering to have him travel so far when he could just for the pleasure of her company. As the weeks passed she finally began to believe that Penry Vaughan meant what he said, that their relationship was important enough to him to nurture with delicacy and care.

But after a while the chaste quality of their relationship grew irksome. Leonora dreamed of the fierce rapture they'd shared on the island and began to long for Penry to want her violently, to stop treating her like a younger sister, and sometimes after he'd gone she'd stare in the mirror in discontent, wishing she

were tall, or voluptuous, or blonde. Anything other than dark-eyed and boyishly slender.

'What's up?' asked Elise one night, as Leonora was trying to find some new, madly attractive way to arrange her hair. 'Mirror, mirror, on the wall, who's the fairest one of all, and so on?'

Leonora turned away, sighing, to slump down on the side of her bed. 'No need to ask that,' she said despondently. 'You are, Elise Fox.'

Elise gave her a hug. 'Darling, what nonsense!' She grinned mischievously. 'It's not me Penry Vaughan drives all this way to see, remember.'

Leonora refused to be consoled. 'Possibly not. Which doesn't stop me wishing I were less unspectacular.'

'The ex-Mrs Vaughan being very spectacular, I take it.'

'Very, from what little he's said about her. So are his sisters. I saw photographs of them.'

'Perhaps it's the contrast Penry finds so appealing——'

'Thank you very much!'

'You know what I mean!' said Elise impatiently. 'Perhaps Dr Penry Vaughan is surfeited with so much glamour and finds your subtler style more to his taste.'

Leonora gave her sister a scornful look. 'Then why doesn't he——' She stopped dead, blushing to the roots of her hair.

'Ah!' Elise nodded sagaciously. 'I see. Dr Vaughan is a shade too platonic for your taste, little sister!'

Leonora shied a pillow at her sister, her face scarlet as she remembered how she'd once pleaded with Penry to make love to her. Next time, she vowed secretly,

Penry Vaughan would do the begging. If there was a next time.

Penry did use persuasion on Leonora next time they met, but it had nothing to do with becoming her lover.

They had just returned to the flat after a long, lazy picnic in the September sunshine, to find Elise out. A note left taped to the fridge informed Leonora that her sister would be back in time for supper.

'Elise goes out a lot on Sundays,' remarked Penry. 'I hope we're not driving her out.'

'No, of course not. It's the only regular free day she has to visit friends. When you're not here I go sailing on Sundays, remember.'

He settled himself on the sofa as he always did, looking fit and rested as he eyed her speculatively. The dark, brooding look about him, so daunting at their first meeting, was missing these days, replaced by a zest and animation she knew must have been the norm for Penry Vaughan before his marriage—or before his divorce, she corrected herself. It was the parting from his wife, unquestionably, which had etched the lines of disillusion on his handsome face.

'Why are you looking at me like that?' asked Leonora.

Penry patted the cushion beside him. 'Come and sit beside me, *cariad*, and I'll tell you.'

Leonora needed no second bidding. These days she was glad of any invitation to proximity, and curled up beside him so promptly that he gave her an amused sidelong glance as he took her hand in his.

'I was just thinking what guts you had to start sailing again after what happened on Brynteg,' he said, surprising her. Brynteg was a subject they never discussed.

She nodded soberly. 'The first time afterwards was

terrifying. When the wind got up, Julian Parker had to get the Enterprise back almost single-handed I was so rigid with fear.'

Penry's eyes narrowed. 'Who the devil's Julian Parker?'

Leonora, deeply pleased at his tone, shrugged airily. 'Just a friend. He crews for me—or I crew for him. But we haven't raced competitively this season because I'm not there regularly enough.'

'Is this where I make the noble suggestion of keeping away at weekends to leave you free to sail as much as you want?' he demanded.

'If you like,' she said cheerfully. 'Are you going to?'

'No, Leonora. I am not.' He paused, then slid his free arm round her shoulders. 'Unless,' he said silkily, 'you specifically request me to do so, of course.'

'The season's almost over now,' she said obliquely, not looking at him, and suddenly the arm descended to pull her against him. Penry released her hand to turn her face up to his.

'I take it that means you're still agreeable to my company when I can make it?'

Leonora longed for his company in much larger doses than he was able to spare, but had no intention of telling him so. She nodded slightly, and he bent his head to give her a kiss which was meant to be fleeting, but which went on and on until they were breathless and shaken when he put her away from him at last.

'Why did you stop?' she whispered.

Penry breathed in deeply. 'You know why!' He smiled at her crookedly, changing the subject with determination. 'Leonora, am I allowed to ask how you feel these days about the ambivalent Mr Ferris? Any hang-ups, or regrets?'

Leonora swung her feet to the ground, disinclined to discuss Guy Ferris. 'No, none.'

He put out a hand to smooth her untidy hair. 'Has he been in touch?'

'Yes.' Leonora sat very still, every nerve-end alight at his touch.

'Did you tell him about me?' demanded Penry.

'No,' lied Leonora shamelessly. 'Should I have?'

Penry frowned, then kissed her again, hard, but Leonora dodged away, scowling.

'What's the matter?' he demanded. 'I've been so unnaturally virtuous lately that you can surely grant me two kisses in one day!'

'I would appreciate it more if this one hadn't been prompted by resentment of another man.'

'If you can call Ferris a man!'

Leonora got to her feet, suddenly and unreasonably furious. She folded her arms across her chest, careless of her untidy hair and sunburned, shiny face. 'I suppose that what you're really saying is that Guy was attracted to me because he could pretend I was a boy!'

'I'm saying nothing of the kind,' snapped Penry, leaping to his feet.

Refusing to be intimidated by the sheer size of him, Leonora glared up into his face. 'Except for that one, never-referred-to night on your island, Dr Vaughan, you're no different. I might just as well be a boy for all the interest you take in me as—as a woman!'

Penry glared at her in sudden fury. 'What the hell do you mean? Are you inferring that my sexual preferences have any remote resemblance to your fancy photographer's?'

'I could be forgiven for thinking so lately,' Leonora

muttered unwisely, then backed away in a hurry from the blaze in his eyes.

'Don't be nervous,' said Penry with dangerous calm. 'I shan't hit you.' He seized her by the shoulders, his fingers biting into her flesh. 'But I'd like to put you over my knee and paddle your behind, young lady. Dammit, Leonora, I thought you understood I was bending over backwards not to rush you.'

Leonora shrugged off his hands with sudden violence. 'Did you have to take a whole summer?' she demanded angrily. 'All you've done, Dr Vaughan, should you be interested, is wreck my self-confidence and give me an inferiority complex about my looks.'

Penry stared at her in silence, visibly pulling himself together. 'How did I manage that?' he asked at last, in a flat, uninflected tone very different from the passionate outburst of a moment earlier.

Leonora let out an unsteady, shuddering sigh. 'It doesn't matter,' she muttered, and turned away, but Penry seized her by the waist and turned her to face him.

'Of course it matters!' He shook her slightly. 'Are you saying that all my bloody unnatural restraint has achieved is to convince you I don't find you attractive?'

She nodded. 'All the women you know are so good-looking. I assumed I was just too ordinary to interest you—in that way.'

'Then why the hell do you think I keep coming to see you?' Penry pulled her down on the sofa forcibly. 'Now sit still, shut up, and listen! Before I got married I led a pretty lively existence where women were concerned, and enjoyed it to the full. I married Melanie, if I'm honest, because she was the only one who'd held out for a wedding-ring.'

'Why are you telling me all this?' asked Leonora, trying to move away.

'Because we need to clear the air, I think, if we're to go on seeing each other.' His eyes narrowed with sudden hostility. 'Unless, of course, you don't want that.'

Leonora shook her head, flushing. 'You know very well that I do. Very much.'

'I'm relieved to hear it. And I took you in my confidence—something, incidentally, I don't do lightly—because I couldn't face another relationship based on misunderstanding. Melanie was like an empty chocolate-box, tempting on the outside, nothing inside—to be blunt, frigid. Yet she was determined to marry me. Beats me why!'

'It's perfectly obvious why!' said Leonora, astonished.

Penry smiled slowly, his eyes lighting up with the gleam she found so irresistible. 'Thank you, *cariad*. You're very good for my ego.'

But Leonora was still thinking over what he'd said. 'Penry,' she said, frowning, 'are you saying you—well, that you wouldn't want a relationship with me if I were frigid, like Melanie?'

Penry shook his head. 'No. I'm not saying that at all. I married Melanie in a rush, for reasons which embarrass me to remember. With you I just wanted to savour the initial stages, step by step, to enjoy just being with you, whatever we were doing Besides,' he added very softly, his fingers stroking the back of her hand, 'you're not frigid, my lovely. I know that beyond all doubt.'

'So you're not sorry you made love to me that night?'

'How could I be? It was a uniquely beautiful experience—for me at least, if not you.'

A weight rolled off Leonora's shoulders. 'It was for me, too. I'll always be grateful to you for that night.'

He picked up her hand and kissed it, then replaced it on her bare brown knee. 'I don't need gratitude for something which gave me such infinite pleasure. On the other hand, if you really feel indebted, Miss Fox, there is a small favour you could do for me in return.'

'Oh, yes?' Leonora eyed him warily. 'What kind of favour?'

'I've been invited to a party next weekend. Will you go with me?'

'Where?'

'That's the snag.' Penry smiled wryly. 'The party's in London. It's to celebrate my sister Clem's tenth wedding anniversary—and my family will be there *en masse*, including my mother, who commands my presence.'

Leonora eyed him in alarm. 'And you want me to go with you? No way!'

He smiled coaxingly. 'Please don't say no, *cariad*. I told my mother I was bringing you. Otherwise one of my sisters will have some unattached female ready to pounce on me. I need you for protection!'

She thought it over uneasily. 'Won't they mind if you bring a stranger to a family party?'

'Not in the least. Nick and Clem will have invited half the world and his wife, anyway. Besides,' added Penry with cunning strategy, 'if you turn me down we shan't see each other for quite a while. I'm tied up at the hospital the weekend after.'

Leonora's heart sank at the prospect of a whole fortnight without him, and as if scenting victory Penry moved closer, his long forefinger caressing her drooping lower lip.

'Is there no way I can persuade you?' he whispered.

Leonora nodded, her eyes bright with mischief. Very deliberately she closed her teeth gently on his fingertip, her eyes holding his, and with a smothered sound Penry jerked his hand away and seized her in his arms, his kiss igniting a response which set them both alight.

Leonora shivered with pleasure as Penry's long fingers caressed the length of brown thigh below her brief denim shorts. Her mouth parting ardently beneath his, she began to unbutton his shirt with unsteady fingers, then slithered lower to kiss his bare brown chest, exulting in the thunder of his heart for a moment before she found herself flat on the sofa as Penry slid her jersey over her head, then dispensed with the scrap of satin beneath. His dark hair brushing her skin, he bent his mouth to each breast in turn, paying such delicately agonising attention to each one that Leonora gasped and thrust her hips hard against him. With a groan Pentry thrust her away then crushed her against his chest, his cheek on her hair.

'This is torture!' he said hoarsely.

She nodded violently, and turned up her face, her eyes sloe-black in her flushed brown face. 'But you're not going to make love to me.'

He let out an unsteady breath, his blue eyes almost as dark as hers. 'No. You must know how much I *want* to make love to you, Leonora, but not here, not like this. I want much, much more than a few snatched moments. Next time we make love I want it perfect, with all the time in the world for each other. Can you understand that, *cariad*?'

Leonora drew in a deep, unsteady breath and nodded. 'Yes.' She glanced at the clock and leapt to her feet, her colour deepening at the look in Penry's

eyes as she pulled her jersey over her head. 'Just as well your particular brand of persuasion came to a halt when it did Dr Vaughan. Elise will be home soon.'

He smiled wryly as he fastened his shirt. 'I know. Otherwise. . .' He sighed with wry regret as he took her into his arms, tipping her face up to his. 'Tell me, Miss Fox, was my persuasion powerful enough? Will you come to Clem's party with me?'

'Yes.' She stood on tiptoe to kiss him. 'Otherwise I'd spend the evening wondering if you were using that particular form of persuasion on someone else.'

'Would you mind?'

'You bet I would!'

# CHAPTER ELEVEN

LEONORA was suffering serious doubts about her sanity by the time the train drew in to Paddington Station the following Saturday evening. She sighed as she folded Elise's cream linen jacket over her arm before making her way along the compartment. An evening spent in the bosom of Penry Vaughan's relatives had all the appeal of Daniel's soirée in the lion's den. Not even the sight of Penry's dark head, clearly visible above the crowds on the platform, had the power to raise her spirits as he forged his way towards her, looking spectacularly attractive in a lightweight grey suit with a white silk shirt striped in Cambridge blue, open at the throat.

'Hello, *cariad*!' He lifted her down from the train, kissed her swiftly, then began to lead her towards the taxi rank. 'I left the car in Parson's Green and came in by Underground so I could hold your hand all the way back.'

Leonora hung back. 'Hello, Penry—hold on. I need to change my clothes first.'

Penry looked at her violet cotton shirt and cream denims in surprise. 'Aren't you wearing that to the party?'

'Of course I'm not,' she snapped.

He eyed her searchingly, then stood still, holding her by the shoulders, oblivious of the crowds which parted to avoid them. 'What's the matter? Sorry you came?'

She nodded vigorously, and he grinned.

'Don't worry, my lovely. I'll protect you. Not that you'll need it. My family are a nice lot by and large.'

'I'm sure they are. How much do they know about me?'

'No details. Your presence tonight won't cause comment, I promise.' He kissed the tip of her nose. 'At one time they'd have thought it odd if I didn't have a girl in tow. It was different when I was married, of course, but I'm not married any more.'

'True. Otherwise my presence wouldn't be necessary!'

'But, since it's not only necessary, but vital, get a move on, *cariad*. If I'm to drive you home afterwards we'll have to leave as soon as we arrive at this rate.'

A few moments later Leonora rejoined Penry, who was prowling around the central bookstall impatiently, looking at his watch. When she tapped him on the arm he turned swiftly, his eyes suddenly narrowed at the sight of her.

'Is this all right?' asked Leonora anxiously. 'Elise said I couldn't go wrong with a little black dress.'

'Little's the word,' he said gruffly, looking her up and down. 'I don't know that I approve of quite so much black silk leg on view, but otherwise you look wonderful.'

She smiled happily. 'Why, thank you, Doctor, you say the nicest things. I wanted to wear my hair up in a knot but Elise said you'd prefer it loose like this.'

'She's right!' Penry put his arm round her to shepherd her towards the moving row of taxis. 'Now get a move on, there's a good girl.'

Leonora felt better once she was in the taxi, particularly since Penry not only held her hand, but kept his arm round her for the entire journey, taking her mind

very successfully off the evening ahead by the sheer joy
of just being with him after a week apart. She gazed
into his face raptly as he described his clinic the day
before at St Mary's and passed on good wishes from
Sister Concepta.

'What's the matter?' he said at last, as he realised
she wasn't paying quite the attention he would have
wished.

'I was just thinking how glad I am to see you,' she
said candidly.

His arm tightened as he bent to kiss her cheek.
'Why, thank you, Miss Fox. I'm very happy to hear it.'

The moment they arrived in Parson's Green Penry
rushed Leonora to the Range Rover, gave her a
moment to fish out a gift-wrapped package from the
bag containing her change of clothes, then stowed the
latter in the car. He fairly hauled her along the street
afterwards, giving her no time for nerves as they
reached a white-painted door with a large brass dragon
for a knocker. Almost at once it swung open to let out
a surge of laughter and music as a tall dark man with a
scar on one cheek clapped Penry on the back and
introduced himself to Leonora as Nick Wood, then
beckoned to a tall, beautiful woman with a mane of
ash-blonde hair, who excused herself from a group of
people to come running to throw her arms round
Penry's neck.

'Hello, you finally made it.' She turned to Leonora
with a radiant smile. 'Welcome to the Wood ménage,
I'm so glad you could come.'

Leonora wished her hosts happy anniversary as she
presented her gift rather shyly. 'I looked up the tenth
anniversary and it said tin, which was a bit limiting. It's
not very original, I'm afraid.'

Her gift was an oblong tin containing a bottle of venerable malt whisky, received with much pleasure by both recipients before Clem swept Leonora away on a round of introductions. At last a man with silvery smiling eyes in a brown face introduced himself as Luiz Santana, husband of Clem's twin, Charity, and took Leonora into the dining-room when Clem was called away to great more arrivals.

'*Queridas*,' he announced, 'this is Penry's guest, Señorita Leonora Fox.' The two women putting finishing touches to the buffet supper turned as one, surprise in the smiles they gave the slender figure standing alone in the doorway. Luiz introduced his mother-in-law and his wife, then excused himself to go off to help distribute drinks.

Leonora smiled diffidently, blinking with surprise at the sight of Charity, who was such a mirror image of her twin that the effect was electrifying. But her real interest lay with the older woman, whose smoke-blue eyes and distinctive bone-structure proclaimed her Penry's mother in a way which made an introduction unnecessary.

'How do you do?' she said shyly, since both women seemed momentarily at a loss for words. 'It was kind of Mrs Wood to invite me.'

'My dear child,' said Mrs Vaughan, a look on her face Leonora could have sworn was relief. She stretched out her hands in welcome. 'How very nice to meet you.'

'Why didn't Pen bring you straight to us?' demanded Charity, adding her own dazzling smile to the warmth of her mother's greeting. 'Honestly, he is the end.'

'Oh, it wasn't his fault!' said Leonora instantly, flying

to Penry's defence. 'Your sister took me off to introduce me to everyone.' She smiled ruefully. 'Not that it
was much use, I'm afraid; I met so many people the
faces were just a blur.'

Charity exchanged a few pleasantries, then, at a look
from her mother, excused herself to go off to the
kitchen, leaving Leonora alone with Mrs Vaughan.

'Penry was rather mysterious about you, my dear,'
said the latter, and patted one of the dining chairs
ranged along the wall. 'Come and sit here and tell me
about yourself. Penry has already given me, and *only*
me I would stress, a brief account of your adventure
on Gullholm. Dear heaven, child, you were so lucky to
survive!'

'I know, Mrs Vaughan,' agreed Leonora soberly.
'Your son saved my life.'

'Thank God he was on hand. The island's usually
left to the gulls at that time of year.' Mrs Vaughan
shuddered slightly, and touched Leonora's hand. 'Fate
was kind to arrange for Penry to be there just when he
was needed most.'

'Someone taking my name in vain?' asked Penry,
coming into the room. 'There you are, Leonora. I see
you've met my mother.'

'No thanks to you,' said Mrs Vaughan in dry reproof.

'Clem spirited her off before I could even get her a
drink.' He handed a glass of wine to Leonora. 'Would
you care for something, Mother?'

'No, thank you, darling,' said Mrs Vaughan, then
met her son's eyes, stiffening, as feminine laughter
rose above the general hubbub in the hall. Penry
turned, his face set, as the door flew open and a tall
woman in a clinging white dress paused theatrically on
the threshold. She moved across the room with an

indolent, hip-swaying saunter, tossing back her shining black hair as she smiled at Penry.

'Hello, Pen. Long time no see.' She turned to Mrs Vaughan. 'Hello, Mrs V, don't look so stern. I couldn't keep away from my darling brother's anniversary party, now, could I? How *are* you—and who's this?'

'Good evening, Melanie,' said Mrs Vaughan shortly. 'What a surprise. Where is—what's his name?'

'Oh, Nigel—on some beastly business trip on the Continent.' She looked at Penry challengingly. 'Haven't you got a friendly little greeting for me, Pen, darling?'

'Good evening,' he said expressionlessly, pulling Leonora to her feet. 'Allow me to introduce you. Leonora, this is Melanie, my ex-wife. Melanie this is Leonora Fox—my fiancée.'

The cruel grip of Penry's fingers conveyed an appeal which Leonora responded to without batting an eyelid at the word 'fiancée'. She smiled serenely. 'How do you do?'

The other woman swept hostile green eyes from the crown of Leonora's curly head down the brief black silk dress and long, slender legs. '*Hello*! Well, well, this is a surprise. I'd no idea you were contemplating matrimony again, Penry.'

'He thought Clem's wedding anniversary an appropriate time to announce the glad news,' said Mrs Vaughan smoothly, and rose to her feet rather stiffly to take Leonora's free arm. 'Come on, Penry. I think Katharine's arrived. She's eager to meet Leonora.' And with a cool, excluding smile for her former daughter-in-law she accompanied her large son and his slender young companion from the room, leaving Melanie staring after them in umbrage.

Leonora was never alone with Penry for a moment. She met Penry's favourite sister Kit and her husband, Reid Livesey, ate some supper, laughed and chatted with more of Penry's friends, and all the time she burned with the need to ask Penry what he was playing at, why he'd thrown down his unexpected announcement like a gauntlet in front of his voluptuous ex-wife.

As the evening wore on, with plenty of opportunity to study Melanie as the latter flitted from group to group, Leonora grew more and more furious with Penry. If his real reason for inviting her was a kind of face-saving operation in front of his former ex-wife, he might at least have had the honesty to say so. He, after all, was the one so determined to do away with sham and misunderstanding. After a couple of hours she was seized with a longing to go home, but Penry, she realised with misgiving, was suddenly nowhere to be seen.

Pressed by Clem and Mrs Vaughan to stay the night, Leonora declined with grateful thanks, hoping her longing to escape wasn't visible to Penry's family, all of whom she would have liked to know better under other circumstances. She went off on a determined search for Penry, but he was still nowhere to be seen. Leonora found a bathroom instead, and spent a few quiet minutes tidying herself up in peace. As she went back along the landing she paused, frowning.

The sound of Penry's unmistakable resonance removed any scruples Leonora might have had about eavesdropping. Through a half-open door she saw a glimmer of white and stiffened, nauseated, as she saw Melanie over Penry's shoulder, her face held up to his in impassioned invitation.

'Please, Pen,' Melanie pleaded, her husky whisper

carrying all too clearly to the girl outside in the hall. 'Just this once. For old times' sake.'

'It's out of the question,' he responded harshly, but Melanie threw herself against him. Red-tipped fingers slid up to encircle Penry's neck and Leonora turned away in blind haste, running downstairs to plunge into the crowd below.

When Penry rejoined her some time later Leonora was the centre of a group discussing the rival merits of various sailing craft. Reid Livesey turned to him with a smile.

'Your lady's a sailor, then, Pen. You must take her over to Rico's place in Portugal.'

'Good idea,' said Penry absently, eyeing Leonora's brittle gaiety with a frown. 'But now I'm afraid it's time we were off. Leonora's determined to make me drive her all the way home tonight.'

There was a flurry of farewells, repeated invitations to Leonora to come again soon, then at last they were in the car and heading out of London.

'What's the matter?' asked Penry at last, breaking a silence which threatened to last all the way to Chastlecombe. 'Didn't you enjoy the party?'

'Not as much as I might have.'

'Didn't you like my family? They certainly took to you!'

'I liked your family very much, but you deliberately gave them the wrong impression about me,' she said angrily. 'Particularly your ex-wife!'

There was a pause. 'Is that what this is all about? Because I embroidered a little and introduced you as my fiancée, or because Melanie was there?'

'I assume the two are interconnected,' said Lenora stonily. 'You conveniently forgot to tell me she was

Nick Wood's sister. You knew she'd be there tonight, which is why you needed me as protective cover. Not that it worked very well, ultimately!'

'What are you getting at?'

'When you were missing I went to look for you. I didn't find you at first, so I went to the bathroom. On my way back downstairs I saw you in one of the bedrooms with Melanie.' Her voice was bitter. 'So absorbed you even forgot to close the door!'

Penry swore under his breath. 'Damn it, Leonora, it wasn't what you thought——'

'I didn't hang about long, but I saw enough to convince me that all that rubbish about Melanie's frigidity was pure invention on your part.'

'Leonora,' began Penry, sounding weary, 'Melanie didn't want me to make *love* to her. She needed a favour from me, which is why she came tonight.'

'Straight into your ever-open arms.' Leonora stared angrily through the windscreen. 'I'm sure she wasn't taken in for a moment about—about me.'

'You're wrong, as it happens. One look at you convinced Melanie of my intentions beyond all doubt.'

'Oh, really. Why?'

Penry hesitated. 'To be blunt, you're the exact opposite of all the other women in my life. Like Melanie they invariably ran to small IQ's and big bust measurements.'

'And one look at my flat chest convinced her I was the love of your life, I suppose!'

'Don't be so childish!' he snapped unforgivably.

As an end to the argument this remark was a great success. To avoid further childishness Leonora took refuge in stony, obdurate silence. Penry made several attempts to break it, but gave up at last, his face like

thunder as he drove at a speed which frightened Leonora to death. By the time they finally arrived in the deserted car park behind the arcade she was trembling from head to foot, racked by every emotion from fear to rage. She yanked her seatbelt free then gave a squeak of protest as Penry pulled her into his arms to kiss her with a ferocity she fought against at first. But the upheaval of the night proved too much for emotions which see-sawed from anger to white-hot response with mortifying speed.

She could hear Penry's heart pounding against hers, as her kisses matched his in utter frenzy. He tore his mouth away at last to rub his cheek against her untidy hair as he crushed her against his chest.

'You're hurting me,' gasped Leonora at last.

Penry held her away a little, his eyes glittering into hers. 'You deserve it,' he said, breathing hard, 'for harbouring such bloody awful suspicions about me. Listen, Miss Doubting Thomas—and listen well. I can't tell you what Melanie was asking me because I don't betray other people's confidences. But one thing I want to make clear once and for all. Even if she had been asking me to make love to her—which she wasn't—the answer would very definitely have been no. For one thing she happens to be another man's wife these days. But there's a *much* better reason than that,' he added, and paused tantalisingly.

'What is it?' asked Leonora hoarsely.

'These days,' he said, looking at her in a way which took away what little breath she had left, 'I have this picture etched in my brain. Of a certain unforgettable night on my island. The experience seems to have rendered all women's attractions null and void. Except yours, Leonora Fox. Do I make myself clear?'

She nodded rapturously, and suddenly the night was beautiful and the moon shone brighter than it ever had before. 'I'm sorry,' she said, hiding her face against him. 'But Melanie's so gorgeous to look at. I was jealous. Horribly.'

Penry crowed softly in triumph then began kissing her again, and she responded ardently, all her anger and hurt melting away in the warmth of his embrace. At last he drew away, his smile rueful. 'I can think of better places to make love, *cariad*.'

'So can I,' she agreed fervently, rubbing her elbow. 'Bits of me keep coming into contact with bits of your car.'

'I'd better let you go in.'

She sighed. 'I don't want to go.'

'Nevertheless, if you have any respect for my blood-pressure, lady, I think you'd better retire to your lonely bed, while I continue my journey to Wales.' Penry kissed her again, lingeringly. 'I wish you were coming with me.'

'So do I.'

They gazed at each other in silence, then Penry touched a finger to her lower lip. 'Leonora, will you come to Wales next weekend? See my house—try it on for size, as it were? I'm tied up at the hospital for a while each day, but we could be together most of the time. Will you come?'

She nodded, her eyes like stars, her pulse racing at the implication in his words. 'I'd love to.'

'Bring Elise, too, if you like.'

'Do you want me to?'

'In a word, no.' He smiled, stroking her cheek. 'But if you're afraid I'll lose my head once we're alone

together, by all means bring a chaperon.'

'I'll think about it,' she said demurely.

Leonora went round in a dream the following week. Fortunately she had an order for a full-length wool coat and dress, and worked in happy isolation in the small room at the back of the shop, her mind lingering on the implication of Penry's invitation as her fingers flew independently to finish the order for a customer due to return to the States a few days later. Penry rang each night, to remind her about the weekend, he said, in case she'd forgotten. Fat chance, thought Leonora, unable to resist keeping him in the dark about whether Elise was going with her.

'As if I would,' said Elise, laughing. 'I've no taste for playing gooseberry to a couple of lovebirds, I assure you. Off you go alone, with my blessing, love, since it seems pretty obvious Penry intends to pop the question.'

'Nonsense,' said Leonora, who had given her sister a very much edited version of Saturday night. 'He's just keen to show me his house.'

'In that case, why not surprise him? Drive to Wales on Friday evening instead of waiting for Saturday. Sue Parker will help in the shop.'

Leonora assented rapturously, keeping her change of plan gleefully secret from Penry. She started out on the Friday evening with suppressed excitement, timing her arrival long before he was likely to make the now nightly telephone call. She sang along with the radio as she drove up through Gloucestershire and crossed into Wales by way of Abergavenny and Brecon, then took the road north towards Builth Wells, to the wooded hills south of the town where Penry's house occupied a

vantage point above the River Wye. His instructions had been so clear, and so often repeated, that Leonora felt she could have found her way blindfolded in the dark. She had no problem in finding the turning which led her along an unadopted road for half a mile before she drove through open gates up a steeply ascending drive past lawns on several different levels until she finally reached a gravelled circle in front of Penry's house. She gazed up at it with a deep sigh of pleasure. Built, as Penry had told her, almost a century before, its mellow brick and gleaming windows blended into the picturesque hillside, welcome in every line of it to the girl who gazed at it in bliss as she turned off the engine.

Leonora jumped out, stood looking up at the house for a few moments more, then ran up the steps to ring the doorbell, laughter bubbling up inside as she antici-pated Penry's surprise at the sight of her. She waited a few moments then rang the bell again, and this time the door opened with maddening slowness. All her joy drained away like water spilled on sand as instead of Penry Vaughan's tall, broad-shouldered figure she came face to face with the woman who'd once been his wife. Melanie smiled lazily, smoothing back her hair, the opulent curves of her body outlined by the satin dressing-gown which was very blatantly the only gar-ment she had on.

'Well, well, fancy meeting you. Leonie, isn't it? Surprise, surprise.'

'My name is Leonora.' Sick and numb with shock, Leonora felt vaguely surprised to hear her voice func-tioning normally.

Melanie took her by the hand and drew her inside.

'Do come in. Pen won't be long. I've been paying him a little visit.'

Leonora snatched her hand away, her eyes hunted as they scanned the large, square hall. 'Is Penry here? He's due back today, from a medical conference.'

Melanie's eyes gleamed. 'Is that what he told you? Naughty Pen. In actual fact we spent last night together, here. We've not long got up. He's just popped out for supplies. Sex does make one so hungry, doesn't it? Or perhaps you don't know about that— goodness, dear, you've gone a very funny colour!'

Leonora gulped, a hand to her mouth, and with an exclamation Melanie hauled her upstairs and through a large bedroom into a bathroom, then left her alone to part with her lunch. It was a pity, Leonora thought with bleak detachment afterwards, that shock always had such an inconvenient effect on her digestive system. After a moment or two to pull herself together and wash her face, she went back through the bedroom, her stomach heaving again when she saw the crumpled disorder of the bed. She shuddered, and ran like the wind down the stairs to escape, but as she reached the hall the door flew open and Penry burst into the house, his face alight at the sight of her.

'Leonora! You came tonight!' he said, pulling her into his arms.

She leapt away. 'Don't dare touch me!' Her eyes flashed coldly as they met the blank astonishment in his. 'I never learn do I? Like a fool I came to surprise you, just like I did once before on Brynteg. Needless to say, the surprise backfired on me. Again.'

Penry stood rigid, his eyes incredulous. 'Can you please tell me what you're talking about?'

'She's talking about me,' said Melanie, emerging

from one of the rooms off the hall, fully dressed now, every shining hair in place.

'*Melanie*? Why the hell are you still here?' demanded Penry wrathfully.

Still? Leonora could take no more. She brushed past Penry, eluding the hand he put out to detain her as she ran outside to the car, deaf to his entreaties as she jumped in the car and started it up with a violent rev of the engine. She reversed in a reckless sweep, scraping the Range Rover with a hideous scream of metal, then tore off down the hairpin bends of the drive, blinking away tears furiously to see where she was going. After a mile or two of expecting the Range Rover in pursuit it finally came home to her that Penry had no intention of following her. The discovery started her crying in earnest, which meant a stop in a lay-by for a while before she was in a fit condition to resume her journey home.

When Leonora finally arrived home, red-eyed and white-faced after a nightmare journey, she found Elise in a terrible state.

'Leonora, what on earth's going on? I've been worried to death! Penry's been on the phone every few minutes to see if you've arrived. He's out of his mind in case you've had an accident or something, but he couldn't come after you because he was due back at the hospital for a clinic.'

Leonora huddled in a little heap on the sofa, pleading for coffee before she'd say a word. Once she'd downed some of the extra-strong brew she gave her sister the bare bones of the story, then turned dull eyes on Elise's horrified face. 'Did Penry say anything about Melanie?'

'No. He just said there'd been a terrible misunderstanding, and you wouldn't listen when he tried to explain.' Elise hugged her sister close.

'What explanation could there be?' Leonora gave a dreary little laugh. 'I saw the evidence with my own eyes, Melanie wearing only a dressing-gown, her hair all over the place. I even saw the bed——' She swallowed hard. 'No, I am *not* going to be sick again,' she added fiercely as Elise eyed her in alarm.

When the telephone rang, right on cue, Leonora started up, wild-eyed. 'If that's Penry tell him I don't want to speak to him or see him again. Ever.'

The following Monday afternoon, shortly after lunch, two customers poring over the jewellery in Fox's Lair looked up in surprise as a tall man came into the shop like a whirlwind and gave Elise a brief, unsmiling greeting.

'Where is she?' he demanded.

'In the office, working. Do go through,' said Elise, unnecessarily, since Penry was already on his way.

He wrenched open the office door then slammed it behind him and stood against it, glaring into Leonora's frozen face.

'What are you doing here?' she said icily.

'I want a word with you. I've come straight from the hospital, and now I'm on my way to St Mary's, where I'm due at five. It was not part of my plan to make a detour via Chastlecombe, but since you won't talk to me on the phone I didn't have much choice. You knew perfectly well I had to stay within reach of the hospital over the weekend. I couldn't get here until now.'

Penry, hostile and intimidating, was too large a presence for the small office. Leonora felt claustrophobic

as he loomed over her. She folded her work carefully and stood up, backing away.

'Elise passed on my message, I know,' she said crisply. 'Perhaps it lost something in translation. I don't want to talk to you. Ever again.'

Penry grabbed her hands. 'Just give me the chance to explain, you obstinate little fool——'

Leonora snatched her hand away, eyes blazing. 'I saw with my own eyes. You don't need to explain. You lied to me about Melanie——'

'I have never lied to you,' he broke in, white about the mouth. 'She was bent on making mischief because I wouldn't do her the favour she wanted, and she bloody well succeeded, didn't she?'

Leonora clenched her teeth. 'Ah, yes, the celebrated favour again. Tell me what it is and just possibly I might believe you.'

The dark blue eyes iced over. 'How extraordinarily good of you, Leonora. Nevertheless I can't do that. Melanie or not, it was still in confidence. All I can say is that I didn't even know Melanie was still there that night. I thought she'd gone. She'd come to persuade me——'

'And succeeded, by the look of the bed!' Leonora turned away blindly, and Penry caught her by the shoulders, forcing her round to face him.

'I did *not* make love to her, Leonora,' he said forcibly. 'Can't you believe me?'

She stared up at him despairingly. 'I want to believe you—but she's so beautiful——'

With a smothered curse he pulled her into his arms and began to kiss her, using a more powerful argument than words as the first touch of his mouth on hers sent everything out of Leonora's head other than the fact

that she loved and wanted this man to the point where she was almost ready to believe that she'd been mistaken. Somehow she found the strength to pull away.

'Tell me why Melanie was there at your house?' she pleaded.

Penry stood back, looking grim and formidable. 'I can't, Leonora. All I can say is that there was an innocent explanation for what you saw. If you can't accept that, and trust me, then there's nothing more I can say.'

Leonora straightened her shoulders, pale and vulnerable in the plain black sweater and skirt she wore in the shop. She saw Penry's eyes on the silver brooch on her shoulder, knew he was remembering their time together on the island, and for a moment she was tempted to throw herself into his arms, to assure him that nothing mattered as long as he loved her, Leonora Fox, not Melanie. Then her resolve hardened. 'I saw what I saw, Penry, and I don't blame you. It's crystal-clear that whatever defects your former wife possesses you're still attracted to her. Who can blame you? When I gatecrashed your life I suppose you thought I might come in useful as some kind of antidote—but it didn't work.' She smiled frostily. 'It was a case of "physician, help thyself". It's not your fault you couldn't, Dr Vaughan.'

Penry heard her out in silence. 'I've had a wasted journey,' he said at last. 'You weren't prepared to listen to a word I had to say, were you?'

Leonora shrugged. 'What was the point?'

'What, indeed?' He gave her a chilling little bow. 'Then I'll say goodbye, Leonora. I hope I didn't shock your customers by barging in so unceremoniously.

'I imagine it made their day.' She felt quite proud of

her composure as she escorted him through the shop, relieved, for once, to see it empty. 'Goodbye,' she said as they reached the door. 'Give my love to Sister Concepta.'

Penry put out a hand, then dropped it, and with a strangled curse turned away to stride off over the cobbles of the arcade, an arresting figure in the autumn sunlight as he went out into the street without a backward glance for the girl watching him go.

# CHAPTER TWELVE

THE winds of late October were lashing Haverfordwest as Leonora left the train. She smiled wearily as Bryn Pritchard came to take her case, blessing his tact when he made no comment on the reason for her visit. He installed her in his battered van, chatting volubly on every subject under the sun other than Dr Penry Vaughan on the journey, but Leonora was hard pressed to make suitable rejoinders, every nerve in her body stretched to breaking-point at the thought of what lay ahead.

When they arrived in Brides Haven Rachel Pritchard welcomed Leonora with a cup of hot, strong tea, but Bryn soon cut across his wife's chatter, pointing out that they must set out at once if he was to make the return trip before dark. His wife packed a box with various goodies for Leonora to take to Penry, then walked with them to the jetty, and waved them off on the *Sea-Fret*, a sturdy fishing-boat a lot newer than Penry's. As the boat crossed the bar into the open sea with a stomach-clenching lurch, Bryn gave his passenger an encouraging smile.

'A bit rough, but nothing to worry about, Miss Fox.'

Leonora, too wrapped up in her thoughts to be afraid, smiled back, unconcerned. 'I'm only sorry I had to bring you out in it.'

Bryn shook his head good-naturedly. 'No trouble at all. The wind's increasing to gale force later, according to the shipping forecast, but I'll be home safe and sound long before then.'

'You didn't phone Dr Vaughan to say I was coming?' asked Leonora anxiously, as Gullholm loomed nearer on the horizon.

'No. Not a word. He said he wanted peace and quiet, mind,' Bryn warned.

Leonora scanned the turbulent stretch of sea anxiously. 'I only intend to stay a few minutes. I hope Dr Vaughan will run me back in the *Angharad*.'

Bryn looked doubtful. 'You'd better not hang about, then.'

Soon the *Sea-Fret* was alongside the jetty at Gullholm and Leonora leapt out nimbly. She received her overnight bag and Rachel's box from Bryn and thanked him warmly. As he headed back across the sound she began to toil up the cliff path, pausing for breath now and then as the wind battered her and tore at her hair, which soon broke free of its restraining scarf and whipped into her eyes, slowing her progress up the wet, slippery path towards the house. Halfway up she paused, fighting for breath, suddenly struck by the enormity of what she was doing. What if Penry took one look at her and threw her out, bag and baggage? She resumed her climb doggedly. He could hardly throw her off the island. The worst he could do was take her back to Brides Haven. Then a fiercer gust of wind almost blew her from the path and she hung on to bag and box like grim death. Bryn was right. The wind was increasing to gale force, and fast. She turned to look towards the shore, relieved when she saw the *Sea-Fret* making good headway back to Brides Haven, then a flock of screaming gulls startled her into resuming her climb, and soon she was on the Neck and starting the last, steep push towards the plateau.

As the path flattened out to lead across the close turf

to the house Leonora's feet slowed. At the sight of windows lit against the gathering gloom she had a sudden desire to turn tail and run, to take refuge below in the *Angharad*. Which, she told herself trenchantly, was nonsense. She'd come this far to say her piece and say it she would, come hell or high water. She smiled at this last. If the weather went on deteriorating at this rate there'd be plenty of the latter around Gullholm.

Sodden by the now driving rain, breathing hard from the climb, Leonora crept round the house to the cluster of outbuildings at the back, where the familiar throb of the generator welcomed her like a friend. Which, she thought drily, was probably the only welcome she'd get. Penry was unlikely to look kindly on someone who landed on his island uninvited twice in a row.

Uncertain whether to knock politely on the kitchen door, or just thrust it open and make a dramatic entry, Leonora dumped her bag on the flagstones and pushed wet rat's-tails of hair back from her face. Somehow it seemed silly to knock. Taking her courage in both hands, she left her bag where it was and turned the knob, pushing open the door into the kitchen which smelled so warm and inviting and blessedly familiar that a lump rose in her throat. She closed the door softly, then advanced cautiously across the room to deposit the box on the counter. The door to the study was half open but the room itself was in darkness. No Penry there. Slipping off her muddy shoes, Leonora went on into the big living-room, every nerve on edge as she crept silently across the familiar worn carpet towards the seductive warmth from the stove, but there was still no sign of Penry. In deference to the generator, presumably, only one of the table lamps was lit, giving the room a shadowy, ghostly look. Steam rose

from her clothes as she hesitated, wondering what to do next. Somehow she'd imagined Penry leaping up from the sofa at the sight of her, angry at her intrusion. Or even smiling in welcome, in some of her wilder dreams. The silence of the deserted room was eerie. There was an open book on the sofa, a basket of ready-chopped wood near the stove, even a half-full glass on a table. Leonora shivered and held out her hands to the stove, then stood motionless as she realised she was being watched. She turned slowly to face the forbidding figure standing in semi-darkness halfway up the stairs.

'They say an Englishman's home is his castle,' said Penry tonelessly, his face invisible in the shadows. 'I'm Welsh, but the principle's the same. I should have fortified myself better against invaders.'

Leonora, wishing with all her heart she'd listened to Elise and telephoned, instead of rushing to the island uninvited, squared her shoulders. 'I've come to say I'm sorry,' she blurted. 'It seemed like the only thing to do before I set out. Now I'm actually here I realise I'm intruding. I'm sorry. It was stupid to barge in here like this.'

Penry walked slowly down the remaining stairs and crossed the room towards her, stumbling over a rug en route. He wore a navy guernsey and salt-stained Levis, and he needed a shave. He needed a haircut, too, noted Leonora with misgiving, and from the look in his eyes he was in a foul mood.

'Are you ill?' she asked sharply.

'I was; but no longer. I've had a drink or two. And if this were any other place I'd tell you to get the hell out of here and out of my life.' He reached over for the glass and swallowed down the rest of its contents, eyeing her malevolently. 'As it is we're on an island

and the bloody weather's deteriorating fast. If I were completely sober I might just manage to get you back to Brides Haven, but I doubt it. In any case, as you can see, I am not sober. So I'm stuck with you, Miss Castaway, yet again. How the hell did you get here?'

'Mr Pritchard brought me.'

'Why the devil didn't he ring me to say you were coming?'

'I asked him not to.' Leonora stuck her chin out. 'I thought you wouldn't let me come.'

'You thought right!'

'I'm sorry. I shouldn't have come.' She looked away. 'I'll ring Mr Pritchard to fetch me in the morning if you'll just let me stay the night.'

'What choice do I have?' he demanded irritably. 'I'm hardly likely to throw you out in this weather.'

'Thank you.' She eyed him cautiously. 'Perhaps you'll let me cook dinner in return for your hospitality.'

'My hospitality!' He eyed her with derision. 'All right, Leonora, let's keep it civilised, by all means. I'd planned a liquid dinner for myself——'

'A square meal would do no harm, by the look of you,' she retorted. 'May I take my jacket off, please?'

'Do what you like,' he said without interest, and stretched out on the sofa. 'I think I'll have a nap.'

In sudden fury Leonora caught hold of his legs and swung them to the floor. 'No, you won't. You'll go upstairs and have a hot bath and a shave. I'll have some black coffee waiting when you get down. It's a good thing your patients can't see you now, Dr Vaughan!'

He staggered to his feet, swaying a little, his eyes like chips of blue ice. 'I happen to be here on holiday, Goody Two-Shoes. A few hard-earned days of R and

R, as the Americans put it, away from everything and everyone—or so I thought. I had a bad dose of influenza, if you must know. My mother wanted to fuss over me in Lanhowell, but somehow I couldn't take that. I needed solitude—so where better to find it than my island? Or so I thought,' he added morosely.

'I see,' she said, unzipping her jacket. 'You obviously haven't been eating properly——'

'And I've had a couple of glasses of Scotch to celebrate finishing a course of antibiotics for a chest infection,' he finished wearily. 'Not exactly a punishable offence. But then, I forgot. Your opinion of my integrity is not exactly high, is it, Miss Fox?'

'I came a long way to say I'm sorry,' Leonora reminded him. 'Go on. Go up and have a bath—even a nap, if you like.'

Penry eyed her broodingly, then shrugged. 'Why not?' he said carelessly, and made for the stairs with the care of someone not absolutely steady on his feet.

Leonora watched him go, frowning, then went to fetch her bag. Alone in the kitchen, she towelled her hair dry and stripped off her wet jeans and socks, draping them on the rack of the Aga with her jacket. In dry denims with a heavy black jersey over her scarlet wool shirt, she looked through the refrigerator and cupboards and began to concoct a dinner likely to appeal to a newly recovered—and fractious—invalid.

Once a pan of vegetable soup was simmering fragrantly on the stove she put potatoes to bake in the oven then sprinkled rosemary and garlic slivers over some lamb chops, ready to grill when her dinner companion chose to put in an appearance. Refusing to let herself think beyond the tasks she was performing, Leonora listened to the radio as she worked, and when

the meal was well advanced she went quietly upstairs to find the bathroom empty, and Penry, fully dressed in fresh clothes, fast asleep on his bed.

She washed swiftly, brushed her drying hair into softer curls, then flicked on some mascara and gave her lips a touch of colour before bearding the lion in his den.

Standing at the foot of the bed, Leonora touched one of Penry's bare brown feet. 'Dinner's almost ready. Shall I bring you up a tray, or will you come down?'

Penry shot upright, yawning mightily as he rubbed eyes which focused on her with a noticeable lack of warmth. 'So you weren't a dream.'

'No.' She smiled cheerfully. 'Do you feel well enough to come down?'

He slid to his feet, stretching. 'Of course I do.' He frowned, surprised. 'In fact I feel very much better.'

'Good. Put something on your feet before you come downstairs,' she ordered as she went out.

'You sound like my mother,' he called after her.

'Thank you,' she shouted as she went downstairs. 'Having met your charming mother I'll take that as a compliment.'

Without anything said a truce seemed to have been tacitly agreed. Penry, obviously very much better after his sleep, admitted that the meal was a great improvement on the one he'd planned.

'I haven't felt much like cooking.'

'I can tell,' said Leonora, removing their soup bowls. 'The fridge is full—so are the cupboards.'

When she returned with the main meal, Penry sniffed ecstatically. 'If this is an apology, Leonora, I accept whole-heartedly.'

'Good. There's some apple tart afterwards, if you like.'

He regarded her with awe. 'Don't tell me you made that, too, while I was sleeping off my drunken stupor?'

'It wasn't a drunken stupor, nor did I make the tart.' She grinned. 'Mrs Pritchard sent it over, along with a pile of Welsh cakes and something she called *bara brith*.'

He nodded, mouth full. 'A sort of tea-bread with currants and so on. She's a great cook. So are you,' he added, then smiled wryly as the wind howled in the chimney like a lost soul. 'This is where we came in first time round, Leonora. Just you and me and a force-ten gale.'

There was a sudden, charged silence which Leonora broke hastily, pressing him to apple tart, but Penry shook his head.

'I'll leave the tart for tomorrow—sinful to cancel the flavour of that lamb.' He stretched luxuriously. 'Coffee would be nice.'

Leonora gave a little bob. 'Certainly sir. Coming up.'

When the meal was cleared away and they were settled before the fire, Penry looked across at Leonora thoughtfully.

'Strange, really. It seems like only yesterday we were here like this before, as if the months in between had never been.' His mouth twisted. 'Which would be a good thing in some ways.'

'Penry,' said Leonora, bracing herself. 'I think that's my cue to explain why I'm here.'

Penry shrugged. 'It isn't necessary.'

'I think it is.'

'You mean you came because you're ready to listen to me now?' He said with sarcasm.

Leonora flushed. 'I wish I could say yes. But I can't.'

'Then what in hell's name made you come all this way in weather like this?'

'Your sister wrote to me.'

Penry stretched out his long legs to glower at his battered espadrilles. 'Which one?'

'Clemency.'

'Ah!'

'She told me Melanie was expecting a baby soon after Christmas.'

He shot a hostile look at her. 'And you assumed I was the father, no doubt!'

Leonora met the look squarely. 'At first reading I did. The word "baby" came off the page like a fist. But as I went on reading I found that wasn't what Clem was telling me at all.' She cleared her throat. 'The favour Melanie wanted was an abortion, wasn't it? And as a doctor it was against your ethics to tell me.'

'Something like that,' said Penry bitterly. 'Melanie always had hysterics at the mere mention of motherhood. Nigel wasn't as forbearing as me. He made very sure she got pregnant. Melanie was furious, and desperate enough to go to any lengths to terminate the pregnancy. She couldn't pay for an abortion herself because Nigel won't let her have a cheque book or a credit card, let alone any cash. She's forced to ask him for everything, loaded as he is. Nigel is by no means the fool she took him for. So Melanie actually had the gall to ask her brother Nick for the money for an abortion that night. At a party to celebrate ten years of marriage to Clem, would you believe? He wiped the

floor with her. Nick's a straight arrow. He wouldn't have anything to do with it.'

'Was she asking you for money?'

Penry's lips curled with distaste. 'No. What you witnessed that night was Melanie trying to persuade me to perform the operation for her—or, failing that, to get someone else to do it as a favour.' He looked Leonora in the eye. 'I gave her short shrift. As you know, I'm sensitive on that particular subject.'

She flushed, her eyes falling. 'Yes. I do. But to continue with Clem's letter—she told me Melanie went to Wales after you to try more persuasion.'

'She did. Melanie was determined to get her own way. She rang up to make an appointment with my receptionist, using a false name. When I found her the other side of my desk I told her in no uncertain terms I wasn't having anything to do with it. I spiked her guns by the simple expedient of ringing Nigel right away, told him the truth, and instructed him to fetch her home and keep her there. I was called away to the hospital so I left her at the house waiting for Nigel to turn up to collect her.' Penry smiled morosely. 'Unfortunately fate delivered you into Melanie's hands before Nigel arrived. She saw you coming up the drive, and hit on the ideal way to take her revenge. She tore off her clothes, made a mess of the bed and—you know the rest.'

Leonora stared at him in horror. 'Why would she do something so horrible? Does she hate you, Penry?'

'No.' Penry shrugged. 'She's terminally immature, that's all. She was furious because I wouldn't do what she wanted and paid me back as spitefully as she knew how. Her punishment is having to bow to the inevitable. Motherhood has overtaken her whether she

wants it or not.' Penry got up to put more logs on the stove. When he sat down again there was a long, tense silence.

Leonora knew perfectly well it was time for her to grovel, but found it difficult to make a start. 'I'm so sorry I wouldn't listen to you,' she said at last.

'I'm sorry, too.' He looked at her curiously. 'Why did Clem take it into her head to write to you?'

Leonora looked down at her hands. 'Your family was worried about your—your frame of mind. Clem seemed to think it was something to do with me.'

'She knew damn well it was something to do with you. I told her that her precious sister-in-law had made a mess of my life yet again, so I suppose she felt obliged to make amends.'

'It wasn't like that at all!' flared Leonora. 'Clem was deeply concerned because you were unhappy, and because she loves you she decided to interfere. Her word, not mine, by the way. I'm glad she did.'

'But if she hadn't you'd never have got in touch.'

'I wanted to, but after the way we parted last time I didn't dare.' She looked at him squarely. 'Do you accept my apology, Penry?'

'Yes. Of course I do.' He held out his hand to help her up. 'But that's enough emoting for tonight. Right now I think it's time you went to bed. You look tired. I've put hot-water bottles in the room next to the bathroom.'

'Thank you.' Leonora eyed him uncertainly. 'Good-night, then.'

'Goodnight.' Penry's eyes were inscrutable as she turned away.

'I'll just collect my bag from the kitchen,' she murmured.

'Shall I carry it up for you?'

'Oh, no. There's not much in it. Just enough for one night.'

'So you definitely expected to stay, then!'

Leonora looked at him levelly. 'Yes, but not here. Mrs Pritchard was going to put me up.'

Leonora felt horribly depressed as she prepared for bed. On the way in the train earlier she had pictured her meeting with Penry over and over again, but none of her imaginings had been remotely like the reality. She'd been a fool to think one polite little apology would be enough to put everything right between them. Penry was a mature, proud man who obviously no longer thought it worth the trouble to cultivate a relationship with someone as jealous and unreasonable as Leonora Fox, spinster of the parish of Chastlecombe.

Perhaps, thought Leonora, turning out the light, she would never have learned the truth if Clem hadn't written. Penry's ethics would never have allowed him to reveal the reason for Melanie's visit to his home. A home, she thought in sudden pain, which I'll never share with him now. Penry had quite plainly lost interest in her. And who could blame him?

Leonora lay hugging a hot-water bottle in the noisy darkness, grateful for the warmth as she listened to the wind howling in counterpoint to the boom of the sea on the rocks below. Her mouth twisted at the thought that this time, at least, there was no danger of a nightmare. Those had vanished since the return of her memory.

She tensed, struck by a sudden brainwave. She lay thinking about it for some time, then decided she had

nothing to lose. Not daring to put on the light, she sat up and felt for the glass of water on the bedside table. For a moment she hesitated, then, her mouth set in a determined line Elise would have recognised with misgiving, set about dampening her cotton nightshirt and then her hair and face to simulate perspiration. Replacing the glass with care, she slid back down in the bed and deliberately conjured up the scene in the *Seren* at the moment the engine cut out and she was about to capsize. The horror of the memory made it all too easy to choke and scream, but to her relief her performance was cut short in seconds as the door burst open, the light snapped on and she was in Penry's arms, held close to his chest, and so glad to be there that not even her guilt could mar the joy of the moment.

'It's all right, it's all right,' said Penry hoarsely, as her tears, hot and flooding in relief, streamed down his bare chest. 'I've got you, my darling, I've got you.'

Leonora held up her face blindly and he crushed her even closer, kissing her until neither could breathe.

'You're wet,' he said at last, and picked her up and carried her into his bedroom. 'I'll find you something dry.'

But when they reached his room Leonora wriggled out of his arms and stood on the bedside rug, hands behind her back, guilt flooding her now in full force at the look in his eyes. 'I didn't have a nightmare,' she blurted, her small breasts rising and falling convulsively under the clinging, damp cotton. 'I doused myself with my glass of water and then I screamed, hoping to bring you running.'

Penry stared at her incredulously, then to her relief the tension drained from his face before her eyes as his

muscular, beautiful torso began to vibrate with laughter. 'You little witch! I *came* running, too, didn't I?'

'Are you angry with me?' she muttered, blushing furiously.

'Only for courting pneumonia,' he said softly and closed the gap between them to lift her face to his. 'Since this nightshirt's damp the sensible course, Miss Fox, would be to remove it, don't you agree?' And slowly and carefully he peeled the garment over her head, his hands unsteady as he completed the task. 'You should dry your hair——' he began, but Leonora shook her head violently and brushed past him to leap into his bed. She held up her arms in entreaty, her eyes glittering darkly in her flushed face.

'Just make love to me, Penry, *please*. If you don't I think I'll die——'

The rest of her sentence died on her lips as Penry took her in his arms with a sound somewhere between a sigh and a groan as their lips met and their bodies flowed together in a deep, primeval need which united them almost at once in a storm of love and need as fierce as the one which raged, unheard, outside.

'Damn,' said Leonora a long time afterwards.

Penry raised his handsome head in enquiry. 'You spoke?'

She gave him a rueful, slumbrous look. 'I made a sort of vow.'

He turned over on his back and drew her up so that her head lay on his shoulder. 'Of chastity? If so, it wasn't much of a success.'

He yelped as she bit him, but Leonora grinned up at him, unrepentant. 'You may remember that I begged you to make love to me the first time, Penry Vaughan! So I made a vow that the next time you'd beg me.'

'And I will. Promise.' He detached a hand to look at his watch. 'But not for half an hour or so—what's the matter?' as Leonora stared at him, wide-eyed.

'I didn't mean tonight,' she muttered, burying her face against his shoulder.

Penry stretched luxuriously, moulding her closely against him. 'Ah, but I did. Unless you object?'

She shook her head emphatically.

He laughed softly. 'I love you so much, you know, my little vixen. You were blazingly angry with me that day at the house.'

'I was jealous. Horribly, mortifyingly jealous of your beautiful wife.'

'Ex.' Penry rubbed his cheek over her hair. 'Leonora, does the fact that I've been married before put you off the thought of becoming my wife?'

'No,' she said decisively, raising her head so that he could see her eyes. 'Nothing could. Are you proposing, Dr Vaughan?'

'Oh, my darling, I am, I am!'

'Then I accept. With great pleasure.'

'I was going to propose to you properly that week-end,' he went on after a long, blissful interval. 'I had champagne chilling ready for a romantic dinner à deux. And when you were in suitably softened mood I was going to tell you how this time I'd found what I'd really been looking for all my life.'

'And only an hour or so ago,' said Leonora wonderingly, 'I was thinking you'd lost interest in me completely.'

'Then I must be a bloody good actor!' He turned her face up to his. 'What's going to happen about Elise and Fox's Lair once we're married?'

'Elise has it all cut and dried already. Sue Parker—

mother of Julian, who's only eighteen, by the way,' added Leonora with a wicked little grin, 'is keen to go into partnership with her, and I can do what I do just as easily after I'm married as before.'

Penry gave her a smile which brought the blood to her cheeks. 'Yes, definitely,' he said softly, brushing her hair back from her forehead.

'I meant knitting!' Leonora giggled, then bit her lip, eyeing him anxiously. 'You must think I was taking a lot for granted, sorting all this out before—well, before I even knew you'd let me on the island, let alone still want me.'

'You knew damn well I wanted you!'

'I didn't! But Elise was absolutely sure you did. She said that if I came here to the island and said I was sorry you'd welcome me with open arms.' She eyed him accusingly. 'You didn't, though. You weren't very welcoming at all.'

Penry opened his arms wide, then closed them about her. 'I couldn't believe my eyes, Leonora, when I saw you standing in the middle of the room down there. I'd been lying on my bed, thinking of you, and suddenly I couldn't bear it a moment longer and jumped off the bed intending to phone you—and there you were, looking half drowned and so nervous I was afraid to put a foot wrong.'

'All you had to do was kiss me, Dr Vaughan!'

'With a day's growth of beard and reeking of Scotch? I could have smacked your bottom for taking me by surprise. If you'd just rung from Bryn's place I could have at least made myself presentable, *cariad*!'

'You looked quite wonderful to me,' she said matter-of-factly, and resisted when he'd have hugged the life

out of her. 'Besides, I was afraid you wouldn't let me come if I phoned.'

'Are you joking? I'd have cast off in the *Angharad* to fetch you the minute I knew you were there!'

'Would you? Really?' Reading the confirmation in his eye, she sighed happily, then detached herself. 'I'm going to tidy myself up. I must look a wreck.'

'Don't go!' Penry drew her back into his arms slowly. 'You look utterly ravishing to me. So much so that I want very much to make love to you again. Are you going to make me beg?'

Leonora shook her head in revulsion. 'No. Not now. Not ever! I love you too much——'

'At last!' said Penry gruffly.

'At last what?'

'You've told me you love me.'

She frowned. 'Of course I love you. I have right from the first. Didn't you know that?'

He shook his head, his eyes blazing with a light which sent everything out of her head. 'Go on,' he prompted after an interval spent in convincing her that her sentiments were returned in full.

'What do you mean?' she asked breathlessly.

'You said you loved me too much—and then stopped.'

Her face cleared. 'Oh. I merely meant that I love you too much to refuse you anything—only I'm probably an idiot to admit it!'

Much later that night, when the storm had died down and they lay at rest in each other's arms, on the verge of sleep at last, Leonora said very quietly, 'Penry.'

'Mm.'

'Will you be offended if I ask you a question?'

He chuckled. 'I won't know until you ask it. Besides, the way I feel now nothing could offend me.'

'Don't count on it. I want to know whether you and Melanie slept in this bed together.'

Penry laughed, cuddling her close. 'No, we didn't. In fact, my little castaway, she never set foot on the island at all—wouldn't come near the place.'

'Great!' said Leonora with satisfaction. 'I'm glad. This is something of yours that belongs just to me, then.'

Penry shook her slightly. 'Correction. Everything I have and am and ever will be belongs to you, Leonora. All of me. Satisfactory?'

'Very.' She gave an ecstatic little wriggle. 'Are you sorry now that I invaded your castle?'

'Haven't I shown you how delighted I am that you did? If you're not sure I'm perfectly happy to convince you again,' he whispered, kissing her. 'It was a lucky day for me when the storm washed you up on my island, my darling.'

'Neither of us had a clue who I was, then!'

'*I* knew who you were, *cariad*. I'm a Celt, remember. I knew I'd met my fate right from the start!'

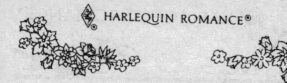

**HARLEQUIN ROMANCE®**

**brings you the
exciting conclusion of**

**THE BRIDAL COLLECTION**

**next month with**

THE REAL McCOY
by Patricia Knoll

**THE BRIDE** ran away.
**THE GROOM** ran after her.
**THEIR MARRIAGE** was over. *Or was it?*

Available this month in
The Bridal Collection
TEMPORARY ARRANGEMENT
by Shannon Waverly
Harlequin Romance #3259

Wherever Harlequin books are sold.

WED-FINAL

**HARLEQUIN ROMANCE®**

welcomes you

# BACK TO THE RANCH

Let your favorite Romance authors take you West!

Authors like Susan Fox, Debbie Macomber, Roz Denny,
Rebecca Winters and more!

Let them introduce you to wonderful women and strong, sexy
men—the men of the West. Ranchers and horsemen and
cowboys and lawmen...

Beginning in June 1993

Wherever Harlequin books are sold.

Following the success of WITH THIS RING and
TO HAVE AND TO HOLD, Harlequin brings you

# *JUST MARRIED*

## SANDRA CANFIELD
## MURIEL JENSEN
## ELISE TITLE
## REBECCA WINTERS

just in time for the 1993 wedding season!

Written by four of Harlequin's most popular authors, this
four-story collection celebrates the joy, excitement and
adjustment that comes with being "just married."

You won't want to miss this spring tradition, whether
you're just married or not!

**AVAILABLE IN APRIL WHEREVER HARLEQUIN
BOOKS ARE SOLD**

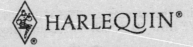 **HARLEQUIN®**

---

# THE TAGGARTS OF TEXAS!

Harlequin's Ruth Jean Dale brings you
THE TAGGARTS OF TEXAS!

Those Taggart men—strong, sexy and hard to resist...

You've met Jesse James Taggart in FIREWORKS!
Harlequin Romance #3205 (July 1992)

And Trey Smith—he's THE RED-BLOODED YANKEE!
Harlequin Temptation #413 (October 1992)

And the unforgettable Daniel Boone Taggart in SHOWDOWN!
Harlequin Romance #3242 (January 1993)

Now meet Boone Smith and the Taggarts who started it all—
in LEGEND!
Harlequin Historical #168 (April 1993)

Read all the Taggart romances!
Meet all the Taggart men!

Available wherever Harlequin Books are sold.

---